W9-AOV-538

Super-Optimum Solutions
and
Win-Win Policy

Super-Optimum Solutions and Win-Win Policy

Basic Concepts and Principles

Stuart S. Nagel

QUORUM BOOKS
Westport, Connecticut • London

H
97
N343
1997

Library of Congress Cataloging-in-Publication Data

Nagel, Stuart S., 1934–
    Super-optimum solutions and win-win policy : basic concepts and
principles / Stuart S. Nagel.
        p.   cm.
    Includes bibliographical references and index.
    ISBN 1-56720-118-0 (alk. paper)
    1. Policy sciences.   I. Title.
H97.N343   1997
320'.6—dc21   96-54284

British Library Cataloguing in Publication Data is available.

Library of Congress Catalog Card Number: 96-54284
ISBN: 1-56720-118-0

First published in 1997

Quorum Books, 88 Post Road West, Westport, CT 06881
An imprint of Greenwood Publishing Group, Inc.

Printed in the United States of America

The paper used in this book complies with the
Permanent Paper Standard issued by the National
Information Standards Organization (Z39.48–1984).

10 9 8 7 6 5 4 3 2 1

Dedicated to great innovators and implementers of public policy:
Franklin Roosevelt on the New Deal and economic policy,
John Kennedy on civil rights and social policy,
Abraham Lincoln on state universities and technology policy,
Thomas Jefferson on the Bill of Rights and political policy.

CONTENTS

FIGURES AND TABLES

Introduction ———————————————

WIN-WIN POLICY

DEFINITIONS AND DISTINCTIONS

Define Policy Problems in Terms of Elements

In this book we are talking about public policy, which means governmental decision making, not private-sector or private-individual decision making. The government is a set of people and rules for making decisions on behalf of the general population of a community or state or nation. The subject matter relates to how people should interact. It is difficult to get away from talking about specific policy fields or social institutions.

The key institutions in this context are economic, social, technological, and political. This means we are talking about how people relate to each other in the context of jobs, families, or government. The social could include families, education, ethnic groups, and social classes. Technology relates to matters like environmental protection, health care, energy, housing, transportation, and communication.

Thus there is not a meaningful way of defining a policy problem without getting into the field of public policy, unless we do so on such an abstract level as to not be very meaningful. Law is frequently defined in terms of government rules as to how people are supposed to interact, and by sanctions or incentives to encourage proper interaction. Public policy might also be concerned with incentives, so there is not much distinction between law and public policy. One could talk about legal problems or public policy problems. Legal problems have a connotation of courts and public policy problems of legislatures. The term "problem" has a connotation that things are not going right. We are not concerned with governmental decision making where there is no or relatively little controversy.

Distinctions

We make a distinction between political, legal, and constitutional. Political mainly refers to government reform and international relations; legal to court procedure and compliance with the law; constitutional to free speech and equal treatment. But again we define those terms by referring to the specific policy fields. In this context legal refers to trial courts, constitutional refers to the Supreme Court, and political refers to legislatures and chief executives.

The best distinction is what we originally had between substance and methods. We can talk about the interaction among the policy fields, though that gets more complicated if we have six fields rather than the usual four. We need to lump political, legal, and constitutional together under governmental. There is also going to be some confusion if we throw in a category called process in addition to methods and substance. Process refers to how policy gets made and implemented. We are not so concerned with that subject. We are mainly concerned with substance and methods of analysis.

Basic Concepts

Public policy is government decision making for dealing with social problems. *Government* means a group of people who make, administer, and interpret laws for a society, which consists of a set of people who live in a given area and have a set of economic, social, technology, political, and political institutions. Laws consist of statements about how people ought to behave, which come from the government and which are backed up by positive and negative incentives.

Decision making refers to processing a set of goals to be considered, alternatives available for achieving them, and relations between alternatives and goals in order to arrive at a best alternative, combination, allocation, or win-win dispute resolution. *Social problems* consist of things that are happening in a society about which there are many complaints and dissatisfactions.

DEFINING WIN-WIN POLICY

Win-win policy refers to public policy that is capable of achieving both conservative and liberal goals simultaneously. Examples could be given from any field of public policy—economic, social, environmental, legal, or political. Win-win policies should be distinguished from compromises, where both sides partially retreat from achieving their goals in order to obtain an agreement.

Win-win policy is sometimes referred to as super-optimizing policy. The concept of win-win means all major sides win, but the concept of winning can be ambiguous. If each side does some winning and some losing, it is sometimes called a win-win solution, but it is really a traditional compromise with a glorifying name. In the context of this book, win-win means all major sides win beyond their best initial expectations. Going beyond the best is what is meant by super-optimum.

Thus if there are two sides and their best expectations are 90 profit units apiece, then a win-win solution means each side achieves beyond 90 profit units. A lose-lose solution means they each achieve a net loss or a negative profit. A win-win solution means one side takes profits, and the other side takes losses. A compromise might involve one side taking 70 profit units, and the other side taking 60 units. In that sense, they both win, but not ahead of their best initial expectations of 90 units each.

ENVIRONMENTAL POLICY EXAMPLE

As a concrete example, the field of environmental policy involves conservative and liberal approaches. Conservatives emphasize the role of consumers and the marketplace in restraining business from engaging in socially undesirable activities, like pollution. Liberals emphasize the role of the government in restraining pollution. Conservatives are especially interested in the goal of economic development, which may be interfered with by government restraints. Liberals are especially interested in the goal of a clean environment, which may not be so effectively achieved by relying on selective consumer buying.

A neutral compromise approach might involve giving business firms partial subsidies to adopt antipollution devices. Doing so would involve some requirements for receiving the subsidies, but less interference than regulation and fines. Doing so would help promote a cleaner environment, but there might still be evasions by business in view of the extra expense and trouble in complying.

A win-win policy alternative might instead emphasize subsidies to universities and research firms to develop new processes (that relate to manufacturing, transportation, energy, and agriculture) which are both less expensive and cleaner than the old processes. Those new processes would then be adopted by business firms because they are more profitable, not because the firms are being forced or subsidized to do so.

The new processes would thus achieve the conservative goals of profits and economic development, even better than retaining the present marketplace. Such a win-win policy would also promote the liberal goal of a cleaner environment, even better than a system of regulation, and without the expense of a continuing subsidy for adopting and renewing antipollution devices.

A specific example of such an environmental win-win policy has been finding substitutes for aerosol propellants and air-conditioning freon that are more profitable to manufacturers and simultaneously less harmful to the ozone layer, and which protect against skin cancer. Another specific example is developing an electric car, which saves money on gasoline and maintenance, while at the same time not generating the exhaust pollution of internal-combustion cars. Developing hydrogen fusion or solar energy may also be an example of a less expensive and cleaner fuel for manufacturing processes.

FEASIBILITY PROBLEMS

Win-win policies may be capable of achieving both conservative and liberal goals in theory, but not in practice. To be meaningful policies, they may have to satisfy various kinds of feasibility. For example, is the policy of developing solar energy for manufacturing technologically feasible? Is there sufficient funding available to subsidize the needed research if the private sector is not so willing, due to the risks, the large amount of money needed, or the long wait before payoffs occur?

Is there insurmountable political opposition from liberals who do not like government subsidies to make business more profitable? What about the opposition from conservatives who do not like government involvement in developing a research agenda? Is the program administratively feasible in terms of built-in incentives, or does it require a lot of obtrusive monitoring? Does the program violate some constitutional rights? Does the program make provision for workers and firms that might be displaced if the policy is adopted?

GENERATING WIN-WIN PROPOSALS

Win-win policies may involve creativity, but developing them is becoming easier as a result of experience with the ideas. We now have many different approaches that can serve as a checklist in leading one to a win-win policy. For example, expanding the resources available can enable conservatives to have more money for defense, and liberals to have more money for domestic programs. The government can sometimes be a third-party benefactor in providing vouchers to enable both landlords and tenants, and also merchants and consumers, to come out ahead.

One can also deal with problems like abortion by getting at the causes. They consist of unwanted pregnancies that could be lessened through more effective abstinence programs and birth control. Thinking in terms of the goals to be achieved, rather than the alternatives to choose among, can stimulate win-win policies. So can thinking in terms of increasing benefits and decreasing costs.

Other approaches deal with early socialization of widely accepted values, technological fixes like the nonpolluting hair spray, and the contracting out of government activities to private firms (which do well as a result of both the profit motive and quality specifications in the contract). Further approaches may involve combining (rather than compromising) alternatives, developing a package with something for each major viewpoint, having international economic communities, adopting a gradual or incremental win-win policy, and arranging for big benefits on one side with small costs on the other.

Part I

BASIC IDEAS

Chapter 1 _____

CONCEPTS AND PRINCIPLES

Super-optimizing analysis refers to dealing with public policy problems by finding an alternative that enables plaintiffs, defendants, conservatives, liberals, and other major viewpoints all to come out ahead of their best initial expectations simultaneously.

An optimum solution is one that is best on a list of alternatives in achieving a set of goals. A super-optimum solution (SOS) is one that is simultaneously best on two separate sets of goals, liberal and conservative. Both sets may share many or all of the same goals, but they are likely to differ in terms of the relative weights they give to the same goals.

This chapter discusses general concepts and principles that relate to super-optimum solutions. It then provides a detailed case study of a minimum wage policy as an example.

The super-optimizing approach fits into the decision-making category of systems and policy analysis. It involves a complex of related goals and costs in the tradition of multi-criteria decision making (MCDM). The key difference between SOS and MCDM is thinking in terms of conservative-liberal goals and alternatives in order to arrive at win-win policy solutions.

MINIMUM WAGE EXAMPLE

In the minimum wage controversy, both liberals and conservatives endorse the goals of paying a decent wage and not overpaying to the point where some workers are unnecessarily laid off because their employers cannot afford the new higher minimum. Liberals, however, give relatively high weight to the first goal and relatively low but positive weight to the second goal, and vice versa for conservatives.

The liberal alternative in the minimum wage controversy might be $4.40 an hour and the conservative might be $4.20. The liberal alternative would thus score higher on the "decent wage" goal, and the conservative alternative lower. On the goal of "avoiding overpayment," the liberal alternative would score lower, and the conservative alternative higher. This real data would thus provide a classic trade-off controversy.

The object in this example is to find a solution that is simultaneously better from a liberal perspective than $4.40 an hour and better from a conservative perspective than $4.20 an hour. One such super-optimum solution would be to provide for a minimum wage supplement by the government of 22 cents an hour to each unemployed person who is hired. The worker would receive $4.41 an hour, but the employer would pay only $4.19 an hour.

The liberal-labor interests would be getting more than their best expectation of $4.40 an hour, and the conservative-business interests would be paying less than their best expectation of $4.20 an hour. The government and taxpayers would be benefiting by virtue of (1) the money saved from otherwise providing public aid to unemployed people; (2) the money added to the gross national product, which increases taxes and provides income to others and an increased base on which to grow in subsequent years; (3) better role models for the children of people who would otherwise be unemployed; and (4) an upgrading of skills if qualifying for the wage subsidy means business has to provide on-the-job training and workers have to participate.

SOS CONTRASTED WITH OTHER SOLUTIONS

Solutions to public controversies can be classified in various ways. First there are *super-optimum* solutions in which all sides come out ahead of their initial best expectations, as mentioned above. At the opposite extreme is a *super-malimum* solution in which all sides come out worse than their worst initial expectations. This can be the case in a mutually destructive war, labor strike, or highly expensive litigation.

Pareto optimum solutions are where nobody comes out worse off and at least one side comes out better off. This is not a very favorable solution compared to a super-optimum solution. A *Pareto malimum* solution would be one in which nobody is better off and at least one side is worse off.

A *win-lose* solution is where what one side wins the other side loses. The net effect is zero when the losses are subtracted from the gains. This is the typical litigation dispute when one ignores the litigation costs.

A *lose-lose* solution is where both sides are worse off than they were before the dispute began. This may often be the typical litigation dispute, or close to it when one includes litigation costs. These costs are often so high that the so-called winner is also a loser. This is also often the case in labor-management disputes that result in a strike, and even more so in international disputes that result in going to war.

Then there is the so-called *win-win* solution, which at first glance sounds like a solution where everybody comes out ahead. What it typically refers to though is an illusion, since the parties are only coming out ahead relative to their worst expectations. In this sense, the plaintiff is a winner no matter what the settlement is, because the plaintiff could have won nothing if liability had been rejected at trial. Likewise, the defendant is a winner no matter what the settlement is, because the defendant could have lost everything the plaintiff was asking for if liability had been established at trial. The parties are only fooling themselves in the same sense that someone who is obviously a loser tells himself he won because he could have done worse.

WAYS OF ARRIVING AT SUPER-OPTIMUM SOLUTIONS

Having the government as a third-party benefactor in the minimum-wage dispute between management and labor interests is one of various ways of arriving at super-optimum solutions. Other ways include (1) expanding the resources available, (2) setting realistically higher goals than what was previously considered best, (3) having big benefits for one side but only small costs for the other side, (4) combining alternatives that are not mutually exclusive, (5) removing or decreasing the source of the conflict, and (6) developing a package of alternatives that would satisfy both liberal and conservative goals.

One procedure for arriving at super-optimum solutions is to think in terms of what is in the conservative alternative that liberals might like; and likewise, what is in the liberal alternative that conservatives might like. Then think whether it is possible to make a new alternative that will emphasize those two aspects. Another technique is to emphasize the opposite. It involves saying what is in a conservative alternative that liberals especially dislike; what is in the liberal alternative that conservatives especially dislike. Then think about making a new alternative that eliminates those two aspects.

A variation on this is to add new goals. The usual procedure starts with the conservative goals as givens in light of how they justify their current best alternative, and it starts with the liberal goals as givens in light of how they justify their current best alternative. This technique says to think about the goals conservatives tend to endorse that are not currently involved in the controversy, but that could be brought in to justify a new alternative. Likewise, what are the goals most liberals tend to endorse that are not currently involved in the controversy, but that could also be brought in. For this technique, a good example is the free-speech controversy where the liberal Group A wants virtually unrestricted free speech in order to stimulate creativity and the conservative Group B wants restrictions on free speech in order to have more order in the legal system. However, liberals also like due process, equal protection, and right to privacy. This raises questions as to whether it might be permissible to restrict free speech in order to satisfy those constitutional rights where the restrictions are not so great, but the jeopardy of those other rights might be great. Likewise, most conservatives like policies that are good for business. They might therefore readily endorse permissive free speech that relates to advertising, to trying to convince workers that they should not join unions, or that relates to lobbying.

One problem with super-optimum solutions is that they look so good that they may cause some people to think they might be some kind of trap. An example is the Camp David Accords. This example is a classic super-optimum solution where Israel, Egypt, the United States, and everybody involved came out ahead of their original best expectations. According to the *New York Times* for March 26, 1989, however, Israeli intelligence at least at first opposed Anwar Sadat's visit to Israel and the Camp David Accords until close to the signing, on the grounds that it all sounded so good that it must be a trap. The Israeli intelligence felt that Israel was being set up for a variation on the Yom Kippur War, whereby Israel got into big trouble by relaxing its guard because of the holidays. They viewed this as an attempt to get them to relax their guard again, and that any minute the attack would begin. They were on a more intense alert at the time of the Camp David negotiations than they were at any other time during Israel's history. This nicely illustrates how super-optimum solutions can easily be viewed by people as a trap because they look so good that they are unbelievable. Traditional solutions are not so likely to be viewed as traps, and they are taken more at their face value, which is generally not much.

RELATIONS TO DECISION-AIDING SOFTWARE

Super-optimizing is an approach to public policy analysis. Policy analysis or policy evaluation can be defined as processing a set of goals to be achieved, alternatives available for achieving them, and relations between goals and alternatives in order to arrive at a best alternative, combination, allocation, or predictive decision rule. Policy analysis can be facilitated by decision-aiding software, which involves showing goals on the columns of a table, alternatives on the rows, and relations as words or numbers in the cells. The overall totals can be shown on a column in the far right, with an analysis that can quickly show how the totals would change if there were changes in the goals, alternatives, relations, or other inputs.

This kind of decision-aiding software also facilitates the finding of super-optimum solutions. It can quickly determine the liberal and conservative totals for each alternative. It can quickly test to see if a proposed super-optimum solution does score better than the best liberal and conservative alternatives using the liberal and conservative weights. Such software also facilitates finding solutions by enabling one to work with many alternatives and many criteria simultaneously. Each side can thereby give on some criteria which are not so important to it, and receive on other criteria in order to arrive at solutions where both sides come out ahead of their best initial expectations. Some of the key literature on decision-aiding software includes Humphreys and Wisudha (1987), Gass et al. (1986), and Nagel (1989).

RELATIONS TO DISPUTE RESOLUTION AND GROWTH ECONOMICS

One stream of inspiration has come from people in the field of mediation and alternative dispute resolution. Some of that key literature includes Susskind and Cruikshank (1987), Goldberg, Green, and Sander (1984), and Nagel and Mills (1987).

Another stream of inspiration has come from people who are expansionist thinkers. This includes the conservative economist Arthur Laffer and the liberal economist Robert Reich. They both have in common a belief that policy problems can be resolved by expanding the total pie of resources or other things of value available to be distributed to the disputants. The expansion can come from well-placed subsidies and tax breaks with strings attached to increase national productivity. This kind of thinking can apply to disputes involving blacks-whites, rich-poor, males-females, North-South, urban-rural, and other categories of societal disputants. Some of that key literature includes Magaziner and Reich (1982), and Roberts (1984).

When the idea of super-optimum solutions was first proposed in the 1980s, people thought it was some kind of funny trick to think one could arrive at solutions to public policy problems that could exceed the best expectations of both liberals and conservatives simultaneously. Since then, the ideas have been presented in numerous workshops where skeptical and sometimes even cynical participants would divide into groups to try to develop super-optimum solutions to problems within their subject-matter interests. They found that by opening their minds to the possibilities and by following some simple procedures, they could succeed in arriving at reasonable solutions. It is hoped that this research will contribute in the long run to decreasing the glamor and excitement of super-optimum solutions by making them almost a matter of routine thinking. There is joy in creating new ideas, but there is more joy in seeing one's new ideas become commonplace.

REFERENCES

Gass, S. et al., eds. *Impacts of Microcomputers on Operations Research*. Amsterdam: North-Holland, 1986.

Goldberg, S., E. Green, and F. Sander, eds. *Dispute Resolution*. Boston: Little, Brown, 1984.

Humphreys, P. and A. Wisudha. *Methods and Tools for Structuring and Analyzing Decision Problems*. London: London School of Economics and Political Science, 1987.

Magaziner, I. and R. Reich. *Minding America's Business: The Decline and Rise of the American Economy*. New York: Harcourt, Brace, 1982.

Nagel, S. *Evaluation Analysis with Microcomputers*. Greenwich, Conn.: JAI Press, 1989.

Nagel, S. and M. Mills. "Microcomputers, P/G%, and Dispute Resolution," *Ohio State Journal on Dispute Resolution*, Vol. 2 (1987), pp. 187–223.

Roberts, P. *The Supply Side Revolution*. Cambridge, Mass.: Harvard University Press, 1984.
Susskind, L. and J. Cruikshank. *Breaking the Impasse: Consensual Approaches to Resolving Public Disputes*. New York: Basic Books, 1987.

Chapter 2 _____

GRAPHING THE CONCEPTS

This chapter deals with super-optimum solutions from the perspectives of bar graphs, trade-off curves, pyramidal shapes, and pie charts. All four perspectives help understand the concepts of conservative best expectation, liberal best expectation, traditional compromise, attempted total victory, and a super-optimum solution.

BAR GRAPHS

Bar graphs are shown in Figure 2–1. We can have a liberal perspective and a conservative perspective. On each perspective there is a vertical scale that measures benefits minus costs.

The horizontal scale shows the different types of solutions:

1. The SOS is the highest for either liberals or conservatives.
2. The liberal best expectation is lower. We could call that the LBE, as contrasted to the SOS. We could also show the CBE for the conservative best expectation.
3. The expected value of either a settlement or going to trial, strike, or war could be shown on the next bar. Normally the settlement would be better. That is the compromise bar.
4. The worst bar is the one that might be labeled "trial, strike, war," or other action designed to smash the other side. What all those activities have in common is the idea of attempted total victory. It could be called ATV.

All this looks better if it starts with the lowest and works its way up. The zero mark need not be shown. All we are concerned with is the relative heights or the rank orders of the bars. The attempted total victory could produce a benefit minus cost score that is negative. Even the compromise could produce a score that is negative but is less negative than the ATV.

Figure 2–1
Bar Graphs Showing Super-Optimum Solutions

A. LIBERAL PERSPECTIVE

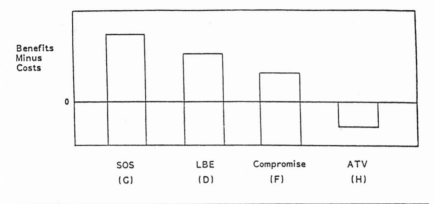

B. CONSERVATIVE PERSPECTIVE

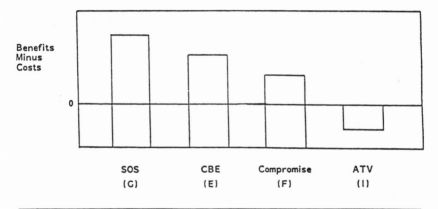

NOTES:

SOS = Super-Optimum Solution.
LBE = Liberal Best Expectation.
ATV = Attempted Total Victory.
CBE = Conservative Best Expectations.
These two bar graphs represent typical relations between alternative resolutions of policy problems and disputes.

TRADE-OFF CURVES

A second graphics perspective comes from the economics of indifference curves and is shown in Figure 2–2. We could put benefits on one axis and costs on the second axis; we then have indifference curves, which gets at the trade-

Figure 2–2
Trade-Off Curves Showing Super-Optimum Solutions

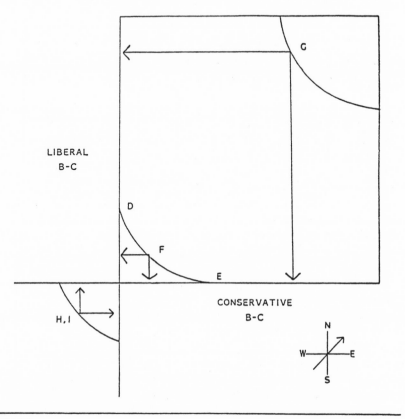

NOTES:

Point G = Super-Optimum Solution.
Point D = Liberal Best Expectation.
Point E = Conservative Best Expectation.
Point F = Compromise.
Points H, I = Attempted Total Victory of Liberals, Conservatives, Respectively.

off idea. We could better put the benefits minus costs of the liberals on one side, and the benefits minus costs of the conservatives on the other side. Then we draw an indifference curve, which shows when the liberals do well the conservatives do poorly, and when the liberals do poorly the conservatives do well.

Any point on that curve represents a compromise except for the extreme points. Point D is where the liberals do the absolute best in that they score extremely high and the conservatives score zero. The second point is where the conservatives do extremely well and the liberals wind up with nothing, which is point E.

Point F is anywhere along the curve between D and E. It is the compromise position where the liberals get something and the conservatives get something. The key thing to note is the trade-off nature of movement along that curve. Whenever the conservatives get more, the liberals get less. Whenever the liberals get more, the conservatives get less.

Points H and I correspond to the ATV bar for liberals in the bar graph and the ATV bar for conservatives. Both sides are likely to come out in the negative, although not necessarily equally so.

The SOS points are anywhere on the curve labeled G. We are thus moving to a different curve, and as we do so we still have a trade-off on each curve, but it is irrelevant because the SOS curve results in liberals and conservatives both doing better. We do not need multiple SOS curves to show that. It is enough at first just to say any curve that is substantially above the original curve. This in a way is like adding a third dimension or at least adding a second dimension. The first curve allows only for movement along a single dimension, namely a line or a curve. The second curve allows for aboveness, which is an important concept in super-optimum solutions. One might note that if we move up to curve G, then it is possible to find a point where both the liberals and the conservatives will be better off than the previous compromise.

What we want is a point where they will both be better off than their best expectations, which are points D and E. At point G, both the liberals and the conservatives are better off than the previous compromise of point F. We could put some numbers on the scale in order to say how much better off. With the previous curve, any movement would be an improvement for only one side, not an improvement for both sides. The new compromise of G is much better for the liberals than former point D, which was the outermost extreme they could do. The new point G is also much better for conservatives than point E, which was the outermost extreme. In other words, point G is not just better than point F as a compromise in the sense of being an improvement for liberals and an improvement for conservatives, but of out-distancing the best expectations on both sides.

We still have not shown how bad the attempted total victory is. We need to indicate on the bar graph that the zero point is normally above the ATV. To further dramatize that, we can show the last bar as hanging upside down to indicate that it is falling below zero. To show this, we need some new letters like H and I. H is the liberal ATV below zero, and I is the conservative ATV below zero. All the curves can be parallel. The curve labeled H, I, just like the bar graph, implies that in the ATV situation liberals and conservatives take a net loss. This is typically true. If an ATV situation is a war, both sides are likely to wind up suffering more costs than benefits. Likewise, if there is a strike the workers wind up losing wages maybe even for months. Management winds up

Figure 2–3
Pyramidal Shapes Showing Super-Optimum Solutions

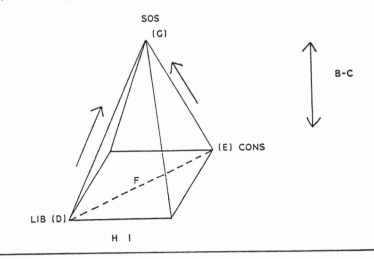

NOTES:

1. As in the other figures, the compromise position is between the liberal and the conservative best expectation.

2. As in the other figures, the super-optimum solution is above both the liberal and the conservative best expectation in terms of their respective benefits minus costs.

3. As in the other figures, the benefits minus costs for each side of attempting a total victory tend to be below or worse than the compromise position.

losing profits for months. Both sides thus take big losses that they may never make up. Also in going to trial, the litigation costs may be so large that it does not make any difference who gets the judgment. Both sides are likely to be losers when the costs are subtracted from the benefits. In some cases, maybe one side makes a profit. These curves are not designed to cover every possible situation, just the typical situations.

PYRAMIDAL SHAPES

Figure 2–3 shows the SOS pyramid and how to interpret it. Point D is the liberal extreme. Point E is the conservative extreme. The moderate or compromise position is point F. The SOS position is comparable to bar G and point G on the curves.

In the pyramid, we do not show the idea of benefits minus costs that are shown in the bars and the curves. The pyramid was originally designed just to position the concepts without having a B-C dimension. It is easy to add a B-C dimension: It is the vertical point from F up to SOS. It can be shown off to the side. It indicates that the SOS solution provides greater benefits minus costs than either the liberal or the conservative solution, but it does not make clear that there are greater benefits minus costs for both the liberals and the conservatives. One can think of the liberals moving up to an SOS solution along the DG line and conservatives moving up to an SOS solution along the EG line.

The graph does not show the concept of a super-malimum solution. For this we would need a point beneath the pyramid, which is not too difficult to draw but may be a little difficult to visualize. It would be a pyramid on top of a pyramid, which has a solid geometry name. A pyramid has four sides and a bottom. It thus has four faces. A cube has six faces because it has the same four sides but has both a bottom and a top because it does not come to a point. Back-to-back pyramids have nine faces, four on top, four on the bottom, and the square that is in between. In geometry it might be called something like a nonahedron, a nine-faced solid geometry shape. Or maybe it is called a back-to-back pyramid (only if it is standing up straight). It may be an octahedron because the floor is not necessarily a plane.

I think there is no need to draw the pyramid at the bottom. One can just say verbally that the ATV is a point underneath the pyramid. One can draw the point that would be H and I without drawing more lines. Pyramids are easy to visualize, but back-to-back or side-to-side ones are not so easy. The line on the inside going from point F to point G can be talked about without being shown. If that internal line has to be printed in a journal or a book in the same color as all the other lines, then it is going to cause confusion. The line that shows the one-dimensional traditional thinking could be a dotted or broken line so it does not mess up the pyramid.

AN SOS PYRAMID RATHER THAN AN SOS TRIANGLE

Why do we use a pyramid rather than a triangle to show relations between the liberal, conservative, compromise, SOS positions? The answer is simply that the triangle implies there is just one liberal dot and one conservative dot. There can be with the pyramid perspective several liberal positions and conservative positions. Under either perspective, there can be lots of compromise and SOS positions unless one defines compromise as right at the midpoint. Then the liberal position would be everything to the left of the midpoint and the conservative position would be everything to the right. This would allow for many liberal and conservative positions.

Under either perspective the SOS is higher than the liberal, the conservative, and the compromise. Under the triangle the traditional ideologies are ordered on a dimension of width. We then add the dimension of height. With the pyramid they are ordered on a plane that is length times width. We still find the SOS in a third dimension of height.

A big drawback to the triangle perspective is that it puts liberal and conservative in a single rut, which leads to zero-sum orientation. The pyramid emphasizes multiple criteria on both sides.

PIE CHARTS

As for other geometric shapes, we could show what is going on with a pie chart, which could be especially relevant to allocation problems. It would mean a separate pie for each type of solution. We could have some traditional pie charts. The first would involve the liberals getting nearly all the pie, maybe saving a sliver for the conservatives. Or at the other extreme, the conservatives get nearly all the pie and liberals get a sliver. The first one is like solution D, the second one is like solution E, the third is the compromise solution like F where they each get about half a pie (see Figure 2–4).

With the expanded pie perspective, we draw the original F. We then just triple it, and everybody comes out ahead. That is not good enough, though; it is just ahead of the compromise position. What we need to note is that in the traditional pie chart we have a 1-inch radius. In the expanded pie chart, we have about a 1.41-inch radius. With a 1-inch radius, the area is about 3 square inches, or to be more exact it is 3.14 square inches. With a compromise, each side gets about 1.57 square inches. With a 1.41-inch pie, we have an area of 6.768 square inches, since the area of a circle is pi times the radius squared.

What we need to improve upon is what the liberals get under D and what the conservatives get under E. What we need is a pie that will give the liberals more than 3.14 and the conservatives more than 3.14. This is a simple algebra problem. We want to know what the radius has to be. All we need to do is have a pie that has a radius that is more than 1.41 inches, and we have a super-optimum pie. People like these pie charts. They relate to the notion of expanded pie analysis. (In China they do not eat pies so we had to call it an expanded cake analysis.) In doing the pie chart, it is not that difficult to get a compass and draw three small pies and then one big pie.

In the expanded pie situation, the liberals wind up with more than what they could get if they got the whole little pie. The conservatives also wind up with more than what they could get if they got the whole little pie. One thing interesting about this is that you do not have to expand the pie very much in order to create an SOS. At first glance, one might think one has to have a big expansion in order to be able to give each side more than they could get if they were previously getting everything. One does not need such a big expansion. All that is needed is a 1.41 increase in the radius. This is just as true if the original pie started out to have a trillion-inch radius. Increasing the trillion-inch radius by 1.41 would give everybody more than they previously had even if they had the whole 3.14 trillion square inches. The general principle is that no matter how big the original pie is, if liberals get all of it or if conservatives get all of it, then all one has to do is increase by 1.41 the radius of the pie. The liberals who were formerly getting all of it will now get even more, and the conservatives who were formerly getting all of it will simultaneously get even more. This can be proven with elementary school arithmetic about areas of circles, even though at first glance it seems contrary to intuitive thinking.

Figure 2–4
Pie Charts Showing Super-Optimum Solutions

A. TRADITIONAL PIE CHARTS

(One-Inch Radius)

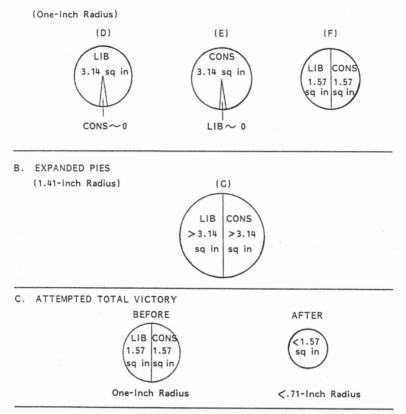

B. EXPANDED PIES

(1.41-Inch Radius)

C. ATTEMPTED TOTAL VICTORY

NOTES:

1. By arranging for slightly more than a doubling of the total resources, it is possible for both the liberals and the conservatives to receive more after the doubling than they received before the doubling, even if the liberals had 100% of the resources before, or even if the conservatives had 100% of the resources before.

2. If an attempted total victory results in slightly more than halving the total resources, it is possible that the liberals or the conservatives will wind up with less than they had before, even if they wind up with 100% afterward, provided that each side had about half the total resources before.

3. These graphs are realistic in the sense that political disputes often involve basically two sides consisting of liberals-conservatives, blacks-whites, females-males, poor-rich, north-south, urban-rural, or other such divisions.

4. These graphs are also realistic in the sense that it is not that difficult to double the total resources of a society, especially if the increase is plowed back into the economy producing a compound rate of growth. It is also not that difficult to halve the total resources of a society, group, or individual as a result of an international war, a destructive strike, or expensive litigation.

5. A key formula is Area $= \pi r^2$. Thus if radius is 1, then area is 3.14. What does r have to be for area to be 6.28? The answer is $6.28 = \pi r^2$, or $6.28/3.14 = r^2$, or $2 = r^2$ or $r = \sqrt{2} = 1.41$. Thus the radius only has to go from 1 to 1.41 and the area will double. Doing so provides more for each of two sides than they could obtain by getting all of the former area.

What does the ATV look like in the pie chart? We have had the experience before that pie charts do not lend themselves to showing negative returns. If someone gets a negative allocation, there is no way of showing that with a pie chart. We can show negatives with bar graphs, trade-off curves, and SOS pyramids, as follows:

1. Any bar that drops below the 0 horizontal axis shows a negative return.
2. Any point in a system of curves that is to the left of 0 on the horizontal axis or below 0 on the vertical axis shows a negative return.
3. Any point below the floor of the pyramid shows a negative return.
4. However, there seems to be no way of showing a negative return with a pie chart. The lowest one can get is 0, which involves showing no sliver at all, as contrasted to a negative sliver.

In Figure 2–4c we add a third section to the pie charts labeled "Attempted Total Victory." This section has two subparts, before and after. The after part is after a war, a strike, or going to trial. The total resources between the liberal and conservative sides then get reduced to about half and each side takes a loss. They now have only a half-inch-radius pie between them. Thus even if the liberals are the winners and wind up with the whole pie in the after period, they have less than they had before when they had to share the pie. This dramatizes how bad resorting to war, strikes, and trials can be. You wind up with the whole pie after the smoke clears, but the whole pie is half or less of what used to exist. Even if you have the whole thing, you have less than what you used to have when you shared the whole pie with the other side. For people who like graphs and pictures, these graphs and pictures are indeed communicative, along with the spreadsheet matrices or tables associated with P/G% (policy/goals percentaging) decision-aiding software.

Chapter 3 ———————————————————

FIELDS OF PUBLIC POLICY

POLICY FIELDS AND SCHOLARLY DISCIPLINES

Six broad topics correspond to various departments on a university campus—economic, social, technology, political, legal, and constitutional (there are only five topics if constitutional is considered part of legal). They illustrate the need for an interdisciplinary policy program.

Prosperity is mainly a concern of economics. Sociology is concerned with poverty, as is social work. Labor and industrial relations are concerned with unemployment. The business school has a big interest in the problems of inflation.

Merit treatment is a concern for the law school and the psychology and sociology departments—also, economics if we get into class discrimination as well as ethnic discrimination. One thing this illustrates is that if one wants to talk about public policy as being an interdisciplinary activity, the better way to do it is not to ask questions as to what political science can contribute. Instead it makes more sense to say we have a set of problems, one of which is prosperity. Where do we look on the campus in order to find people who have something to contribute on that subject? How about merit treatment? Technological innovation?

On technological innovation, the law school is concerned with intellectual property, patents, copyrights, and trademarks. The law school has an interest in all policy subjects. Policy is law and vice versa, although the law school emphasizes the legalistic approach to policy rather than a socialistic approach. Under public policy we could mention the law school concern for the Uniform Commerce Code and facilitating interstate commerce, or bankruptcy procedures that are equitable to creditors and debtors. Technological innovation primarily means the engineering school, with every engineering department concerned with innovation, including electrical, environmental, mechanical, civil, nuclear, aeronautical, and industrial. Political science has a concern with all the problems, or at least public administration does, just as law does. A school of public policy, of course, would be concerned with all of these. We are talking not about intellectual innovation, such as developing a new theory of human evolution, such as Marxist theory—it is not technological. We could talk about genetic and biological engineering, and agricultural developments. Architecture gets close to humanities, just as the industry gets close to social science.

On the matter of democracy, political science is especially relevant. Democracy includes majority rule and electoral process. Psychology is concerned with influencing voters. The part of democracy that relates to free speech is of interest to people in library science, the law school, literature, and art. Freedom of religion would be of interest to the religious studies program. Due process relates to criminology within sociology, and also to criminal law in the law school. Due process, though, may be more a part of law compliance than it is of democracy, just as equal treatment is more a part of merit treatment than it is of democracy.

World peace and other international matters are subjects of interest to all area studies people, especially political science, international economics, and international sociology, which deals with migration and demography. The cross-national concerns of the language departments are also relevant, although they show an interest in policy by way of participating in the area programs.

Law compliance is a special interest of the law school, but also of sociology regarding criminology, of the business school and economics if we talk about wrongdoing, and of political science if we talk about violating the Constitution and government corruption, or selling legislative votes.

OUTLINE OF THE FIELDS

   A. ECONOMIC POLICY (Promoting Prosperity)
      1. Economy as a Whole
         a. Inflation and Unemployment
         b. Taxing, Spending, and the Deficit
         c. Organizing the Economy
      2. Factors of Production
         a. Land and Agriculture
         b. Labor and Management
         c. Business and Consumers
   B. SOCIAL AND PSYCHOLOGICAL POLICY (Promoting Merit Treatment and Personal Development)
      1. Groups
         a. Ethnic and Gender
         b. Poverty and Public Aid
         c. Families
      2. Personal Development
         a. Education
         b. Leisure

C. TECHNOLOGY AND SCIENCE POLICY (Promoting Innovation)
  1. Physical Planning
     a. Environment
     b. Housing
     c. Transportation and Communication
  2. Applied Science
     a. Energy
     b. Medical Care
     c. Technological Innovation
D. POLITICAL POLICY
  1. Domestic Politics (Promoting Democracy)
     a. Governmental Reform
     b. Electoral Policy
     c. Political Process
  2. International Politics (Promoting World Peace)
     a. World Peace
     b. Trouble Spots
     c. International Trade
E. LEGAL POLICY (Promoting Law Compliance, Especially Constitutional Law)
  1. Compliance with the Law
     a. Traditional Crimes
     b. Business Wrongdoing and Incentives
     c. Governmental Wrongdoing and Judicial Review
  2. Bill of Rights
     a. Freedom of Speech and Assembly
     b. Freedom of Religion
     c. Fair Criminal Procedure
     d. Fair Civil Procedure
  3. More Recent Rights
     a. Merit Treatment and Lifetime Learning
     b. Privacy and Reproductive Freedom
     c. Business Entry and Economic Growth

BIBLIOGRAPHY

Economic Policy

Unemployment and Inflation

Okun, Arthur. *The Political Economy of Prosperity* (Norton, 1970).
Pierce, Lawrence. *The Politics of Fiscal Policy Formation* (Goodyear, 1971).
Stein, Herbert. *The Fiscal Revolution in America* (University of Chicago Press, 1969).

Poverty

James, Dorothy (ed.). *Analyzing Poverty Policy* (Lexington-Heath, 1975).
Steiner, Gilbert. *Social Inequality: The Politics of Welfare* (Rand McNally, 1966).
Wilcox, Clair. *Toward Social Welfare: An Analysis of Programs and Proposals Attacking Poverty, Insecurity, and Inequality of Opportunity* (Irwin, 1969).

Social Policy

Family

Hula, Richard and Elaine Anderson (eds.). *Family Policy* (Greenwood, 1991).

Levitan, Sar, Richard Belous, and Frank Galio. *What's Happening to the American Family: Tensions, Hopes, Realities* (Johns Hopkins, 1988).

Peden, Joseph and Fred Glahe (eds.). *The American Family and the State* (Pacific Research Institute for Public Policy, 1986).

Education

Ziegler, Harmon and Kent Jennings. *Governing American Schools* (Duxbury Press, 1974).

Gove, Samuel and Frederick Wirt (eds.). *Political Science and School Politics* (Lexington-Heath, 1978).

Masters, Nicholas, Robert Salisbury, and Thomas Elliot. *State Politics and the Public Schools* (Knopf, 1964).

Technology Policy

Environmental Protection

Grad, Frank, George Rathjens, and Albert Rosenthal. *Environmental Control: Priorities, Policies and the Law* (Columbia University Press, 1971).

Nagel, Stuart (ed.). *Environmental Politics* (Praeger, 1975).

Rosenbaum, Walter. *The Politics of Environmental Concern* (Praeger, 1973).

Technological Innovation

Kuehn, Thomas and Alan Porter (eds.,). *Science, Technology, and National Policy* (Cornell University Press, 1981).

Roessner, David (ed.). *Government Innovation Policy: Design, Implementation, Evaluation* (Macmillan, 1988).

Lambright, Henry and Diane Rahm (eds.). *Technology and American Competitiveness* (Greenwood, 1991).

Political Policy

Government Reform

Nagel, S. (ed.). *Public Policy and Government Structures* (Symposium Issue of the *International Political Science Review*, 1986).

Sundquist, James. *Constitutional Reform* (Brookings, 1986).

Aranson, Peter. *American Government: Strategy and Choice* (Winthrop, 1981).

World Peace

Harkavy, Robert and Edward Kolodziej (eds.). *American Security Policy and Policy Making* (Lexington-Heath, 1980).

Merritt, Richard (ed.). *Foreign Policy Analysis* (Lexington-Heath, 1975).

Rosenau, James. *The Scientific Study of Foreign Policy* (Free Press, 1971).

Legal Policy

Criminal Procedure: Right to Counsel

Fellman, David. *The Defendant's Rights Today* (University of Wisconsin Press, 1976).
Gillers, Stephen. *Getting Justice: The Rights of People* (Basic Books, 1971).
Nagel, Stuart (ed.). *The Rights of the Accused: In Law and Action* (Sage, 1972).

Crime Reduction

Levine, James, Michael Musheno, and Dennis Palumbo. *Criminal Justice: A Public Policy Approach* (Harcourt Brace Jovanovich, 1980).
Taft, Donald. *Criminology: A Cultural Interpretation* (Macmillan, 1950).
Walker, Samuel. *Sense and Nonsense about Crime: A Policy Guide* (Brooks/Cole, 1989).

Constitutional Policy

Equal Treatment under the Law

Emerson, Thomas, David Haber, and Norman Dorsen. *Political and Civil Rights in the United States* (Little, Brown, 1967).
Palley, Marian and Michael Preston (eds.). *Race, Sex, and Policy Studies* (Lexington Books, 1979).
Rodgers, Harrell, Jr. (ed.). *Racism and Inequality: The Policy Alternatives* (Freeman, 1975).

Free Speech

Dorsen, Norman, Paul Bender, and Burt Neuborne (eds.). *Political and Civil Rights in the United States* (Little, Brown, 1976).
Schauer, Frederick. *Free Speech: A Philosophical Inquiry* (Cambridge University Press, 1983).
Spinrad, William. *Civil Liberties* (Quadrangle Books, 1970).

Part II _____

BASIC COMPONENTS OF WIN-WIN POLICY

Chapter 4 ⎯⎯⎯⎯⎯⎯⎯⎯⎯⎯⎯⎯⎯⎯⎯⎯

CONSERVATIVE AND LIBERAL GOALS

A GENERAL SET OF VALUES

In anthropology and sociology courses, human beings are frequently referred to as involved in six sets of institutions designed to organize more systematically the ways in which humans interact with each other. The lists vary across textbooks, but they generally talk about:

1. Economic institutions, which relate to the production and consumption of goods.
2. Social institutions, which relate to the interaction of family members, families, ethnic groups, genders, clubs, and other groupings as well as to the training of the young.
3. Technology and science institutions, which relate mainly to new inventions and products for being more productive or for understanding nature.
4. Political institutions, which relate to how decisions are to be made, interpreted, and implemented on behalf of the society of people.
5. Intersocietal relations, which relate to how one society or collectivity of people is supposed to relate to other collections of people.
6. Legal institutions, which relate to getting people to comply with rules on how they are supposed to interact with each other in the economic, social, technological, political, and intersocietal realms.
7. Other institutions, such as those designed to promote music, visual arts, and literature. If we are going to emphasize controversy, then art institutions become controversial by way of political institutions that try to repress or impose certain art forms.

Each of these six sets of institutions corresponds to an important policy controversy. The six corresponding controversies might vary across policy studies people, but the list might generally include:

1. Prosperity, especially reducing inflation, unemployment, and poverty.

2. Merit treatment, especially in terms of abilities as they relate to different job opportunities independent of one's race, gender, age, or other groupings.

3. Technological improvement, especially in terms of encouraging useful technological innovation and dispersion while providing for displaced workers and firms.

4. Democracy, including majority rule with universal adult voter eligibility, and minority rights to try to convert the majority.

5. International interaction that involves nonviolent relations, buying and selling of goods, and free exchange of ideas.

6. Law compliance, including compliance with laws against violence, theft, consumer fraud, workplace abuses, and environmental pollution.

Other important public policy issues can be incorporated into the above categories. Energy and health policy, for example, are largely matters of improving and spreading technology to provide less-expensive energy sources and more-effective forms of medical treatment.

Table 4–1 is entitled "Universal Values and Win-Win Public Policy." Column 1 lists the six general policy controversies corresponding to the six basic human institutions. Both conservatives and liberals would probably agree that those policy issues are indeed quite important. They are, however, likely to disagree on the intermediate *goals* to seek in order to achieve better functioning on the basic institutions and issues. Both sides are especially likely to disagree as to what policy *alternatives* are best for achieving either the intermediate or higher goals.[1]

THE SPECIFIC VALUES

Prosperity

Column 2 of Table 4–1 summarizes the general conservative goals and alternatives on each issue; column 3 summarizes the general liberal goals and alternatives. For example, on the issue of prosperity, conservatives tend to be especially oriented toward the goal of reducing inflation, with reducing unemployment as an important but secondary goal. Liberals tend to be especially oriented toward the goal of reducing unemployment, with reducing inflation as an important but secondary goal. Conservatives advocate increasing interest rates as a major means of reducing inflation. Liberals advocate decreasing interest rates as a major means of reducing unemployment. There is thus a conflict or trade-off that tends to result in compromises on setting interest rates.

Column 4 refers to super-optimum solutions. These are win-win solutions since all major sides gain, including conservatives and liberals in general. Such solutions are a special form of win-win in the sense that the gain exceeds the best initial expectations of each side, and thus excludes a nonsubstantial gain.

Table 4-1
Universal Values and Win-Win Public Policy

ISSUES	CONSERVATIVE	LIBERAL	SUPER-OPTIMUM SOLUTIONS
1. PROSPERITY (esp. inflation and unemployment)	*- Inflation* + INTEREST RATES	*- Unemployment* - INTEREST RATES	Economic growth through 1. Training 2. Technology 3. Competition 4. Exports 5. Capital
2. MERIT TREATMENT (esp. race and gender)	*+ Productivity* 1. COLOR-BLIND HIRING 2. GENDER-BLIND	*+ Equity allocation* 1. PREFERENCES 2. AT LEAST TEMPORARY	Outreach hiring 1. Enterprise zones 2. Advertising 3. Equal opportunity employer 4. Valid tests Outreach training 1. Needs test 2. Toward merit hiring and training
3. TECHNOLOGY INNOVATION (esp. patents)	*+ Profits* 1. PRESERVE PATENT SYSTEM 2. ABOLISH STRICT LIABILITY	*+ Competition* 1. ABOLISH PATENTS 2. RESEARCH GRANTS	1. Focused grants 2. Required licensing 3. Reasonable royalties 4. Government insurer
4. DEMOCRACY (esp. voter turnout)	*- Double voting* LEAVE AS IS	*- Eligible not voting* TINKER, E.G., MOTOR-VOTER, POSTCARD	1. Same day registration 2. Multiple places 3. Multiple days 4. Invisible ink monitoring
5. WORLD PEACE (esp. role of UN)	*Save U.S. $ and lives* MINIMUM U.S. INVOLVEMENT	*+ World peace, prosperity, and democracy* SUBSTANTIAL U.S. INVOLVEMENT	1. Volunteer UN force 2. - Trade barriers 3. Trade + democracy
6. LAW COMPLIANCE (esp. drugs)	*- Drug dealing* MILITARY AND POLICE	*- Side effects of drug enforcing* 1. Other crimes 2. Corruption 3. Money 4. Health damage 5. Poverty 6. Int. comp. LEGALIZATION	Deprofitize drug sales 1. Confirmed addicts as sick people 2. HMO coverage 3. No incentive to hook children 4. Severe prosecuting of illegal drugs 5. Accept non-cures

NOTES:
1. In the column on "Issues," the concepts are goals that correspond to economic, social, technology, political, international, and legal institutions. - = Decrease. + = Increase.
2. The items in italics are conservative or liberal goals. The items beneath the goals in roman type are conservative or liberal alternatives.
3. The alternatives or policies in the SOS column are capable of exceeding the goal-achievement of conservative alternatives on conservative goals and the goal-achievement of liberal alternatives on liberal goals.

In the context of reducing inflation and unemployment simultaneously, economic growth through increased productivity can be such a solution. Productive economic growth can come about through training, new technologies, competition, exports, and government capital where private enterprise is reluctant to get involved.

This five-part program can promote an increase in productivity which in turn results in an increase in the gross domestic product (GDP). If there is a productivity growth in the GDP, then that means more goods are available. Inflation means too many dollars chasing too few goods. Thus by having more goods competitively available, prices tend to go down. Increased production can thus reduce inflation better than increasing interest rates, because increasing interest rates has the effect of reducing the GDP and increasing unemployment.

Likewise, if there is a productivity growth in the GDP, then that means the population has more money available to spend. Increased national income means increased national expenditure. If the population does have more to spend, then the increased spending helps to create new jobs, thereby more than offsetting the previous unemployment or the unemployment that is caused by worker displacement as result of productivity downsizing.

Merit Treatment

Turning to the second row and the issue of merit treatment, conservatives talk about the importance of productivity and how color-blind and gender-blind hiring is relevant to having a productive economy. Liberals talk about equity or fairness in the allocation of jobs. To them, this may mean at least temporary preferences to redress past overt discrimination, especially where those hired are qualified, where the tests are subjective, and where the gap is small between the score of the minority applicant who is given a preference over the competing applicant from the dominant group.

The win-win or SOS proposal that may be capable of achieving both high productivity and high fairness for minorities is a program of outreach training. This means seeking individuals who have potential capability *if* given the proper intensive training, and who have *not* received adequate training previously as a result of a lack of expenditures per student in the school systems they attended. Such people would be hired or admitted to a certain university only if they score above the hiring threshold. There would thus be no preference in hiring, and there would be an ability test and a needs test for getting into the training program. The Reagan administration advocated outreach hiring, rather than outreach training, as a compromise between color-blind policy and preferences. Outreach hiring does not work so well, mainly because it assumes there are trained and qualified minorities available to be hired, which may not be so.

Technological Improvement

On technological innovation, conservatives are oriented toward increasing profits. Liberals want to increase competition. They both want to increase innovation. Conservatives want to preserve the patent system. Liberals want to replace the patent system with research grants. The SOS involves focused grants, required licensing, reasonable royalties, and the government as an insurer.

Democracy

A key issue with regard to democracy is voter turnout. Conservatives are especially worried about double voting. Liberals are especially worried about eligibles not voting. Conservatives want to leave the system as it is, which has four elements that come up in the SOS. Liberals want to tinker with such ideas as postcard registration or motor voter. Some neutral approaches involve precinct registration or no purges of the voter rolls. The SOS is same-day registration, multiple precincts, multiple days, and the invisible ink security method.

World Peace

World peace is in the context of the United Nations peace-keeping. The conservative goal is to save U.S. dollars and lives. The liberal goal is to promote world peace, prosperity, and democracy. The conservative approach is minimum U.S. involvement. The liberal approach is substantial U.S. involvement. The SOS approach is to endorse a volunteer UN force.

Law Compliance

In law compliance we are mainly talking about what to do about drugs. The conservative goal is to reduce drug dealing. The liberal goal is to reduce the side effects of drug enforcement. This includes other crimes, corruption, great expenditure of dollars, health damage, poverty, and reduced international competitiveness. The conservative approach is military action and police. The liberal approach is legalization. A neutral approach is traditional treatment and education, or separate marijuana from cocaine. The SOS is deprofitize drug sales, which involves various aspects: (1) treating addicts as sick people, (2) HMO coverage for addicts, (3) no incentive to hook children, (4) severe enforcement of illegal drugs outside the HMO system,[2] and (5) accept the reality that some addicts will never be cured and will be on drug maintenance for the rest of their lives, like diabetics are on insulin.

SOME CONCLUSIONS

Looking back, we can see this chapter is designed to be an introduction to win-win policy analysis, as applied to widespread policy problems. The next logical step is to provide greater detail on everything that has been presented, including:

1. More principles and examples of how to generate win-win proposals.
2. More principles and examples of the feasibility problems which win-win proposals tend to encounter.
3. A lot more examples as applied to economic, social, technology, political, international, and legal policy.
4. A lot more examples as applied to Africa, Latin America, Asia, Eastern Europe, Western Europe, North America, and the countries within those regions.
5. Generalizing across specific policy problems and generalizing across places.

The concept of super-optimizing as a policy management tool is quite new. It does not appear in the literature of public policy or public administration until about 1990. It is a new way of thinking as compared to:

1. Win-lose policy, where one side wins and the other side loses.
2. Compromise policy, where both sides lose to some extent in order to generate an agreement.
3. Lose-lose policy, such as a mutually destructive war or mutually harmful tariff-raising.
4. Unambitious win-win policy, where each side comes out slightly ahead, and maybe only slightly ahead of their worst expectations.
5. Super-optimum solutions, whereby all major sides or viewpoints can come out ahead of their best initial expectations simultaneously.

Although the concept of super-optimizing is quite new, it is being increasingly popularized as in the international dispute resolution of Jimmy Carter, or some of the 1992 campaigning of Bill Clinton and Al Gore. What is needed is for scholars of public policy and public administration to develop further the theory, principles, and examples. Practitioners like Carter, Clinton, Gore, and others can then apply the ideas toward bringing about such universal values as prosperity, merit treatment, technological improvement, democracy, world peace, law compliance, and others.[3]

NOTES

1. For further details on win-win policy, see Lawrence Susskind and Jeffrey Cruikshank, *Breaking the Impasse: Consensual Approaches to Resolving Public Disputes* (Basic Books, 1987); and such Stuart Nagel books as *Policy-Analysis Methods and Super-Optimum Solutions* (Nova Science, 1994); *The Policy Process and Super-Optimum Solutions* (Nova Science, 1994); and with Miriam Mills, *Developing Nations and Super-Optimum Policy Analysis* (Nelson-Hall, 1993).

2. For further details on each of the six values or goals, see the following:

Prosperity: Lee Bawden and Felicity Skidmore (eds.), *Rethinking Employment Policy* (Urbana Institute Press, 1989).

Merit treatment: Norman Dorsen, Paul Bender, Burt Neuborne, and Sylvia Law (eds.), *Political and Civil Rights in the United States: Volume II* (Little, Brown, 1979).

Technological innovation: Michael Goldhaber, *Reinventing Technology: Policies for Democratic Values* (Routledge & Kegan Paul, 1986).

Democracy: Charles Dunn, *American Democracy Debated* (Scott, Foresman, 1982).

World peace: David Felder, *How to Work for Peace* (Florida A&M University Press, 1991).

Law compliance: James Levine, Michael Musheno, and Dennis Palumbo, *Criminal Justice: A Public Policy Approach* (Harcourt Brace Jovanovich, 1980).

3. On the matter of public accountability, this concept usually applies to keeping public administrators from sins of commission, fraud, waste, arrogance, and related forms of wrongdoing. The concept should be broadened to put more emphasis on sins of omission, including the failure to adopt win-win or super-optimum policies when they are available. In the past, policy managers could argue that they were unaware of win-win or super-optimum policies. As the literature builds, public administrators can be held accountable to higher standards to take advantage of opportunities, including opportunities to adopt and implement win-win policies.

Chapter 5

RELATIONS BETWEEN GOALS AND POLICY ALTERNATIVES

REPUBLICAN INCONSISTENCIES

One can define hypocrisy as not practicing what one preaches. This means giving examples where Republicans are advocating some policies that run contrary to their goals, or professed goals. Their actual goals may be different than their professed goals. We'll also give examples on the side of the Democrats.

The best way that this probably can be approached is not by talking in terms of economic, social, technology, political, foreign, and legal issues, but instead by talking in terms of a list of about five major Republican goals and five major Democratic goals, and then give examples of policies that are in conflict (see Table 5–1).

A major Republican goal is *free competitive enterprise*. Policies that conflict would include Republican opposition to government policy designed to require the leasing of electric, telephone, and cable television networks in order to provide competition. The counterargument is that it is really a form of deregulation because as of now there are monopolistic franchises awarded to electric companies to keep out competition, generally at the state level, as well as monopolistic franchises to cable television at the city level. At the federal level, telephone companies are given monopolistic franchises by the Federal Communications Commission. None of those companies have monopolies simply because they are so wonderfully efficient and low priced that nobody can compete with them.

Delegating to the states rather than the national government. A good example of hypocrisy on this is the Republican legislation designed to wipe out common law rules and statutory rules that exist in all 50 states in favor of one federal rule that practically immunizes business from being sued. Nearly all 50 states provide, without exception, for strict liability in workplace injuries and product liability. All 50 states will be wiped out, especially on product liability and

Table 5-1
Inconsistencies Between Republican Goals and Policies

GOAL	POLICIES
1. Free Competitive Enterprise	1. *Electricity* 2. *Phoning* 3. *Cable TV*
2. Delegating to States	1. *Tort liability* 2. *Criminal sentencing 85%*
3. No Government Interference and Right to Privacy	1. *Search and seizure* 2. *Drug crackdown*
4. Holding Families Together	1. *Taking children away, not neglected or abused* 2. *Only aid to one-parent families*
5. Encouraging Work	1. *Failure to provide job facilitators* 2. *100% deduction for earnings*
6. Complying with Framers of the Constitution	1. *Prayer amendment and flag burning* 2. *Tort liability*
7. Reducing Spending	1. *More defense spending* 2. *School vouchers* 3. *More prison dollars* 4. *Welfare dollars*
8. Reducing Tax Burdens	1. *VAT tax* 2. *Flat % tax*
9. Saving Fetuses	1. *Less prenatal nutrition dollars* 2. *Child cut-off* 3. *Oppose research on miscarriages*
10. National Defense	1. *Dollars for dismantling nuclear weapons in Russia* 2. *Dollars for aid to promote trade and prosperity*

generally on workplace liability, as a result of Republican legislation that requires the proving of negligence, setting caps on the damages that can be collected, and totally abolishing the right to sue if a product was made more than 15 years ago, including machine tools that injure workers. Also, with regard to criminal sentencing, states are not going to be allowed to get prison funds unless they provide for serving all sentences at least 85% of the sentence handed down. The inconsistency is that by depriving states of prison funds (to get them to increase sentences), the result will be decreased sentences due to lack of prison funds.

Another Republican goal is to *leave things up to the individual, without government interference.* This clearly conflicts with preaching government interference for issues that have to do with victimless crimes and abortion. These issues should have a right to privacy from government interference. The Republicans' proposal to weaken search and seizure conflicts with the right to privacy. Some Republicans are no longer pushing an abortion amendment. So this cannot be used to show hypocrisy. They are pushing for a stronger drug crackdown, including a crackdown on marijuana, rather than a legalization approach or a medicalization approach. The examples of Republican hypocrisy should come especially from the Republican Contract with America rather than from anything that is not that recent. This includes provisions that relate to the balanced budget, crime, welfare, education, tax cuts, national defense, senior citizens, regulation, tort changes, and congressional term limits. Not letting people sue is an interference with private activity, since it is not the government that is doing the suing. The Republicans can argue, though, that the government is providing the courts in which the suing occurs and the government is authorizing the suing. When they talk about leaving it up to consumer sovereignty, they mean that an injured consumer should simply not buy the product anymore, and not that the injured consumer should have a right to sue.

A fourth goal would be *holding families together*. The hypocritical policy is taking children away who are not neglected or abused. A previous argument that still has some weight is allowing public aid only to a one-parent family, which causes the father to leave. Aid is now provided for the two-parent family under earned income tax credit.

Encouraging work rather than welfare. The failure to provide job facilitators runs contrary to that goal. The Republicans argue that the best job facilitator is to be cut off of aid. The proof, though, is in the data that show that cutting off does not facilitate getting jobs as much as a combination of cutting off and training, day care, wage subsidies, and job placement. The old argument of hypocrisy was the 100% deduction for earnings. Republicans are not pressing that so much because it is so obviously contradictory, although the old justification was that the nastier the government treats welfare recipients by taking their money, which they earn, then the more they will want to quit being on welfare.

Complying with the Framers of the Constitution. One example on this is pushing the prayer amendment. Conservatives would argue that the Supreme Court has misinterpreted the First Amendment and that the prayer amendment will restore the Framers' intent. The prayer amendment certainly runs contrary to Jefferson's agnosticism and separation of church and state. Also, the Framers of the Constitution, according to John Marshall, left it up to the Supreme Court as to what the First Amendment means, they did not leave it up to Pat Robertson to decide. A lesser example would be changing the jury system. Changing search and seizure fits better under right to privacy. The Republicans also argue that the Framers indicated a negative attitude toward illegal searches, but they never said the illegally seized evidence could not be used as evidence. The right to appeal may go contrary to the Fifth and Sixth Amendments. The right has not been completely abolished; the Supreme Court may still uphold it. Cutting off public aid not only conflicts with holding families together, it may also conflict with discouraging abortions. Also, providing no governmental public aid goes contrary to what existed as of 1789. The Republicans can argue that they are not totally eliminating public aid; they are just giving it to the states.

Reducing spending. There are at least four or five things in the Contract with America that involve increased spending, such as increases in defense spending and prison spending. There will be an increase in welfare spending as a result of cutoffs that lead to foster care and orphanages. Advocating school vouchers is another expensive program.

Reducing tax burdens. Some of the Republican proposals would greatly increase burdens on the middle class, and reduce taxes only on high income brackets such as having a value-added tax, which is worse than a national sales tax, or a flat tax, which does not take ability to pay into consideration. Even though it is a flat percentage tax, it does not provide for a higher percentage for higher incomes.

DEMOCRATIC INCONSISTENCIES

We will do the same thing with at least five major Democratic goals, where things that the Democrats advocate conflict with Democratic proposals—although the conflict may involve a segment of the party, which is also true of the Republicans. Not all Republicans endorse the prayer amendment or search and seizure restrictions, or a value added tax. Nearly all of them endorse the goals, but some of the goals are also endorsed by Democrats, but not as much relatively speaking.

One Democratic goal is to *promote low prices to consumers*. This conflicts with labor liberals opposing tariff reduction. It also conflicts with environmental liberals opposing competition in the electricity business, for reasons that have to do with increasing consumption, decreasing conservation spending, and putting out of business electric companies that use exotic fuels.

The Democrats normally advocate *preserving jobs*, but then they advocate a lot of things that take away jobs, such as tariff reduction, defense conversion, productivity increases, and jobs for people on welfare or the elderly. It would not be hypocrisy if the Democrats made more provision for displaced workers, but that frequently is not done.

A lot of the Democratic failures are more sins of omission in the sense of advocating something and not following up on it, such as advocating world peace and not doing anything to promote the *United Nations volunteer force or American involvement*.

Advocating new technologies. Here it is worse than a sin of omission. The Clinton administration has cut out lots of money for new technologies, especially new sources of energy. For a while the Democrats were being called the Atari Democrats because they were so much in favor of high-tech solutions. The prevailing sentiment now is to cut spending for any new technologies that could not be online by the next congressional election.

The Democrats can also be accused of slowness. This is not the same as hypocrisy, nor are sins of omission. An example of slowness is talking about *training vouchers* and not having any bill drafted or hearings being held, even though that was such a fundamental part of the Democratic tax cut.

The Democrats do advocate a *cleaner environment*. They have not done anything to make it any worse, so cannot be blamed for anything that especially relates to current air pollution, water pollution, radiation, noise, toxic waste, solid waste, or wilderness conservation. Clinton has been accused by some environmentalists of being too willing to compromise, but that may be on issues where nothing was being accomplished under the previous noncompromise po-

Table 5–2
Inconsistencies Between Democratic Goals and Policies

GOALS	POLICIES
1. Low Prices to Consumers	1. Labor opposing tariff reduction 2. Environmentalists opposing electricity competition 3. Anti-trust liberals lose economics of scale
2. Preserving Jobs	1. Tariff reduction 2. Defense conversions 3. Productivity downsizing 4. Welfare and elderly 5. Immigrants 6. All without considering displaced workers
3. New Technologies	Cutting dollars for post-1996 technologies
4. Free Trade	1. Retaliatory tariff against Chinese competition in publishing 2. Also keeping out foreign airplanes
5. Free Speech	1. Feminists want anti-women porno and verbal sex harassment regulations 2. Good government limit linterest groups
6. Equal or Merit Treatment	Minority Democrats want preferences
7. High Wages	1. Fighting automation, e.g., featherbedding 2. Strengthening strikers in productivity downsizing
8. Due Process Justice	1. Feminsits in rape and physical molesting 2. Consumer liberals oppose due process jury, appeal, consent
9. Peaceful Resolution of International Disputes	Belligerent treatment of 1. Iraq, Iran 2. Cuba, Vietnam, China, North Korea
10. More Goods, Especially to Poor, Especially Quality Goods	1. Price control too low, food, housing, health care 2. Socialistic housing (vs. vouchers), medicine

sition, such as toxic waste cleanup. Clinton has not authorized an increase in toxic waste. He has authorized accelerated cleanup by having the government participate in the cost rather than expecting business to pay for it all, and by cleaning up only to the point of no substantial danger. One area where Clinton has been a hypocrite is in arguing in favor of free trade, and then he does such things as trying to raise tariffs against China because they want to manufacture products for their domestic and foreign markets. And they are willing to pay royalties. This is a retaliatory tariff, not because China has violated human rights, but because they want to be more competitive. It is a retaliatory tariff against Chinese competition in publishing.

Keeping foreign airplanes from servicing the American market. Clinton could argue that he did lessen the restrictions on Canadian planes flying from Canada to the United States or back from the United States to Canada, but they cannot fly from one American city to another, offering passenger service to Americans. One could say that that is an act of omission to fail to remove the restrictions. An act of omission is failing to pass a statute that provides for training vouchers. It is an act of commission to preserve restrictions on free trade.

INCONSISTENCIES AND HYPOCRISY

Hypocrisy and spite tend to go together. The explanation might be that one wants to hurt the other side, even if it is contrary to one's goals. Thus we have

two reasons for hypocrisy: because the real goals are not the same as the professed goals, and for spite, which means that one of the real goals is revenge.

We have two liberal goals that relate to labor: jobs and high wages. We could
have two goals that relate to consumers: low prices and more goods. Democratic
policies can conflict with more goods, such as price control that is too low. This
was mentioned in the context of interfering with getting low prices. It should
be better mentioned in the context of getting more goods, such as food and
housing, and maybe health care. Socialistic housing decreases the supply available to the poor, as contrasted to a voucher system. The same thing is true with
regard to socialistic medicine. It cuts down on access to doctors, partly because
few doctors want to be salaried employees of the government. A voucher system
enables health care consumers to go to any doctors, not just those who are
working for the government. Both socialized medicine and socialized public
housing do run contrary to the idea of providing more goods, especially to the
poor, although this gets into pricing, but also quality goods. The voucher system
is partly privatization. It does run contrary to traditional philosophy that favors
(or used to favor) public housing and socialized medicine for at least low-rise
public housing, and the single payer system. The big disadvantage of the single
payer medical system is that it is so expensive, not that it discourages doctors.
Some of them could get discouraged if the paperwork was too much, which
explains why many American doctors will not handle Medicaid or Medicare
patients.

Maybe conservatism is naturally more hypocritical than liberalism because
conservatism is not so popular with the masses, and therefore conservatives have
to lie or distort in order to get their policies adopted, which means coming up
with phony goals. This is untrue. Conservatism has been unpopular in the United
States relatively speaking, from about 1930 to at least 1994, but it was very
popular from about 1860 to 1930. During that time period the idea of the marketplace was something endorsed by the wave of immigrants, including black
immigrants going north, poor white immigrants going north, everybody going
west, European immigrants coming to the United States; and later Asian and
Hispanic immigrants. It was a time of mobility.

However, the frontier ended about 1900. Immigration also got cut off as of
World War I, and especially in the 1920s. A depression set in in the 1930s. All
these things added up to greatly decreased mobility. People then began to look
to the government to provide better workplaces. In the old days one would just
quit and go west. People began to look more to the government to provide
social security and public aid, especially in times of depression when jobs were
not so available.

In the period from 1860 to 1930, the Democrats and liberals may have had
a tendency to exaggerate and distort their goals. This is shown by William
Jennings Bryan, the leading liberal Democrat of about 1900. He basically represented the last attempt to organize debtors as a meaningful political party.
Thomas Jefferson could talk about debtors versus creditors, but that concept

became meaningless by about 1900. It was nonsense for Bryan to talk about the masses being crucified on a cross of gold. The masses were no longer small farmers borrowing from the banks to get seed and other materials until the fall harvest. They were now factory workers, who were not borrowing from anybody. Credit cards did not exist. The new concepts were labor versus management, not debtors versus creditors.

This is why people like Bryan got pushed aside by people like Franklin D. Roosevelt. Bryan's last gasp was in the Scopes trial of 1926, when Roosevelt was governor of New York. Bryan was moving down and Roosevelt was moving up. It was not a matter of personalities. It was the end of an old liberalism and the beginning of a new liberalism. The new liberalism lasted from at least 1930 until 1994, and is not necessarily over.

We seem to be in a state of flux with regard to what comes next. Maybe it will be a win-win philosophy rather than anything confrontational between labor and management, debtors and creditors, merchants and landed aristocrats. The merchants versus the landed aristocrats was never much of a controversy in the United States, although it was between the 13 colonies and England. It never played a part in domestic American politics. The Republicans included farmers and commercial people under their umbrella. The farmers, though, were not landed aristocrats; they were largely homesteaders rather than dynastic plantation owners.

What this means is that neither Democrats nor Republicans have any inherent reason for being more or less hypocritical than anyone else. They are both about equally hypocritical in the sense that they both have a tendency to espouse popular goals that will get them elected to office. Their policies may, however, be more directed toward narrow constituencies who pay the campaign bills. Both parties would like to get votes from all segments of the population, but campaign money to the Republicans mainly comes from business interests. The Democrats get campaign money from labor unions and various other organizations that do not have a lot of money but tend to side with the Democrats, like environmental, consumer, and feminist groups.

There are Democrats who are revenge-oriented and would like to hurt the Republicans, even if it runs contrary to achieving Democratic goals. They are the antibusiness Democrats. There are the Republicans who are revenge-oriented, even if it means hurting Republican goals. They are the Republicans who are antilabor, or who may be antigay or antiminorities in general. If we get into why this hypocrisy exists, the answers are in order to get votes and partly out of spite, although vote getting is more important.

INCONSISTENCIES AND CONFLICTING GOALS

Inconsistency could mean inconsistency between goals. Or it could mean inconsistency between policies. Hypocrisy is inconsistency between policies and goals, or between what one practices and what one preaches.

Inconsistencies Between Republican Goals

There is an inconsistency between the right to privacy goal and the goal of saving fetuses. Win-win solutions by definition are solutions that enable one to achieve two inconsistent goals simultaneously, which means they really are not totally inconsistent. Fetuses could be saved without interfering with the right to privacy by facilitating the avoidance of unwanted pregnancies. This means making relevant information and birth control more available.

Another inconsistency is that Republicans advocate balancing the budget, which conflicts with reducing taxes.

Another inconsistency is promoting competition, which may interfere with profit making of each firm. Although the total profits of the industry might go up, Republicans do not like to talk about promoting business profits as a goal, even though that might be an actual goal. It sounds too mercenary.

Inconsistencies Between Democratic Goals

An example of inconsistency among Democratic goals is preserving jobs and promoting new technologies. This can be resolved through more vigorous programs to find jobs for displaced workers.

There is also an inconsistency between free trade and preserving jobs.

Another inconsistency is between promoting minority interests and maybe allowing free speech to organizations like the Ku Klux Klan. The win-win solution relates to socialization that deprives antiminority groups of a voluntary audience. Prosperous times can also promote both free speech and minority interest.

Inconsistencies Between Policies

An example of an inconsistent policy would be the U.S. Department of Agriculture (USDA) trying to reduce farm productivity by giving subsidies for growing less. At the same time, they give subsidies to schools of agriculture to develop techniques for making farms more productive.

Another frequently mentioned policy inconsistency is the Department of Health and Human Services trying to discourage smoking to promote health at the same time the USDA is giving subsidies to tobacco farmers to grow more tobacco.

Chapter 6

RELATIONS AMONG GOALS OR POLICIES

ECONOMIC POLICY AS A CAUSE AND EFFECT

Economic growth policy as a cause has five categories (see Figure 6–1 and Table 6–1):

Social policy. If there is unemployment, this causes family breakup. The breadwinner in the family who is unemployed may leave the family so it can qualify for public aid. There should be more funds for education and reducing group friction.

Unemployment or a recession has an adverse effect on technological innovation. Business firms are not spending so much on research and development when business is bad.

Political policy, which includes world peace. Peace is possibly jeopardized if there is worldwide unemployment. This may cause governments to engage in aggressive action against other countries, partly to distract the citizens of the first country from their unemployment problems. Also, war activity gives people jobs. A bad economy decreases democracy versus dictatorship.

Legal policy includes crime reduction and due process. In times of unemployment people are more likely to be committing crimes against property to supplement their incomes and crimes against person out of frustration of unemployment.

Constitutional policy, including equal treatment under law, gets jeopardized when people are unemployed. They are more resistant to equal opportunity and free speech for minorities.

Economic growth policy as an effect has those same five categories (see Figure 6–1 and Table 6–2): If now we go in the other direction and say unemployment is an effect, we can start out by saying that education and training help reduce unemployment by increasing employability in new fields.

Figure 6–1
Economic Policy as a Cause and Effect of Other Policies

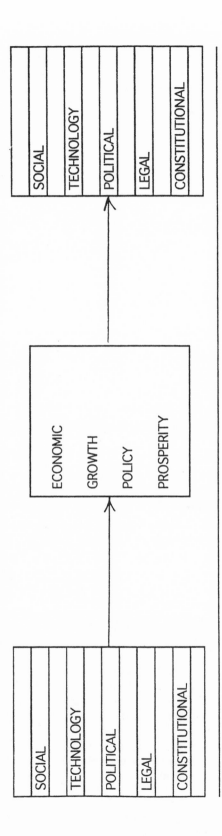

Table 6–1
Policies as Causes of Other Policies

CAUSES	EFFECTS	RELATIONS
1. PROSPERITY	1. Merit treatment 2. Innovation 3. Democracy 4. World peace 5. Law compliance	1. Concessions 2. Funding 3. Concessions 4. Decrease conflict 5. Decrease deprivation
2. MERIT TREATMENT	6. Prosperity 7. Innovation 8. Democracy 9. World peace 10. Law compliance	6. Productivity 7. Rising up in technology 8. Rising up in government 9. Rising up in world peace 10. Decrease deprivation
3. TECHNOLOGICAL INNOVATION	11. Prosperity 12. Merit treatment 13. Democracy 14. World peace 15. Law compliance	11. Productivity 12. Physical equalizer 13. Communication 14. Transportation, communication, trade 15. Detection monitoring
4. DEMOCRACY	16. Prosperity 17. Merit treatment 18. Innovation 19. World peace 20. Law compliance	16. Ideas circulate 17. Swing vote 18. Free speech 19. Decrease war 20. Respect for law
5. WORLD PEACE	21. Prosperity 22. Merit treatment 23. Innovation 24. Democracy 25. Law compliance	21. Waste 22. Scapegoat, paranoia, excuse 23. 80 s 24. Abridge freedom 25. Black market, anarchy
6. LAW COMPLIANCE	26. Prosperity 27. Merit treatment 28. Innovation 29. Democracy 30. World peace	26. Crime dollars 27. Anti-discrimination laws 28. Patent laws 29. Redistricting 30. International law

NOTES:

1. The first line of this table can be read as saying that prosperity (as a cause) stimulates merit treatment (as an effect) by way of the explanation that during prosperous times dominant groups are more willing to make concessions to groups that might otherwise be discriminated against.

2. The more general format for reading a line is: "The _____ cause stimulates the _____ effect by way of the _____ relations."

3. Sometimes it is more meaningful to think in terms of the opposite of the causes or effects. Thus instead of prosperity, merit treatment, technological innovation, democracy, world peace, and law compliance, one can talk in terms of depression-inflation-poverty, discrimination, technological stagnation, dictatorship, war, and crime.

Technological innovation and diffusion can increase the gross national product (GNP) and increase spending, which makes for more jobs. Some technological innovation may dislocate more workers, at least in the short run, than can be easily offset by increased productivity.

World peace promotes employment opportunities because it facilitates the buying and selling of goods. This kind of exporting helps make additional jobs. Domestic democratic policy causes diverse ideas.

Legal policy regarding reducing crime can affect employment by providing jobs such as police or people working with prisons. Crime reduction can be a big source of employment. Reducing crime reduces business expense and helps make businesses more internationally competitive, thereby providing more jobs and more dollars available for the economy.

Equal treatment may reduce unemployment because some unemployment may be based on discrimination.

Table 6-2
Policies as Effects of Other Policies

EFFECTS	CAUSES	RELATIONS
1. PROSPERITY	1. Merit treatment 2. Innovation 3. Democracy 4. World peace 5. Law compliance	1. Productivity 2. Productivity 3. Ideas circulate 4. Waste 5. Crime dollars
2. MERIT TREATMENT	6. Prosperity 7. Innovation 8. Democracy 9. World peace 10. Law compliance	6. Concession 7. Physical equalizer 8. Swing vote 9. Scapegoat, paranoia, excuse 10. Anti-discrimination laws
3. TECHNOLOGICAL INNOVATION	11. Prosperity 12. Merit treatment 13. Democracy 14. World peace 15. Law compliance	11. Funding 12. Rising up in technology 13. Free speech 14. 80 s 15. Patent laws
4. DEMOCRACY	16. Prosperity 17. Merit treatment 18. Innovation 19. World peace 20. Law compliance	16. Concessions 17. Rising up in government 18. Communication 19. Abridge freedom 20. Redistricting
5. WORLD PEACE	21. Prosperity 22. Merit treatment 23. Innovation 24. Democracy 25. Law compliance	21. Decrease conflict 22. Rising up in world peace 23. Transportation, communication, trade 24. Decrease war 25. International law
6. LAW COMPLIANCE	26. Prosperity 27. Merit treatment 28. Innovation 29. Democracy 30. World peace	26. Decrease deprivation 27. Decrease deprivation 28. Detection monitoring 29. Respect for law 30. Black market, anarchy

NOTES:

1. The first line of this table can be read by saying that prosperity (as an effect) is partly stimulated by merit treatment (as a cause) by way of the explanation that non-discrimination leads to greater productivity by workers and managers.

2. The more general format for reading a line is: "The _____ effect is stimulated by _____ cause by way of the _____ relations."

THE IMPACT THAT EACH FIELD HAS ON THE OTHER

If we think in terms of six fields—economic, social, technology, political, foreign, and legal—then we have six times five divided by two relations, which is 15 relations. We have 30 relations if we do not divide by two in order to give each cause or topic an opportunity to be a cause and an effect. We could number the relations 1 to 30. We might discuss economic policy as an influence on the other five; then social policy as an influence on the other five; and likewise with technology, political, foreign, and legal. Numbering them 1–5 may not be as meaningful as numbering them continuously.

We also need to note the subdivisions, which are the economy as a whole, the factors of production, groups, education, physical planning, applied science, government reform, world peace, international trade, compliance with the law, and constitutional rights. This converts 6 topics into 11.

First we need to clarify the key goal under each topic.

1. The key goal of economic institutions is to promote *prosperity*.

2. The key goal of social groups is *merit treatment* whereby everyone is considered as an individual and not as a group member.

3. The key goal of *technology* is *innovation* and dispersion.

4. The key goal of political institutions is *democracy*.

5. The key goal of foreign policy is *world peace* or maybe peace and trade.

6. The key goal of legal institutions is *law compliance* and rights.

Looking at Tables 6–1 and 6–2, here is how the above six key goals affect the other goals.

Prosperity promotes merit treatment. In time of depression the dominant economic group or class group is not so willing to allow for merit treatment. Ethnic groups get along much better in times of prosperity.

Prosperity provides the funding for technological innovation.

Prosperity promotes democracy. Depression leads to dictatorship; so does runaway inflation.

Prosperity promotes peace. A country that is in a state of depression may have a tendency to get involved in warlike interaction with other countries in order to distract domestic public opinion and to somehow achieve prosperity through conquest.

Prosperity promotes compliance with the law. People are more likely to be committing crimes in a time of depression out of a need for income and out of frustration. There is no need to mention rights because they are covered under merit treatment with regard to equal protection and under democracy with regard to free speech. There may also be no need to mention international trade separate from prosperity, since prosperity can pertain to domestic and international prosperity.

Merit treatment is good for prosperity. If people are treated in accordance with their abilities, they are more likely to be more productive and add more to the GNP, which provides income and jobs.

Merit treatment leads to technological innovation. If people are allowed to rise up in accordance with their abilities, then people who are members of minorities or low-income people have a better chance of developing creative ideas that can lead to Nobel Prizes and new products. This helps explain why the United States has done well on these matters, although we also have a good higher education system and ambitious immigrants.

Democracy does not mean as much without merit treatment. It means that people choose leaders by way of all adults having one vote, with minority rights that allow minority viewpoints to try to convert the majority. Merit treatment means that no minority or no segment of the population is excluded. Excluding them would miss out on the ideas that they could contribute and the skills that they have.

Merit treatment leads to world peace. It enables people with good ideas for improving world conditions to rise up to become leaders of their respective countries and international organizations like the United Nations. The United Nations has been well served by some good people from developing nations like Uthant of Burma, Javier Perez de Cuellar from Peru who was the secretary general before Boutros Boutros-Ghali from Egypt. They are all possibly better than Kurt Waldheim from Austria. The other UN secretary generals were Trygve Lie of Norway and Dag Hammarskjold of Sweden.

There is a relation between merit treatment and law compliance. A good deal of noncompliance with the law in the United States and elsewhere is sometimes disproportionately by an underclass of people who may rightfully perceive, although with possible exaggeration, that they are discriminated against. They then violate the law partly out of resentment. They also violate the law because if they are really discriminated against, they may not have good access to education and job opportunities that causes them to get into illegal activities.

Technological innovation definitely promotes prosperity by developing new techniques for creating products more efficiently at lower prices and higher quality. Selling those products makes for greater prosperity.

Technological innovation has facilitated merit treatment. New automated technologies like typewriters and computers have provided opportunities for women and elderly people as contrasted to human labor for hunting or pulling a plow. New technologies are greatly diminishing the importance of physical power.

Innovation is good for democracy. This includes new forms of communication like TV, radio, books, newspapers, and magazines that inform the public what is going on and provide ways of converting the public to new viewpoints or getting feedback from the public.

Innovation makes for world peace partly by improving world transportation and communication, which facilitates trade and business. Countries that buy and sell from each other are less likely to go to war with each other.

Innovation improves law compliance partly by way of better detection techniques to catch wrongdoers. This means better monitoring including police cars, TV cameras, walkie-talkies, and the like.

Democracy promotes prosperity because it allows ideas to circulate freely and therefore arrive at better ideas for promoting economic well-being.

Democracy promotes merit treatment partly because in a democracy minorities are more likely to have some influence. They don't have enough influence to be in the majority, but a democracy tends to mean a two-party system and minorities can be pivotal or swing votes in determining which party will be elected. Therefore the parties show sensitivity to merit treatment because antagonizing minorities could throw them over to the other party.

Democracy promotes innovation partly because under a democracy ideas are allowed to circulate freely. This includes innovative ideas that might otherwise antagonize someone who is attached to things as they are. We need to note that democracy does not just mean majority rule. It also means free speech and minority rights. These two concepts are almost in opposition but they can exist simultaneously.

Democracy promotes world peace. Dictatorships are more likely to go to war just as countries in depression are more likely to go to war. People resist going to war. If put to a vote, war is less likely to occur.

Democracy promotes respect for the law if people feel that they play a part in shaping the legal system. The jury system is an example.

World peace promotes prosperity. In time of war there is a terrible waste of resources that could be going into training and technological innovation for making more prosperity.

World peace is good for merit treatment. When a country is at war, minorities are likely to be abused, partly looking for scapegoats if the war is not going well or out of paranoia fears of subservience or as an excuse to discriminate in ways that wouldn't be tolerated in peacetime.

World peace is good for innovation. Some people think that war develops new products. That is a myth. There were a lot less patented new products between 1940 and 1945 than between, say, 1985 and 1990 at about the end of the cold war when tremendous developments were occurring with regard to computers, communications, and new energy forms. That was definitely peacetime and one of the most innovative time periods.

There is a relation between world peace and democracy—peace definitely promotes democracy. Countries at war abridge a lot of freedoms, such as abridging habeus corpus during the Civil War or locking up suspected subversives in World War I. Merit treatment refers to ethnic groups. Democracy refers to political viewpoints.

Peace is good for law compliance. In time of war, especially in a country that is losing, anarchy may break out. Even a country that is winning has black market activity. The war dislocates the economy and values.

Law compliance promotes prosperity. A big factor reducing prosperity is spending a lot of money for crime.

Law compliance promotes merit treatment, especially with regard to compliance with antidiscrimination laws. Most societies do treat people equally or on a merit basis as far as the letter and spirit of the law are concerned. It is enforcement or law in action rather than law in the books where discrimination occurs.

Law compliance promotes innovation, including compliance with the spirit of patent laws. People who violate other people's patent rights discourage innovation. Worse are those who own a patent and abuse it by trying to keep out competition.

There is the effect of law compliance on democracy. One big drawback to American democracy over the 20th century has been noncompliance with the basic constitutional principle of one person/one vote. The states refuse to redistrict state legislatures and state delegations. This kind of noncompliance with the law definitely hurts democracy. Noncompliance with the Constitution is the worst kind of noncompliance as compared to mere shoplifting, although it is undesirable too.

There is an impact of law compliance on world peace. Here we are talking about international law and the need for countries of the world to abide by international tribunals, mediation, and arbitration and other legal approaches to resolving disputes rather than going to war.

CAUSAL RELATIONS AMONG THE FOUR BASIC POLICY FIELDS

Figure 6–2 shows the causal relations among the policy fields. *The economy affects technology.* When the economy is prosperous, business firms spend more money on research and development and less money in times of recession, as is currently occurring in Japan.

Prosperity affects social relations. This includes the divorce rate and the crime rate. Also, people may have more leisure time in times of recession because of unemployment. Prosperity has a mixed effect on education. In a time of recession, people may go to school instead of trying to find a job, if they can afford to go to school. It may have an adverse effect on staying in high school if one needs to work to support the family in hard times.

Prosperity has an effect on political problems. People turn more readily to extreme politics in times of depression or runaway inflation.

Technology affects social relations. Reproductive technology can affect family planning. New technology means new education devices such as television, videotapes, and computers. New technology may affect methods used by both criminals and the police. New technology also influences how people spend leisure time, such as television and videotape technology.

Technology affects politics by providing new ways of campaigning for office and thereby creating campaign finance problems.

Social relations affect politics. Thus the occurrence of abortions, crime, leisure, and the need for education has an impact on public policy. A key social relation consists of ethnic relations. They influence how people vote.

The big impact of *technology* on the economy is to *increase productivity* but to *displace workers* in the process.

Ethnic relations and immigration have an uplifting effect on the economy but also a displacing effect. Education is important for uplifting the economy. Crime, such as drug-related crimes, can have an adverse effect on the economy by diverting a lot of resources.

Politics and public policy can stimulate the economy, especially by way of stimulating new technologies and education.

Social relations affect technology. This includes especially education, which makes it possible to benefit from new technologies and to invent them in the first place. Inventiveness may begin at an early age, before formal education.

Figure 6–2
Causal Relations Among the Four Basic Policy Fields

CAUSE

	ECONOMIC	TECHNOLOGY	SOCIAL	POLITICAL
ECONOMIC		7	8	9
TECHNOLOGY	1		10	11
SOCIAL	2	4		12
POLITICAL	3	5	6	

EFFECT

Politics affects technology by way of the patent system, government subsidies, and tariffs to protect infant industries.

Politics can affect social relations by way of public policy toward the family, schools, crime, and leisure.

Part III

DEVELOPING AND IMPLEMENTING WIN-WIN IDEAS

Chapter 7 —————————————————

WIN-WIN SOCIETAL
FACILITATORS

The following political, economic, sociological, and psychological institutions or ways of doing things in a society are conducive to innovative and effective public policy making. This includes public policies that can enable conservatives, liberals, and other major viewpoints to all come out ahead of their best initial expectations simultaneously.

POLITICAL METHODS

Competitive Political Parties

This is a key facilitator since the out-party is constantly trying to develop policies (including possibly SOS policies) in order to become the in-party. The in-party is also busy developing new policies in order to stay the in-party. New policies are developed largely as a result of changing domestic and international conditions, not just for the sake of newness. Without the stimulus of an out-party, the in-party would have substantially less incentive to be innovative. More important, without the possibility of becoming the in-party, the out-party would lose its incentive to be innovative. More innovation generally comes from the out-party than the in-party (all other factors held constant), including the possibility of SOS innovations.

Better Policy Analysis Methods and Institutions

SOS solutions are likely to be facilitated by policy analysis methods that deal with multiple goals, multiple alternatives, missing information, spreadsheet-based decision-aiding software, and a concern for successful adoption and implementation. Better policy analysis institutions refer to training, research, funding, publishing, and networking associations. These institutions can be part of the activities of universities, government agencies, and independent institutes in the private sector. The extent to which these policy institutions deal with super-optimizing analysis will make them even more relevant to facilitating SOS solutions.

ECONOMIC POLICIES

Competitive Business Firms

Competition among political parties may be essential for facilitating SOS public policy. Competition among business firms may be essential for facilitating a prosperous economy and a prosperous world through international business competition. Numerous examples can be given of nations that failed to advance and collapsed due largely to a one-party system, such as the former Soviet Union. Likewise, numerous examples can be given of business firms that failed to advance and virtually collapsed due largely to lack of substantial competition such as the American steel industry. The American automobile industry has not collapsed, but it did fail to develop small cars, cars that resist style changes, safer cars, less expensive cars, and more durable cars in comparison to the international competition that was not taken seriously until almost too late.

Well-Targeted Subsidies and Tax Breaks

In the context of super-optimum solutions, this tends to mean subsidies and tax breaks that increase national productivity and international competitiveness. Such subsidies and tax breaks are the opposite of handouts that provide a dis-incentive to increased productivity on the part of either welfare recipients or big business. Good targeting in this regard especially refers to upgrading skills and stimulating technological innovation and diffusion. A dollar invested in those kinds of subsidies is likely to pay off many times over without necessarily having to wait very long for the results.

Increased National Productivity

All these facilitators are important. Economists might rightfully consider in-creased national productivity to be especially important. It leads to an increased gross national product or national income, which means an increased tax base to which the tax rate is applied. If increased productivity increases the tax base, then tax rates can be lowered and still produce more tax money for well-targeted subsidies that produce further increases in national productivity. These increases, however, are not an end in themselves. The increased national income can fa-cilitate finding and implementing SOS solutions that relate to employment, in-flation, agriculture, labor, business, poverty, discrimination, education, families, the environment, housing, transportation, energy, health, technological innovation, government structures, government processes, world peace, international trade, and every other public policy field. In other words, with more money and resources available, SOS solutions are facilitated, but SOS solutions often draw upon creativity that is associated with doing much better on relevant goals with constant or decreasing resources.

SOCIOLOGY: CHILDHOOD SOCIALIZATION

In the SOS context, this refers to creating a frame of mind that causes adults to do what is socially desired because the alternative is virtually unthinkable. This can be contrasted with a less effective emphasis on deterrence, whereby socially desired behavior is achieved through threats and bribes. Examples include childhood socialization to reduce adult behavior that is violent, alcoholic, drug addictive, and hostile toward constitutional rights.

PSYCHOLOGY OF SOS SOLUTIONS

Innovative Risk Taking

This is an important SOS facilitator because many SOS solutions involve technological fixes. In order to develop these new technologies, many people usually had to risk substantial amounts of money, time, effort, and other resources. There may have been a strong possibility that it would have all been wasted. An SOS society needs more people who are willing to take such chances. Classic examples include Marie and Pierre Curie who sacrificed about 30 years of work plus their health to develop radium and thus radioactivity, which is part of the basis for nuclear energy. Thomas Edison frequently not only risked his resources but his whole reputation by announcing inventions before he had developed them in order to give himself an ego risk as a stimulus to quickly inventing what he falsely said he had already done.

Sensitivity to Opportunity Costs

This means either through socialization or an appropriate incentive structure trying to get decision makers to be more sensitive to the mistake of failing to try out a new idea that might work wonders, as contrasted to being so sensitive to sins of commission rather than omission. Both wrongs are undesirable. One can, however, say that a police officer who wrongly beats a suspect is doing less harm to society than a president who wrongly fails to adopt a new health care program that could save numerous lives or a new education program that could greatly improve productivity and the quality of life. A person who is sensitive to opportunity costs tends to say "nothing ventured, nothing gained," whereas an insensitive person tends to say "nothing ventured, nothing lost."

We need more of the former in order to facilitate the generating, adopting, and implementing of SOS solutions.

An SOS Combination of Pessimism and Optimism

This does not mean a balance or a compromise between being pessimistic and being optimistic. It means being 100% pessimistic or close to it regarding how bad things are and how much worse they are going to get unless we actively do something about them including developing SOS solutions. It simultaneously means being 100% optimistic or close to it regarding how good things can get in the future if we do vigorously work at them including developing SOS solutions. This is in contrast to those who say the present is wonderful and needs little improvement. It is also in contrast to those who say the present may be wonderful or not so wonderful but some invisible hands or automatic forces of Adam Smith. Karl Marx, or God will automatically improve the future.

Constantly Seeking Higher Goals

This list is in random order. Some of the items overlap or interact, but it is better to overlap than leave gaps in this context. It is appropriate perhaps to have the last facilitator relate to constantly seeking higher goals. Traditional goal-seeking leads to compromises. Worse, it can lead to one side trying to win 100% and the other side losing 100%, but the war, strike, litigation, or other negative dispute resolution leads to both sides losing close to 100%. Obviously seeking higher goals is more likely to result in higher goal achievement than seeking lower goals, including SOS goal achievement. The counterargument sometimes made is that higher goals lead to frustration because of the gap between goals and achievement. There may be more frustration in fully achieving low goals that provide a low quality of life when others are doing better. High societal goal-seeking (including SOS solutions) is facilitated by all of the above factors, but it is a factor in itself because high goal-seeking tends to become a self-fulfilling prophecy.

THE MISSED OPPORTUNITIES PROBLEM

What are the ways of encouraging policy makers to avoid missed policy opportunities? This gets into the SOS facilitators, including such things as: A two party system, which provides more than one source of partisan ideas for dealing with policy problems. Separation of power, which provides more than one branch of government for suggesting ideas. Federalism, which provides more than one level of government for suggesting ideas. Elections, which enable the public to punish the incumbents and challengers who do not solve problems, and reward the challengers or incumbents who offer ideas that sound like they can solve problems.

Facilitating multiple interest groups as sources of ideas; or at least allowing them to have virtually unlimited free speech to advocate and inform. Encouraging policy programs with universities as sources of ideas, with articles and book writing and paper presenting. Encouraging think tanks, with contracts and grants and contributions for developing policy ideas.

In Chapter 22 of *Professional Developments in Policy Studies* (Greenwood, 1993), we talk about improving policy analysis institutions. One source of ideas that needs to be mentioned is having each government agency have a unit within it that deals with policy evaluation and the development of new policy ideas. Those units now exist in all cabinet-level departments and in many subdepartment units. There are also evaluation programs associated with Congress, like the Congressional Budget Office, the Office of Technology Assessment, the Congressional Research Service, and the General Accounting Office (GAO). The White House has the domestic policy staff, the Office of Management and Budget. The courts have the judicial research and evaluation unit at the federal level.

Associations that deal with public policy—including social science, political science, public policy, public administration—have members who are academics and practitioners. Publishing entities or firms publish relevant books and journals and newsletters. There are funding sources that put money up for policy research, like the Ford Foundation, the Rockefeller Foundation, the National Science Foundation, the Carnegie Corporation.

We mentioned think tanks, which tend to be independent institutes. There are also research institutes that are associated with universities that are separate from teaching programs, like the Institute for Government and Public Affairs at the University of Illinois. There are also associations of governments, like the United Nations, the European Union, the North American Free Trade Association, the General Agreement on Tariffs and Trade, or the World Health Organization. They all are concerned with trying to develop policies for dealing with world problems in their fields of interest, including the International Labor Organization, the Food and Agriculture Organization, and other organizations that are regional, like the United Nations Economic Commission on Africa. The World Bank is also involved.

There should be technology transfer or ideas transfer at entities. This includes the U.S. Agency for International Development or the U.S. Information Agency on an international basis. Within the United States the relevant organs would include the National Conference on State Legislatures, which exchanges information by way of publications and annual conferences. This is not an academic association, but more an association of state governments.

All of these are fairly neutral ways of encouraging policy ideas. One could say that the conservative approach is to rely on the private sector more, which would include private-sector think tanks, although they are nonprofit rather than commercial, like the American Enterprise Institute. Liberals would rely more on government agencies as a source of ideas, like the GAO.

Chapter 8 _____

WIN-WIN CREATIVITY AND GENERATORS

There are about ten different ways of arriving at super-optimum solutions. The list could be used as a checklist to prod one's mind into thinking of solutions to specific problems. This chapter will discuss the generators in random order.

MORE RESOURCES TO SATISFY ALL SIDES

Expanding the Resources

An example might include well-placed subsidies and tax breaks that would increase national productivity and thus increase the gross national product and income. Doing so would enable the tax revenue to the government to increase even if the tax rate decreases. This would provide for a lowering of taxes, instead of trying to choose between the liberal and conservative ways of raising them. It would also provide for increasing both domestic and defense expenditures, instead of having to choose between the two.

Third-Party Benefactor and Well-Placed Incentives

Some situations involve a third-party benefactor that is usually a government agency. An example is government food stamps, which allow the poor to obtain food at low prices, while farmers receive high prices when they submit the food stamps they have for reimbursement. Another example is rent supplements, which allow the poor to pay low rents, but landlords receive even higher rents than they would otherwise expect.

MORE EFFICIENCY IN ACHIEVING GOALS

Setting Higher Goals

An example of setting higher goals than what was previously considered the best while still preserving realism might include the Hong Kong labor shortage with unemployment at only 1%. Hong Kong is faced with the seeming dilemma of having to choose between foregoing profits (by not being able to fill orders due to lack of labor) and opening the floodgates to mainland Chinese and Vietnamese (in order to obtain more labor). A super-optimum solution might involve adding to the labor force by way of the elderly, the disabled, and mothers of preschool children. It also would provide more and better jobs for those who are seasonally employed, part-time employed, full-time employed but looking for a second job, and full-time employed but not working up to their productive capacity.

Decreasing the Causes of the Conflict

An example of removing or decreasing the source of the conflict between liberals and conservatives, rather than trying to synthesize their separate proposals, would be concentrating on having a highly effective and acceptable birth control program to satisfy both proponents and opponents of abortion, since abortions would then seldom be needed. Another example would be concentrating on a highly effective murder-reduction program to satisfy both proponents and opponents of capital punishment. Such a murder-reduction program might emphasize gun control, drug medicalization, and reduction of violence socialization.

Redefining the Problem

Quite often a highly emotional controversy between liberals and conservatives may be capable of being resolved beyond the best expectations of each side through the approach of redefining the problem. They may be arguing over how to deal with a problem that is really relatively unimportant in terms of achieving their goals, as contrasted to a more important problem on which they might be likely to get mutually satisfying agreement. This involves seeing beyond a relatively superficial argument to the higher level goals that are endorsed by both liberals and conservatives, although possibly not to the same relative degree.

Increasing Benefits and Decreasing Costs

There are situations where one side can receive big benefits but the other side incurs only small costs. An example is in litigation where the defendant gives products that it makes. The products may have high market value to the plaintiff, but low variable or incremental cost to the defendant, since the defendant has already manufactured the products or can quickly do so.

Early Socialization

The socialization matter could be discussed across every field of public policy. If one is going to have a super-optimum society, then it is important what kinds of attitudes children have with regard to discrimination, poverty, world peace, crime, education, consumer-merchant relations, labor-management relations, free speech, and fair procedure. One could even say that the key purpose, or a key purpose of public policy, is to provide for a socialization environment in which children have socially desired attitudes on every field of public policy. If that is done properly, then a good deal of the problems of what policies to adopt will take care of themselves because the need for public policy will be lessened. If children, for instance, are imbued with more of the idea of judging each other in terms of their individual characteristics rather than in terms of ethnic characteristics, then we have less need for public policies dealing with racism because there is likely to be a lot less racism.

The Technological Fix

The second level of insight is to communicate a recognition that such super-optimum solutions are realistically possible and not just conceptually possible. A good example relates to the ozone problem and the use of fluorocarbons in hair sprays and other aerosol containers. As of about 1985, such devices represented a serious threat to depleting the ozone layer and thereby causing a substantial increase in skin cancer throughout the world. The solution was not to rely on an unregulated marketplace, which normally provides almost no incentives to manufacturers to reduce their pollution. The solution was not regulation or prohibition, which tends to be evaded, is expensive to enforce, and is enforced with little enthusiasm given disruptions that might occur to the economy. The most exciting aspect of the solution (although the problem is not completely solved) was the development of new forms of spray propellant that are less expensive for manufacturers to use and simultaneously not harmful to the ozone layer.

This kind of solution tends to be self-adopting since manufacturing firms, farmers, and others who might otherwise be polluting the environment now have an important economic incentive to adopt the new low-polluting methods because they reduce the expenses of the business firm. This approach does require substantial research and substantial government subsidies for research and development as contrasted to paying the polluters not to pollute, which is even more expensive and often not so effective, because they may take the money and pollute anyhow. The business firms generally do not have capital for that kind of research and development, or the foresight or forbearance which public policy and governmental decision-making may be more capable of exercising. This includes international governmental decision makers, as well as those in developing nations.

Contracting out to Multiple Firms with Societal Strings Attached

As for how the super-optimum solution operates, it involves government ownership, but all the factories and farms are rented to private entrepreneurs to develop productive and profitable manufacturing and farming. Each lease is renewable every year, or longer if necessary to get productive tenants. A renewal can be refused if the factory or farm is not being productively developed, or if the entrepreneur is not showing adequate sensitivity to workers, the environment, and consumers.

As for some of the advantages of such an SOS system, it is easier not to renew a lease than it is to issue injunctions, fines, jail sentences, or other negative sanctions. It is also much less expensive than subsidies. The money received for rent can be an important source of tax revenue for the government to provide productive subsidies elsewhere in the economy. Those subsidies can be used especially for encouraging technological innovation-diffusion, the upgrading of skills, and stimulating competition for market share, which can be so much more beneficial to society than either socialistic or capitalistic monopolies. The government can more easily demand sensitivity to workers, the environment, and consumers from its renters of factories and farms than it can from itself. There is a conflict of interest in regulating oneself.

International Economic Communities

An exciting new development with regard to international interaction to deal with shared policy problems is the international economic community (IEC). It involves a group of countries agreeing to remove tariff barriers to the buying and selling of goods among the countries as a minimum agreement to constitute an IEC. The agreement may also provide for removal of immigration barriers to the free flow of labor, and a removal of whatever barriers might exist to the free flow of communication and ideas. The European Economic Community is a good example, but other examples are developing in North America, Africa, Asia, and East Europe.

The alternative of having an economic community does well on the conservative goal of preserving national identity, since no sovereignty is lost in an IEC, as contrasted to the sovereignty that is lost in a world government or a regional government. The IEC may also add to the national stature of the component parts by giving them the increased strength that comes from being part of an important group. Thus, France may have more national stature as a leader in the European Economic Community than it has alone.

Likewise, the alternative of having an economic community does well on the liberal goal of promoting quality of life in terms of jobs and consumer goods. Jobs are facilitated by the increased exporting that the IEC countries are able to do. Jobs may also be facilitated by free movement to countries in the IEC that have a need for additional labor. Consumer goods are facilitated by the increased importing that the IEC countries are able to do without expensive tariffs.

MORE COMBINATIONS OF ALTERNATIVES

Big Benefits on One Side, Small Costs on the Other

An example of this kind of SOS will be discussed in Chapter 18—the case of growers versus farmworkers in Illinois. The essence of the solution is that the growers agree to deposit $100,000 to begin an employee credit union. Depositing $100,000 costs nothing to the growers since it is insured by the federal government and can be withdrawn after an agreed-upon time period, possibly even with interest. The $100,000, however, serves as the basis for the beginning of an economic development fund that enables the workers through real estate leveraging to obtain a mortgage for building over $500,000 worth of housing as a big improvement over their current housing. The existence of the credit union also enables them to avoid having to get advances from the growers, which generates a lot of friction as a result of alleged favoritism in giving and collecting the advances. There are other elements involved, too, such as new grievance procedures and reports regarding compliance with other rules governing the working conditions of migratory labor. The essence of the solution, though, is that both sides come out ahead of their original best expectations.

Combining Alternatives

An example of combining alternatives that are not mutually exclusive is combining government-salaried legal-aid attorneys with volunteer attorneys. Doing so could give the best of both public-sector and private-sector approaches to legal services for the poor. Another example is combining tax-supported higher education plus democratic admission standards with contributions from alumni and tuition plus merit standards. Doing so results in universities that are better than pure government ownership or pure private enterprise.

Developing a Multifaceted Package

One can develop a package of alternatives that would satisfy both liberal and conservative goals. An example is pretrial release where liberals want more arrested defendants released prior to trial, and conservatives want a higher rate of appearances in court without having committed a crime while released. The package that increases the achievement of both goals includes better screening, reporting in, notification, and prosecution of no-shows, as well as reduction of delay between arrest and trial.

Sequential SOS

We can put the land reform example in with sequential SOS. The current verbalization does not say anything about encouraging the landless peasants to subsequently upgrade their skills to be able to take on nonagricultural work, or to upgrade the skills of their children. We could change the SOS definition to say simultaneously or sequentially. One drawback is that there is subjectivity and favoritism as to which alternative goes first. Simultaneity has an air of equality and equity; doing it sequentially may be essential in terms of developing feasibility. It is not so feasible to do various alternatives or goals simultaneously.

JURY-SIZE EXAMPLE

We could go down the list of approaches to generating SOS solutions and see how they apply here to the jury-size example (see Table 8–1; Chapter 21 also discusses jury size in detail).

Expand the resources available. There is a limited pool of stenotypists; they have to be able to stenotype over 200 or 225 words per minute. It is a difficult program to get into, and especially to pass. The videotape machine in effect creates many instant expert people who are better than the stenotypists.

Videotaping does involve setting higher goals by saying that we want every word exactly as it was said, with no ad-libbing. We also want to be able to see and hear. It provides big benefits at lower costs.

The idea of a third-party benefactor is not so relevant. The government is paying for the videotaping, but the government was paying for the stenotyping before. The government comes in as a third-party benefactor when there is a low-income litigant who wants to appeal. Such a person cannot afford to buy an expensive transcript, so the government pays for it. The money goes to the stenotypist. It is like a voucher. The videotaping eliminates the cost of transcribing, which occurs instantly when the taping is occurring. The government pays for the taping for rich people and poor people. Everybody is better off in that sense.

Every approach to generating an SOS solution does not have to apply to every solution. There is no way of combining a 6-person jury and a 12-person jury unless two juries sit in on every case for experimental purposes. This would not make sense, nor would alternating the juries.

Removing the source of the conflict is not relevant here, except in the sense of decreasing litigation. Then one does not have to decide how to structure trials if litigation is way down. This can be done by moving a lot of civil cases into

Table 8–1
6-Person Versus 12-Person Juries

CRITERIA ALTERNATIVES	C GOAL Convict the Guilty	L GOAL Acquit the Innocent	N TOTAL (Neutral Weights)	L TOTAL (Liberal Weights)	C TOTAL (Conservative Weights)
C ALTERNATIVE 6-Person Juries	4	2	12	10	14*
L ALTERNATIVE 12-Person Juries	2	4	12	14*	10
N ALTERNATIVE Between 6 and 12 or < unanimity	3	3	12	12	12
SOS ALTERNATIVE Videotaping or Note-taking	5	5	20	20**	20**

NOTES:

1. Videotaping allows judges and juries to view during deliberations what was said at the trial. Doing so facilitates accurately resolving disputes over the evidence so as to increase the probability of convicting the truly guilty, and simultaneously increase the probability of acquitting the truly innocent.

2. Note-taking may also improve recall and the accuracy of decision-making, as can allowing jurors to ask questions of the judge or the lawyers, or providing special training to jurors as to the meaning of relevant phrases and procedures.

3. Those matters are likely to do more for convicting the truly guilty than switching from 12- to 6-person juries. They are also likely to do more for acquitting the truly innocent than retaining the 12-person jury. This is an example of redefining the problem in terms of the goals, rather than the alternative.

 * = The winning alternative before considering the SOS alternative.

** = The alternative that simultaneously does better than the conservative alternative on the conservative totals, and better than the liberal alternative on the liberal totals.

a speedy administrative proceeding and decreasing criminal cases by taking the profits out of drug-dealing.

The package of alternatives provides a set of ways of increasing the accuracy of jury decision making, including videotaping, notetaking, asking questions of the judge or the lawyers, advanced training programs, and right to counsel on both sides.

Redefining the problem in terms of the goals means how to improve both convicting the guilty and acquitting the innocent. The intermediate goal is getting an accurate transcript at low cost.

METHODS FOR GENERATING ADDITIONAL POLICY ALTERNATIVES

The following list contains a variety of methods for generating policy alternatives or nonpolicy decisional alternatives. The list can also be used for generating criteria, although generating alternatives is more an act of creativity than generating the criteria for judging the alternatives.

The list is organized in terms of pushing factors, facilitators, and pulling factors. This three-part organization comes from Frederick Jackson Turner's analysis of the causes of people moving west in the 1800s. The pushing factors included undesirable aspects of the east, such as crowdedness, lack of jobs, and debts. Facilitating factors included wagon trails, railroads, river systems, and other means of transportation. Pulling factors included attractions in the west, such as free land and business opportunities.

This chapter is not based on the kind of number crunching as found in so many social science articles, although it is based on years of participant observation. It is not based on seeing how many citations can be included as found in many legalistic articles, although it has a reference list of useful and relevant books. Nor is it based on personal anecdotes as so often occurs in the writing of practitioners, although each principle can be supported by case studies. The chapter emphasizes general ideas about generating ideas, which may be the most important skill to be developed by public administrators, social science scholars, or anybody.

Pushing Factors

Other People

Talk with someone else about generating alternatives. Trying to explain alternative ways of achieving something with an audience listening stimulates more ideas than either talking or thinking to oneself. Put one's head together with someone else who is trying to come up with ideas. The interaction of two or more people trying to generate ideas tends to work better than one person alone.

Have contact with stimulating colleagues via correspondence, conventions, informal campus relations, or other on-the-job relations. Work with graduate students and undergraduates to develop dissertations, seminar papers, and term papers. Work with different people to provide a variety of interaction.

Arrange to be asked questions by people with a variety of orientations, including sincere inquiry, skepticism, cynicism, and even a touch of malice. Try to operate in an interdisciplinary environment for a greater variety of perspectives. Apply one's creative ideas to see what happens in practice.

Commitments

Accept a commitment to write an article, a book chapter, or a conference paper on how to deal with a policy problem. This is likely to generate new alternatives.

Teach in those fields in which one wants to generate policy alternatives. Take on obligations to coauthor articles, chapters, or papers. Take on obligations to do consulting work that involves generating alternatives. Prepare grant proposals. Arrange for competitive situations as a stimulus to developing new ideas.

Facilitators

Literature

Consult the literature in the field. There may be many alternatives already suggested. There are some software checklists that might be worth trying, such as "Trigger" published by Thoughtware (2699 S. Bayshore Drive, Suite 1000a, Coconut Grove, FL 33133) and the "Idea Generator" published by Experience in Software, Inc. (2039 Shattuck Avenue, Suite 401, Berkeley, CA 94701).

Keep up with the newest ideas in various policy fields. Read thought-provoking literature. Know the general literature in the fields in which one is interested. Read some of the literature on creativity, including the list of references attached to this chapter.

Have theoretical frameworks that can serve as checklists and prods for developing alternatives. Be familiar with the methods of knowing, including how to inductively generalize, how to deduce conclusions, how to determine what authorities hold, and how to do sensitivity analysis. Think about ways of generating ideas like this list, or adding to this list.

Working Style

Talk out loud about the possible alternatives. Dictating is better than thinking in generating ideas. Delegate work to others in order to have more time to think. Have a pencil and paper handy at all times or dictating equipment to write or dictate ideas that come to one's mind before they are lost.

Schedule time periods for creative development and implementation of ideas. The more time periods the better. Occasionally travel in order to provide a variety of environments.

Have good assistance on matters that relate to office management, data processing, library work, secretarial help, computer programming, and the like. Take a break and then come back to a problem, especially after a night's sleep, which may bring forth new ideas. Clarify to oneself the general areas in which one wants to be creative. Think positively about one's capability to develop alternatives and answers.

Multi-Criteria Decision Making

Try listing some alternatives, even if one or two come to mind to begin with. Merely trying to generate a list tends to result in more items being listed than one originally had in mind or thought one had in mind. After generating some alternatives, then generate some criteria for evaluating them. This will lead to more alternatives. After generating alternatives and criteria, then generate some relations between the alternatives and criteria. This will lead to more alternatives. After generating alternatives, criteria, and relations, then generate some initial conclusions. This may lead to more alternatives. After generating alternatives, criteria, relations, and initial conclusions, then do various forms of sensitivity analysis designed to determine what it would take to bring a second- or other-place alternative up to first place. This may generate still more alternatives.

If there is a situation where there are two conflicting sides, each one favoring a different alternative, look to see what kind of alternative might satisfy the goals of both sides. If there is a situation where there are conflicting sides, each favoring a different alternative, look to the possibility of a compromise alternative that will partially satisfy each side if it is not possible to find an alternative that will fully satisfy both sides.

When observing how the alternatives score on the criteria, ask how each alternative can be improved. Try to convert the alternatives, criteria, relations, tentative conclusions, and sensitivity analysis into a publishable table with notes. This may generate new alternatives.

Pulling Factors: Rewards

Be motivated to want to generate alternatives. Arrange to be in situations where one is rewarded for generating alternatives. Explicitly think about the benefits one receives from generating alternatives, such as recognition, grants, publishing opportunities, graduate students, consulting opportunities, and so on. Nonintellectual rewards can also be arranged for. These might include money, power, love, food, sleep, pure recreation, and so on. Operate in a permissive environment that encourages experimentation and new ideas. The earlier one can get into such an environment the better, preferably starting at birth.

Some people use heredity as an excuse for not being brighter or more creative. In both areas, there is a substantial range in which each person can operate. If one is more determined, then one can operate closer to the top (rather than the bottom) of one's inherited range. Creativity is probably less a matter of heredity than intelligence is. It is more susceptible to the kind of pushing, facilitating, and pulling factors mentioned above. Thus one can more easily arrange to be a more creative person than one can arrange to be a brighter person by seeking more favorable occurrences of those factors. Doing so can be rewarding in itself, as well as producing the kinds of rewards mentioned above. The broader rewards accrue not only to the individual, but also to the many potential beneficiaries of individual creativity. It is an ability well worth stimulating by both society and by oneself.

REFERENCE LIST OF BOOKS DEALING WITH CREATIVITY RELEVANT TO GENERATING DECISIONAL ALTERNATIVES

Baker, Sam. *Your Key to Creative Thinking: How to Get More and Better Ideas* (Harper & Row, 1962).

Campbell, David. *Take The Road to Creativity and Get Off Your Dead End* (Center for Creative Leadership, 1977).

Gabriel, H. W. *Techniques of Creative Thinking for Management* (Prentice-Hall, 1970).

Hare, Paul. *Creativity in Small Groups* (Sage, 1981).

Koestler, Arthur. *The Art of Creation* (Macmillan, 1964).

Lasswell, Harold. *The Future of Political Science* (Atherton, 1963). See the two chapters on "Cultivation of Creativity."

Lichtgarn, Fred. *Basic Components of Creativity* (Aim Publications, 1979).

Nierenberg, Gerard. *The Art of Creative Thinking* (Simon & Schuster, 1982).

Osborn, Alex. *Applied Imagination: Principles and Procedures of Creative Problem Solving* (Scribner's, 1963).

Rothenberg, Albert. *The Emerging Goddess: The Creative Process in Art, Science, and Other Fields* (University of Chicago Press, 1979).

Stein, Morris and Shirley Heinze. *Creativity and the Individual: Summaries of Selected Literature in Psychology and Psychiatry* (Free Press, 1960).

Taylor, Calvin and Frank Barron (eds.). *Scientific Creativity: Its Recognition and Development* (Wiley, 1963).

Zaltman, Gerald, Robert Duncan, and Jonny Holbek. *Organizations and Innovation* (Wiley, 1973).

Zeleny, Milan. *Multiple Criteria Decision Making* (McGraw-Hill, 1982). See the chapter on "Invention of Alternatives and Conflict Dissolution."

Chapter 9

WIN-WIN METHODS

The essence of super-optimizing methods can be summarized in the following seven elements or steps that relate to alternatives, goals, relations, total scores, and internal consistency from conservative, liberal, and neutral perspectives. The seven elements also include finding a super-optimizing alternative and subjecting it to a what-if analysis.

THE INPUTS

For a given policy controversy, what is the conservative alternative or *alternatives?* What is the liberal alternative or alternatives? What is a neutral or compromise alternative between the conservative and liberal alternatives?

What goal or *goals* are conservatives seeking to achieve in the policy controversy? What goal or goals are liberals seeking to achieve? Are there some neutral goals that are about equally accepted by conservatives and liberals?

How does each *alternative score on each goal*, using a 1–5 scale where 5 = highly conducive to the goal, 4 = mildly conducive, 3 = neither conducive nor adverse, 2 = mildly adverse, and 1 = highly adverse to the goal?

THE OUTPUTS

What is the *total score for each alternative* when the goals are neutrally or equally weighted at 2 on a 1–3 scale, where 3 = relatively high importance, 2 = relatively middling importance, and 1 = relatively low importance? What is the total score for each alternative when the goals are given conservative weights? A 3 is a conservative weight for a conservative goal, and a 1 is a conservative weight for a liberal goal if no better information is available. What is the total score for each alternative when the goals are given liberal weights?

A 3 is a liberal weight for a liberal goal, and a 1 is a liberal weight for a conservative goal.

Is there *internal consistency* in the table such that the conservative alternative wins on the conservative totals, and the liberal alternative wins on the liberal totals? If not, why not?

SUPER-OPTIMIZING

What *super-optimum alternative* or alternatives might be suggested that would score high enough on each of the goals so the SOS alternative would win over the conservative alternative on the conservative totals, and simultaneously win over the liberal alternative on the liberal totals?

What *defects* might exist in the proposed super-optimum alternative that might require changing the proposal? How well can the SOS alternative do if we change the alternatives or goals so as to add, subtract, subdivide, or consolidate alternatives or goals?

SOS TABLES IN GENERAL

Symbols in these tables include: C = conservative, L = liberal, N = neutral, S = super-optimum, #1 = group 1, #2 = group 2.

The 1–5 scores showing relations between alternatives and goals have the following meanings: 5 = the alternative is highly conducive to the goal, 4 = mildly conducive, 3 = neither conducive nor adverse, 2 = mildly adverse, 1 = highly adverse.

The 1–3 scores showing the relative weights or multipliers for each goal have the following meanings: 3 = this goal has relatively high importance to a certain ideological group, 2 = relatively middling importance, 1 = relatively low but positive importance.

A single asterisk shows the winning alternative on this column before considering the SOS alternative. A double asterisk shows the alternative that simultaneously does better than the conservative alternative on the conservative totals, and better than the liberal alternative on the liberal totals (see Table 9–1).

CHINA EXCESS POPULATION PROBLEM

Relevant causes of excess children in the China population context include: (1) The need for adult children to care for their elderly parents, which could be better handled through social security and/or jobs for the elderly. (2) The need for extra children to allow for child mortality, which could be better handled through better child health care. (3) The need for male children in view of their greater value, which could be better handled through providing more opportunities for females. (4) The lack of concern for the cost of sending children to

Table 9-1
A Simplified SOS Table

CRITERIA ⟍ ALTERNATIVES	C GOAL C =3 L=1	L GOAL C=1 L=3	N TOTAL (Neutral Weights)	C TOTAL (Conservative Weights)	L TOTAL (Liberal Weights)
C ALTERNATIVE	2	4	12	14*	10
L ALTERNATIVE	4	2	12	10	14*
N ALTERNATIVE	3	3	12	12	12
SOS ALTERNATIVE	>3.5	>3.5	>14	>14**	>14**

Table 9-2
Super-Optimizing Analysis Applied to the China Excess Population Problem

CRITERIA ⟍ ALTERNATIVES	C GOAL Small Families	L GOAL Reproductive Freedom	N TOTAL (Neutral Weights)	L TOTAL (Liberal Weights)	C TOTAL (Conservative Weights)
C ALTERNATIVE Strict One-Child Policy	4	2	12	10	14*
L ALTERNATIVE Flexible on Family Size	2	4	12	14*	10
N ALTERNATIVE One child with exceptions allowed	3	3	12	12	12
SOS ALTERNATIVE Remove Causes of Excess Children	5	5	20	20**	20**

college, which could be better handled through a more vigorous program of recruiting rural children to college (see Table 9–2).

It is not a super-optimum solution to provide monetary rewards and penalties in this context because: (1) The monetary rewards for having fewer children enable a family to then have more children. (2) The monetary punishments for having more children stimulate a family to have still more children to provide offsetting income. (3) The monetary rewards and punishments are made meaningless by the simultaneous policies that are increasing prosperity in rural China.

SEVEN ELEMENTS PER ISSUE

For each issue, we need seven elements: (1) what is the issue, (2) the conservative alternative, (3) the conservative goal, (4) the liberal alternative, (5) the liberal goal, (6) the SOS alternative, and (7) possible defects in the SOS alternative. The last point is important. Otherwise the system looks too dogmatic. An SOS alternative is not a perfect alternative. It may have imperfections that especially relate to different kinds of feasibility. If the feasibility problems can be overcome, then by definition it is capable of achieving both conservative and liberal goals simultaneously, or at least a compromise alternative.

SUPER-OPTIMIZING BIBLIOGRAPHY

For further details regarding win-win or super-optimizing policy evaluation, see the following books:

Levine, David. *Reinventing the Workplace: How Business and Employees Can Both Win* (Brookings Institution, 1995).

Nagel, S. *Legal Scholarship, Microcomputers, and Super-Optimizing Decision-Making* (Quorum Books, 1993).

Nagel, S. *Policy-Analysis Methods and Super-Optimum Solutions* (Nova Science, 1994).

Nagel, S. *The Policy Process and Super-Optimum Solutions* (Nova Science, 1994).

Nagel, S. and Miriam Mills. *Developing Nations and Super-Optimum Policy Analysis* (Nelson-Hall, 1993)

Nagel, S. and Miriam Mills. *Professional Developments in Policy Studies* (Greenwood, 1993).

Noyes, Richard (ed.). *Now the Synthesis: Capitalism, Socialism, and the New Social Contract* (Holmes & Meier, 1991).

Susskind, Lawrence and Jeffrey Cruikshank. *Breaking the Impasse: Consensual Approaches to Resolving Public Disputes* (Basic Books, 1987).

Chapter 10

WIN-WIN FEASIBILITY

There are at least seven potential feasibility obstacles that need to be taken into consideration in trying to move a win-win or super-optimum solution from a conceptual proposal through the political process into an adopted and implemented public policy. These potential feasibility obstacles in random order include the following:

Technological feasibility refers to whether the alternative is capable of being developed in view of obstacles that relate to the principles of physical science, biological science, or other scientific principles: for example, environmental protection such as cleaner and less expensive processes; energy sources such as safe nuclear or massive solar energy; and an AIDS cure or vaccine.

Adoption or *political* feasibility refers to whether the alternative is capable of being passed by a relevant legislature and not vetoed by the relevant president or other chief executive: for example, drug medicalization, on-site registration.

Implementation or *administrative* feasibility refers to whether the alternative is capable of being monitored and enforced: for example, toxic waste (standards and settlement), contracting out schools (test scores, drop-out rates, time needed).

Economic feasibility refers to whether there is enough money available to finance the alternative: for example, health care, jobs for public aid recipients.

Constitutional feasibility refers to whether the alternative is capable of being judged by the courts as being in conformity with the Constitution. A related kind of feasibility is legal feasibility that refers to whether the alternative conforms with relevant statutes, administrative regulations, court precedents, or other applicable law besides the U.S. Constitution: for example, PAC restrictions. "Don't ask, don't tell," housing sweeps consent.

Psychological feasibility or changing people's attitudes: for example, judicial review, free speech, sexual harassment.

Displaced workers and businesses.

EXAMPLES BY TYPE OF FEASIBILITY

The best example of technological feasibility might be to use energy or environmental protection—more specifically, finding new technologies that are both cleaner and less expensive. The energy examples relate to finding new energy sources that are safe and can provide long-term energy. The safety problem is not so much a factor with solar energy or nuclear fusion, only with uranium atomic energy. Technological feasibility in this context does not mean that a problem is possible or impossible, but how long it might take. We can also talk about an AIDS vaccine or cure as an example of technological feasibility. The examples we want to use are those that have been suggested as SOS solutions. This does include safe nuclear energy and massive solar energy.

With regard to political feasibility, a good example might be drug medicalization. It is an SOS that has a lot of emotional public opinion obstacles, more so than any of the other political feasibility problems. It is not a problem of technology or economics or constitutionality. Another emotional problem might be skin implants to prevent teenage pregnancy. That, however, is a voluntary matter. The bigger problem is the cost, which needs to be reduced. The skin implant might be available if the cost comes down enough as part of the Clinton health maintenance organization (HMO) program. It would be a very small part of the coverage. If an emotional issue can sneak into a small part of a big statute, the political feasibility problem might be overcome. This was done in Illinois by legalizing various forms of sexual behavior among consenting adults by putting it into a total criminal code rather than making it a separate statute. This might be easier than trying to somehow educate the public.

For a good example on administrative feasibility, we might use an SOS that is subjective to apply, such as the cost sharing on toxic waste dumps, or the concept of cleaning up so there is no substantial health danger. Both of these involve some administrative problems. We could point to administrative and political problems on virtually every SOS. We could look at the review from a previous year to see where administrative problems were especially mentioned. Another good example might be electoral reform with regard to political action committees (PACs). The SOS is some kind of public funding. Meaningful rules can be developed as to who gets it and how. Administering the UN peacekeeping effort may be a problem, because it must be adopted before it runs into administrative problems trying to make sure the contract specifications are complied with. Another example is the contracting out of public schools where there is controversy over what standards should be used to determine whether the contracts are being performed well. They have already been adopted.

On economic feasibility we can mention both health care and jobs for public aid recipients. Both programs are faced with problems as to where the money is going to come from. The cigarette tax might not be enough for the health care subsidies. The money saved by getting people off of public aid might not be enough to set the public aid programs, especially since the jobs have to come before the public aid money is saved.

Constitutional feasibility gets into SOS alternatives that are questionable on whether the Supreme Court would allow them. An example might be public housing sweeps. Another example might be restrictions on campaign expenditures as part of the PAC reform. If we are going to talk about constitutional feasibility we could have a free speech example, using campaign expenditures, of a due process example using the consent provisions in the public housing contracts. The consent ideas is Clinton's SOS. There are a number of constitutional issues before the Supreme Court, but they are not testing the constitutionality of SOS solutions. One is: bans of gays in the military. The SOS solution on a sequential basis is "don't ask, don't tell." The Supreme Court may throw it out.

We have mentioned psychological feasibility, which is closely associated with political feasibility because we are talking about public opinion not being sufficiently supportive. Thus, these six kinds of feasibility are probably sufficient.

EXAMPLES BY POLICY PROBLEM

Abortion

An easy example is to take a single policy problem and show how any of the kinds of feasibility could apply, such as the abortion problem. Constitutional feasibility means that the seeking of an outright prohibition on abortion at the state or congressional level looks like it will not get passed in the Supreme Court. Political or adoption feasibility might relate to the free choice bill like the Equal Rights Amendment. Congress will not touch it for fear of antagonizing too many emotional voters. They will also argue that there is no need to do so since the Supreme Court has provided for free choice and equal gender rights.

An example of administrative feasibility is trying to prohibit abortions and make it stick, because back-alley abortions do not seem capable of being wiped out. The technological feasibility might relate to coming up with a form of birth control that would not involve anything that would be considered unnatural, but could possibly be handled as a dietary matter. This may not be technologically feasible. In developing nations the pill and even the condom lack economic feasibility.

Drug Crimes

It is constitutionally unfeasible to provide the death penalty where there is not murder involved. It is politically unfeasible to talk about legalization at the present time. It is administratively unfeasible to cut off the supply. There is no technological substitute for cocaine as methadone is for heroin. Economic feasibility comes up in the context of whether we can afford cocaine treatment programs. They would be expensive but they would save a lot of money in comparison to what is spent in trying to cut off supply and trying to deal with drug-related crimes.

Health Care Legislation

There is political feasibility in terms of getting legislation through Congress or some other legislature and getting the president's signature. We can use the health care bill as an illustrative example. It lacked political feasibility because of the employer mandate arousing too much opposition. The mandate should have been dropped and replaced by low-cost quality health insurance that employers and others would want to voluntarily buy. The mandate idea is traditional regulation. Talking in terms of incentives is a more modern win-win approach.

Health care has political feasibility given strong opposition from businesses that do not want to pay the mandate, from fee-for-service doctors who do not like the HMO competition, from insurance companies who also do not like the HMOs, and from pharmaceutical manufacturers and other health care providers that have to compete with HMOs. They are all afraid that the alliances, which are designed to represent health care consumers and get as good a health care insurance deal as possible, will choose the HMOs because they are so obviously better on both cost and quality. The motivation behind the opposition has never been communicated by the Clinton administration. Instead they have tried to appease the opposition by deemphasizing the HMOs. Clinton is trying to communicate to the public about the crime bill and maybe a little about health care, but he has some big political feasibility problems when public opinion is so far off as to what both kinds of legislation provide for, especially health care.

Regarding economic feasibility, the program had a drop from 100% to 95% and possibly 92% because there is not enough money available for subsidies that would guarantee 100% coverage. The subsidy idea in the form of a voucher is a win-win approach, meaning a partial subsidy or, more important, meaning a certificate that entitles one to buy a private-sector product. The trouble with how economic feasibility is handled in health care is that it never addressed the possibility of getting enough money by a reallocation from other governmental activities, such as defense, drug enforcement, or paying interest on the debt. It only talked about reallocation of health care expenses, like diverting money wasted on Medicare and Medicaid. It is also not politically feasible to raise income taxes, but it is acceptable to raise cigarette taxes. This did not provide enough funds.

On economic feasibility, there may not be enough money to cover the subsidies to have universal coverage if the government has to rely on a cigarette tax and a tax on luxury health care programs. The whole health care universality may be in jeopardy unless Clinton can get through the employer mandate or come up with a tax increase to make up the difference.

Administrative feasibility could be a big problem if the government were to own and operate health care facilities. It is being delegated to the private sector, especially the HMOs. There are still administrative problems, in trying to decide who is eligible for a subsidy. The criteria need to be worked out. Anybody with a family income per person above a certain amount gets no subsidy. The figure for the poverty line is about $14,000 for a family of four. The figure for a health care subsidy should be about twice that, meaning $28,000 for a family of four. Any family earning less than that would be eligible for a subsidy. A chart would be needed to indicate how much of a subsidy. If the family income is only $14,000, then there would be 100% subsidy because that would be like Medicaid; $21,000 is a 50% subsidy. One could work out a formula for using simple extrapolation: 14 is 100%, 28 is 0%, 21 is 50%, and so on for the other amounts. This is designed to show that there is an administrative problem, but it is feasible.

On administrative feasibility, there is an argument that the situation will be very difficult to administer because it covers so many people and so many health care providers and treatments. The administration is primarily through HMOs, which are generally well managed. This is part of what is meant by managed competition. It is not administration by some kind of socialized medicine with government doctors. That kind of system does tend to get very sloppy because the salaried government doctors do not have adequate incentives for efficient administration. The HMOs do; any waste on their part cuts into their profits and salaries.

There are technology problems in trying to develop new ways of manufacturing that are both cleaner and more profitable. Health care is not so designed to develop any new technologies. It is designed to spread existing technologies to people who otherwise cannot afford them. It is up to the HMOs to decide which existing technologies get included. The government may specify a certain minimum of coverage, like X rays for lung problems once a year, but CAT scans only under specified circumstances. The HMOs compete in the services they offer. The more important incentive to use modern diagnostic technology is to decrease the treatment cost.

On technological feasibility, there is nothing technologically difficult or complicated. New medical technologies are covered by HMOs unless they are extremely exotic and expensive. One can obtain the latest kinds of biomedical technology, including various kinds of transplants, all kinds of magnetic resonance imaging (MRI) and CAT scans, although not unnecessary MRIs, and not technologies that have not yet been reasonably well developed, like brain transplants. It used to be a joke to talk about penis transplants. The Bobbitt case shows that it can be done by an HMO almost as an outpatient basis at a very low cost. This is a very dramatic form of modern technology. Also on the business side one might note that the HMOs can make use of the latest computerized recordkeeping, invoicing, medical diagnosis—all of which may involve computers. They can do it better than a small fee-for-service doctor's office.

Constitutional feasibility is not so much an issue in the current legislation, but it could be if there are still important class differences. The legislation is designed to lessen those differences. That is what universality is all about: It is universality in terms of people covered, though not treatment covered. Some treatments will still be available only to the rich. This has never successfully raised the constitutional issue. It should be noted, though, that legal services available only to the rich are unconstitutional. Poor people are entitled to free legal help in criminal cases by way of the Sixth Amendment, but there is no clause about free medical help to the poor or to the middle class.

On legal and constitutional feasibility, there is nothing questionable in this legislation. The closest thing might be if people are denied certain treatments, would the denial be considered an arbitrary classification contrary to the equal protection clause. The answer is definitely yes if the denial is based on race, gender, economic class, or region. Economic class could come up. A certain kind of bypass or heart transplant may be available only to rich people. The HMO contract would probably specify that nobody gets that kind of bypass whether they are rich or poor under the $2,000/year insurance. A rich person can go to a private fee-for-service doctor and get the treatment outside of the insurance, and pay his or her own money. This may have some elements of unfairness and inequity, but it is not government discrimination. The courts have never held that the government has an obligation to do any equalizing like that. The government has an obligation to provide lawyers to the poor, but not doctors, especially not doctors for highly expensive surgery. There is no constitutional right to medicine, but if the government does provide medical treatment to some people, it cannot arbitrarily exclude others with meaning based on race, gender, class, or region. The government cannot discriminate, but the government does not have to equalize when there is discrimination in the private sector. Some business firm might argue that forcing it to pay is like taking property without just compensation. The court doesn't see this as a constitutional problem. The government has a right to force people to pay taxes so long as doing so is not discriminatory. The element of force in a nondiscriminatory way does not raise constitutional issues. Forcing someone to give up property they own does mean being compensated, but not forcing the payment of taxes.

Regarding psychological feasibility, people sometimes confuse the group practice of HMOs with collectivism or socialism, especially if encouraged to do so by fee-for-service doctors and traditional insurance companies.

Displaced workers are included under fee-for-service doctors and other health care workers who cannot compete with HMOs.

JURY DECISION-MAKING AS A DETAILED EXAMPLE

Feasibility

We can go down the list of feasibility aspects as a good checklist. On political feasibility, this is not a matter on which Democrats or Republicans are divided. On economic feasibility, the cost is low and money would be saved since stenotypists cost more than videotaping.

On administrative feasibility it is just a matter of setting up a permanent videotape machine in the back of the courtroom that can see and hear. It would have a six-hour tape and not have to be changed very often. There could be some kind of an alarm that goes off if it is not working. The worst scenario is that the machine breaks down and nobody knows about it and thus part of the trial is not recorded. No harm is done unless somebody appeals and needs a transcript. If that happens, then a new trial would have to be ordered. Thus, we would not want an alarm because the loser would always appeal knowing that a new trial would be granted. Maybe it could be a silent alarm that rings in a court clerk's office who then comes in quietly and replaces the machine. The technology is there, although it did not exist previously.

In terms of constitutionality it is not like having disruptive television cameras. This would be no more obtrusive and maybe less so than a stenotypist. Even television in the courtroom has been upheld as not disruptive to a fair trial. Psychological feasibility is the temporary obstacle. This means just plain inertia. For example, a stenotypist took down everything that was said at the city council hearing. It could have been done easier with a videotape, with more accuracy in terms of seeing and hearing what was going on and getting all the words accurately without ad-libbing or the cost of transcribing.

Regarding displaced workers, some stenotypists would be out of jobs. Maybe they could still use their skills in taking depositions, but these can be done with videotaping too. Stenotypists' skills could be used in taking dictation, although there is no instant replay. Lots of downsizing occurs as a result of new technologies. This would be an example. There should be programs for retraining that also involve job placement, wage subsidies, and day care. People should not be retained in favor of a procedure that costs less and gets a better quality product. Provision should be made to facilitate displaced workers getting new jobs.

Devil's Advocate Points

What about the cost of videotaping? The initial costs of the machine or the tapes are not very high. The cost of running the machine is less than a stenotypist. It may require no operator.

What about stenotypists being out of jobs? There are plenty of opportunities for stenotypists to work in offices, including doing dictation typing.

There is still a need for answering the question as to what the jury size should be. We do not want to evade that question. The jury size can be anything between 6 and 12, supplemented by videotaping, notetaking, and other approaches to improve the accuracy of jury decision making.

Why has videotaping not yet been adopted? It is a relatively new technology. There has been more concentration on the trade-off controversy as far as jury size is concerned. And videotaping has been viewed as a money saver rather than for improving accuracy.

There are other approaches to the 6-person versus 12-person jury problem. One could rely on anecdotes, which tend to say there is no difference.

In states that have 6-person juries the law may make it easier to convict. Or the people may be different or the cases may be different. The problem is not solved by just comparing with more states.

The approach of relying on experimental juries is defective because it might depend too much on a single case that could be biased. It might require videotaping 50 trials and playing them to 50 12-person juries and 50 6-person juries, which would be too expensive.

A deductive model may be helpful but it has the defect of emphasizing trade perspectives and possibly faulty assumptions.

MINIMUM WAGE AS A DETAILED EXAMPLE

Feasibility

From a political feasibility perspective, we can think in terms of seven sets of people who represent potential opposition, including three groups on the left, three on the right, and the general public in the middle. There are four benefits to the general public: (1) the money saved from otherwise providing public aid to unemployed people; (2) the money added to the gross national product, which increases taxes and provides income to others and an increased base on which to grow in subsequent years; (3) better role models for the children of people who would otherwise be unemployed; and (4) an upgrading of skills if qualifying for the wage subsidy means business has to provide on-the-job training and workers have to participate. It is clear how workers and employers in the program benefit. Other workers can join and other employers can join. It is open-access. On the general left is a feeling that this is a handout to business and abuses the workers with subminimum wages. The answer to that is the workers are being paid more than the minimum and business is not getting a handout. Businesses provide a quid pro quo in the form of hiring unemployed workers and providing on-the-job training (OJT), which they would not do without the program. On the right it could look like a handout to the unemployed, like public aid. The answer to this is that the workers have to work and do well enough (not to be fired) on the job and in the training program.

The key question then is why hasn't the system been more widely adopted?

The key answer is that it costs money, meaning there are economic feasibility problems. Even though the payoff may be substantially more than the money invested, the money may still not be appropriated. The difficulty of getting policies funded that have future payoffs can be indicated by the news items on tax cuts rather than using the state surpluses for investment purposes. Economic feasibility relates to both adoption and implementation. The program may never get adopted in view of the unwillingness to appropriate the money.

There may be some administrative problems, but not many because the program is delegated to private-sector employers. It is not the kind of administrative program that requires any complicated tax collecting or imaginative discretion. All the employers have to do is hire people who were otherwise unemployed and provide them with OJT, which after six months should enable them to get off the subsidy and be worth the current or raised minimum wage. This could be a one-year program. The administrative agency might be the unemployment compensation offices or the jobs program offices. This is private-sector employment, though, not working for government agencies where administrative problems can ruin the program, especially since government employers have no profit motive and may be willing to hire relatively unproductive people just to provide them with jobs. The private sector is not going to do that. The productivity aspect is in a sense self-enforcing.

On the matter of technology, one reason for unemployment is that new technologies displace workers. Another technology aspect is that OJT may especially lead to trained workers who can handle the new technologies.

There is no constitutional problem. It is not an arbitrary classification of people to say only unemployed people are eligible for these minimum wage subsidies. They represent greater hardship cases than those who already have jobs. It might be more meaningful to use the minimum wage instead of switching to health care or maybe even both.

Sources of Opposition

The key feasibility question is political feasibility, especially support for the voucher from the general public and from management and labor. Labor could be divided into the workers who are covered by the vouchers and other workers. There is also opposition from a general right wing and a general left wing that are broader than the immediate employers and workers.

The general public benefits from the strings attached to the vouchers, which require management to hire unemployed workers and provide OJT. Workers are required to take the job and the training and to perform acceptably. This results in saving taxes and various forms of public aid that would otherwise go to the unemployed workers. Other benefits to the general public include adding to the GNP as a result of doing productive work, which has multiplier effects for many other people who receive income as a result of the spending, and also by paying taxes on income received. This makes money available to cover the vouchers.

Also, there is the positive role model for one's children or grandchildren. There are lower costs from a reduction in antisocial activities that are associated with people being unemployed. The positive role models are an intergenerational effect. There is also a compounding effect if taxes are paid, which enables the taxes to be considered like interest on the increased national debt so that the government has the money available for reinvestment. That's like interest on the increment, which leads to further growth.

Other workers are also eligible for OJT so that they can increase their productivity and wages. The workers in the program are getting jobs and training. The employers are getting workers at less than the minimum wage, with their training being increased. The workers are getting paid more than the minimum wage. The right wing might object on the grounds that this is a handout program, but it is not. The unemployed workers have to perform well on the job and in the training program or else they get fired. We can think of the opposition as being the general left (intellectual liberals rather than workers), other workers, workers in the program, general public, employers in the program, other employers, and general right (intellectual conservatives rather than employers). That's seven possible sources of opposition. A good political feasibility analysis should take all of them into consideration.

Other employers who might object can always enter the program, although they may not want to hire workers that are so unskilled. This kind of program, though, could be used for any level of skill. A worker who is a lawyer, who would otherwise get paid maybe $100/hr, but who is unemployed, could get a wage supplement. This means that if the supplement is worth 20% of the market price and the market price is $100, then in theory the government pays $20 and the employer pays $80 in order to provide an incentive to hire the unemployed lawyer. In practice, wage supplements make sense mainly or exclusively for people who are unemployed who need a wage supplement in order to make them employable at the minimum wage. We have plenty of people like that, or close to it, who are on public aid or displaced workers due to tariff reduction, downsizing, defense conversion, or other reasons. The program needs to concentrate on people who would otherwise be on public aid. Unemployed lawyers and doctors are not likely to be on public aid. The unemployed lawyer can go to work generally at well above the minimum wage by doing nonlaw work for a business firm. The unemployed public aid recipient does not have much in the way of options. He may have no employer willing to hire him without a subsidy. The term "subsidy," though, should not be used in referring to these minimum wage vouchers. The worker is not getting a handout, but is doing a job. Likewise the employer is not getting a handout for hiring somebody who does nonsense work.

The general left-wing opposition does not like the idea of a substandard minimum wage or handouts to business. But this is not a substandard minimum wage, since the workers are getting paid more than the minimum wage, except the government is making up the difference. It is also not a handout to business.

They are agreeing to provide jobs to workers who would otherwise be unemployed, and to provide on-the-job training. It all adds up to a good example of a win-win solution that takes into consideration lots of different sources of opposition and political feasibility. It also illustrates the mechanics of a scoring process. In terms of a what-if analysis, one might raise the question as to whether this would be a win-win solution if management were allowed to pay only $3 an hour and the workers were to get $7 an hour. This would mean a supplement of a lot more than $4 an hour and would no longer be an SOS, because the taxpayers would be paying out a lot more than they would be getting back in terms of less public aid and other benefits, especially the saving on taxes. These workers would be paying taxes on what they earn, but substantially less than what they would be receiving.

Devil's Advocate Positions

If the management side refuses to pay more than about $1 an hour and the labor side demands about $7 an hour, then the supplement would be $6.02 an hour and the general public would definitely not be getting its money's worth. Thus, the system works only if the gap between the conservative and liberal sides is small enough so that the wage supplement, or the rent supplement in the case of landlords and tenants, can be cost-effective. This means that the cost is not so high that it exceeds the benefits that the general public would be receiving in terms of increased productivity on the part of otherwise unemployed people.

If the unemployed workers receive a supplement that causes their wages to exceed the previously employed workers who are doing the same kind of work, then those previously employed workers are going to feel rather resentful:

The newly employed workers are required to enter into an OJT program that the previous workers are not required to enter. The previous workers, though, may consider being in that program to be a benefit, not a cost. They should also therefore have access to the program if they want to be in it.

The previously employed workers are probably going to demand and succeed in getting a wage increase. It would be hard for management to justify paying the previous workers less than the new workers if they are doing the same work. The justification that management would offer would be that it is the government's money, not management money. It would be difficult for the government then to justify paying extra money for the same type of work.

In reality, there are not likely to be very many workers who are making just barely above the minimum wage to complain. The workers who are most likely to complain are unionized workers who make substantially more than the minimum wage. They have the most capability of complaining successfully because they are organized, but they are not likely to have anything to complain about since their wages are already substantially higher than the minimum wage.

Also, even the workers whose wages are substantially higher are in a better position now to demand still higher wages if people are being brought in at a new higher figure. This has a buoying-up effect on wages further up the line.

Workers should always welcome new workers being brought in at extremely high wages because it tends to raise the wage scale of the previous workers. The disparity is only temporary. Academics who are not short-sighted welcome their department adding a few new faculty members at $100,000 or $200,000 apiece in view of that buoying-up effect. Or in this case, it would be a pulling up, rather than a pushing up effect.

Another argument made against the minimum wage supplement is that it forces on an employer relatively incompetent aged people, disabled people, mothers of preschool children, and the traditionally unemployed.

However, it does not force anything on anybody. No employer has to accept the subsidy. The employer is paying from his pocket less than the minimum wage, in recognition of the fact that these people may (until they receive further training) not be as competent as previous employees. The OJT may make them even more competent than the previous employees.

The employer may object on the grounds that OJT is too expensive to provide. The government is in effect paying for part of it by way of the subsidy. This is a rather short-sighted position, since OJT will make the workers more productive and thereby enable the employer to get more out of them and thus make better profits in the long run, which may occur very quickly.

The workers may object that they do not like having to be in an OJT program. They can quit. Nobody is forcing them to be in the program. This is not a criminal sentence. If they do not want to receive the subsidy, they can go back to doing whatever they had been doing previously. Most workers, though, would welcome the opportunity to take on a subsidized job with free OJT, especially where completing the training means that one moves into a higher-paying job category.

This is not a program designed to solve all the problems of unemployment and a lack of updated worker skills. It is a minimum-wage policy in recognition of the fact that some workers may not be worth the minimum wage, at least in the eyes of the employer, unless their skills are upgraded. It is also a recognition of the fact that if the government is going to give out a subsidy to workers and employers, it may as well ask for some useful strings or repayment in the forms of hiring the unemployed and offering and accepting on-the-job training.

There may be some objection from people who feel that this is a reward to lazy people who are unemployed. This is a matter of semantics. It is an incentive to accept a job and OJT, it is not a reward. One could even view it as a form of punishment if one emphasizes the obligation to accept employment in return for public aid. It makes more sense to emphasize the opportunity to have employment and OJT. There are those who feel that the way to deal with unemployment is to punish the unemployed rather than to provide incentives to the unemployed to get jobs, and especially to potential employers to hire them. This punishment attitude might be considered not a major viewpoint that a super-optimum solution needs to appease, but it just happens that it does help to satisfy it by presenting the policy to such conservative audiences as a workfare program rather than a job opportunity program.

Part IV ———————————————

BROAD APPLICATIONS
OF WIN-WIN ANALYSIS

Chapter 11 ——————————————————

CONSTITUTIONAL LAW

GOVERNMENT STRUCTURES

Branches of Government

Line-Item Veto

The line-item veto allows the president to veto portions of a bill, rather than veto all or nothing. Having such a veto strengthens the president; not having such a veto strengthens Congress; a compromise would be to have it only for appropriation bills. A super-optimum solution might be to allow the line-item veto, but lower the override from 67% to 60%. Allowing the veto strengthens the president; lowering the override strengthens Congress. (See Table 11–1 for all of the government structures issues.)

Presidential versus Parliamentary Government

Presidential government serves for a fixed number of years. This provides for smoother continuity than a government that can be thrown out of office at almost any time. The continuity appeals to conservatives. Parliamentary government serves only until there is a vote of no confidence in the parliament or until about five years has passed. This provides for a more responsive government. The responsiveness appeals to liberals.

Presidential and parliamentary governments are equally desirable unless one weights continuity heavier than responsiveness, or vice versa. Another alternative is to redefine continuity as not meaning stability or predictability, but instead meaning expansion at a nearly continuous rate of growth, especially economic growth. Responsiveness can also be redefined in a modern way to mean that the government is responsive to the need of the people to constantly have their skills upgraded.

To better assure upward economic growth and the upgrading of skills, modern

Table 11-1
Government Structures

ISSUES	CONSERVATIVE	LIBERAL	NEUTRAL	SUPER-OPTIMUM SOLUTIONS
1. LINE-ITEM VETO	1. Strengthen president -- 1. Allow line-item veto	1. Strengthen Congress -- 1. No line-item veto	-- Only for appropriations	1. Allow but lower the override 2. from 67% to 60%
2. PRESIDENTIAL vs PARLIAMENTARY GOVERNMENT	1. Continuity -- 1. Presidential government	1. Responsiveness -- 1. Parliamentary government	-- Compromise	1. Right to continous economic growth 2. Right to upgrade work skills
3. UNFUNDED MANDATES	1. Pro-States -- 1. Requirement of funds	1. Pro-Fed -- 1. No requirement of funds	-- Recommendation or exceptions	1. Have money for federal and states through economic growth
4. CENTRALIZATION vs DECENTRALIZATION	1. Economic prosperity -- 1. States decentralize	1. Civil liberties -- 1. Federal power	-- Share power	1. Well placed subsidies and tax breaks to stimulate both economic prosperity and civil liberties
5. JUDICIAL REVIEW	1. Majority rule in civil liberties -- 1. No judicial review	1. Sensitivity to minority rights -- 1. Judicial review	-- 1. Judicial review with 2/3 concur 2. Elected judges 3. Fixed terms	1. Restrained judicial review 2. Sensitize legislators, administrators, and the public

constitutional rights should include both economic growth and skills upgrading. The constitution can also specify the establishment of institutions to assure the achievement of these goals, such as institutions like the Ministry of International Trade and Industry of Japan.

By providing for expanded continuity and responsiveness, the SOS alternative should exceed the best expectations of conservatives and liberals, regardless of the less important issues of government structure.

Levels of Government

Unfunded Mandates

The issue here is whether there should be a requirement for federal funding wherever Congress mandates the states or cities to comply with guidelines governing the environment, schools, highways, workplaces, consumers, criminal justice, or other matters.

Those in favor of the requirement talk in terms of helping the states and having decentralized government. Those who oppose the requirement talk in terms of obligations the states have for enforcing laws of the United States. The neutral position is to (1) have a recommendation rather than a requirement, (2) have a requirement with big loopholes, or (3) have a requirement for matching grants.

The issue is further complicated by the fact that conservatives want federal money for anticrime projects and projects that are helpful to business such as highways, airports, and freight-train facilities. Conservatives view the requirements as decreasing liberal legislation when it has to be funded. Liberals view the requirement as facilitating the administration of liberal legislation.

Economic growth is an SOS alternative that can provide more tax revenue for both the federal government and the states to conduct whatever functions are democratically decided. If the GNP grows, then there will be more tax revenue to all levels of government, even if income and sales tax rates are held constant. The democratic process can allow the Senate, House, and president to decide what allocation of funding they consider best, although with a strong recommendation for federal funding, since the federal government does have the most tax revenue by virtue of the federal income tax.

Centralization versus Decentralization

When conservatives advocate state power, a key purpose is often to aid business in dealing with labor. When liberals advocate state power, a key purpose is often to aid labor in dealing with business. Likewise, there is a segment of conservatives who advocate decentralization, and a segment of liberals who also do so. Their purposes, however, are different in terms of what economic interests they are seeking to benefit.

There is considerable controversy over whether economic prosperity benefits more from state power or from decentralizing. State power in the form of well-placed subsidies and tax breaks can be helpful, but decentralizing to get away from repressive regulation is also helpful.

Likewise, civil liberties can benefit from state power in the form of Supreme Court decisions designed to restrict the states from interfering with free speech, due process, and equal treatment, but decentralization can be helpful to get away from a central government that is repressive of civil liberties.

The super-optimum solution is well-placed subsidies and tax breaks to stimulate both economic prosperity and civil liberties.

Judicial Review

Judicial review means allowing the courts in a nation or province, especially the higher courts, to have the power to declare null and void governmental acts that the courts find to be contrary to the constitution. No judicial review means that the legislators and chief executives shall decide for themselves whether they are complying with the constitution. As of the 1990s in the U.S. context, this issue tends to apply only to civil liberties cases. It formerly applied to economic regulation cases, but not since the 1930s.

The conservative goal in civil liberties matters tends to endorse majority rule regarding free speech, due process for people accused of crimes, and equal treatment for groups that have been discriminated against. Conservatives as of the 1990s therefore tend to advocate judicial restraint, rather than vigorous judicial review.

The liberal position advocates a more activist judicial review in terms of nullifying governmental acts that conflict with constitutional rights. A neutral position might advocate judicial review subject to having a two-thirds concurrence rule, elected judges on the Supreme Court, or fixed terms to make the courts more responsive to the majority.

An SOS might involve educating the majority better than has been done in the past as to how the majority benefits from free speech, due process, and equal opportunity. By sensitizing legislators, administrators, and the general public to the importance of civil liberties, more might be done to protect these rights than can be done through judicial review alone.

This analysis assumes that both conservatives and liberals endorse constitutional rights, but differ as to the need and desirability for judicial review to protect such rights. The idea of supplementing restrained judicial review with appropriate socialization should appeal to both conservatives who emphasize majority rule in civil liberties and liberals who emphasize minority rights.

Restrained judicial review means that the courts follow such rules as *not* declaring a law unconstitutional (1) if it can be found to be illegal on other grounds, (2) if the law is not presented in the form of a case that involves a litigant who is being hurt by the enforcement of the law, or (3) if the benefit of the doubt does go in favor of the legislature in a close case.

CIVIL LIBERTIES

First Amendment

Evaluating Ways of Handling Freedom of Speech

The neutral position does well on both liberal and conservative totals, better than a more liberal or conservative position. This may be so because free speech is not an issue that divides liberals and conservatives the way economic issues do.

A policy that involves government funding and facilitates for minority viewpoints would encourage creative ideas and constructive criticism of government, but it seems politically unfeasible since the Supreme Court does not require it and a majoritarian Congress is not so likely to appropriate funds. The closest provision is probably requiring radio and TV stations to give minority parties free time when the major parties receive free time, and likewise with federal presidential funding, provided that the minority parties are substantial.

Unlimited free speech would allow invasions of privacy, prejudicial publicity, and unlimited campaign expenditures, which neither the courts nor Congress endorse. Those rights of privacy, due process, and minimum equality in political campaigning are the fundamental rights that allow free speech limitations under the neutral goal.

Examples of limitations under the liberal goal include child pornography, libel, false pretenses, and advocacy that leads to physical harm. All these free speech exceptions have been substantially limited over the last 20 or so years.

The super-optimum solution may be to have virtually unrestricted free speech with the exceptions under the neutral alternative emphasizing conflicts with other rights in the Bill of Rights. To win support from the conservative business community, it is important to allow for free speech in advertising products, prices, and services, especially among the professions, union organizing, and business competition. (See Table 11–2 for all of the civil liberties categories.)

Ku Klux Klan Rallies

The terms "conservative" and "liberal" are used here to refer to narrowing free speech rights versus broadening them. The terms have nothing to do with endorsing Klan purposes.

The conservative approach is to prohibit or attack the Klan rally in order to prevent it from occurring. The liberal approach is to have a counterrally or demonstration in order to show that anti-Klan feeling is stronger and more meaningful than pro-Klan feeling. A neutral approach might be to try to ignore the rally. This has the effect of allowing it to go unchallenged, and thereby to make it appear that pro-Klan opinion is stronger than anti-Klan opinion.

The conservative position is seeking to minimize the extent to which the Klan has an audience or outlets to obtain an audience. The liberal position is seeking

Table 11–2
Civil Liberties

ISSUES	CONSERVATIVE	LIBERAL	NEUTRAL	SUPER-OPTIMUM SOLUTIONS
1. FREE SPEECH	1. Government stability -- 1. Restricted free speech	1. Creative ideas -- 1. Unrestricted free speech	Some restrictions for equal protection, due process, and privacy	1. Free speech for business and labor with access 2. Socialization
2. KU KLUX KLAN RALLIES	1. Minimize disruption to society -- 1. Prohibit or attack	1. Allow diverse ideas -- 1. Counter rally	Ignore	1. Remove causes 2. Prosperous economy 3. Childhood socialization
3. RELATIONS BETWEEN GOVERNMENT AND RELIGION	1. Avoid resentment -- 1. "Pro" religion	1. Encourage creativity and diversity -- 1. "Anti" religion	Some pro aid, some anti interference	1. No aid 2. No interference
4. SCHOOL PRAYER	1. Stimulate religiosity and ethical behavior -- 1. Prayers and Bible reading	1. Avoid dogma and stimulate creativity -- 1. No prayers or Bible reading	Student led	1. Ethical training 2. Minute of meditation 3. Before and after hours 4. Prayer to oneself
5. RIGHT TO COUNSEL	1. Politically feasible -- 1. No free counsel or only volunteers	1. Accessible to poor -- 1. Salaried government lawyers	1. Reimbursed judicare, salaried criminal, volunteer civil	1. Salaried base 2. Clearinghouse 3. Training program
6. SCHOOL INTEGRATION	1. Save taxes and minimize disruption -- 1. No government-imposed racial integration	1. Improve education -- 1. Government-imposed integration, especially busing	Some busing for racial integration	1. Economic integration 2. Especially line drawing

to allow diverse ideas and is fearful that prohibiting some ideas on the basis of content can set a bad precedent regarding the prohibition of other dissident ideas.

The SOS position may endorse the counterrally in the short run. As a long-run solution, the SOS position may seek to remove the causes of Klan support by either participants or an audience. This can be done partly through having a prosperous economy that does not generate hatred against minorities as scape-goats for lack of jobs and other opportunities. It can also be done through childhood socialization and education that emphasize the importance of judging people on the basis of individual merit in order to have a productive and co-operative society.

Evaluating Ways of Handling Relations Between Government and Religion

Like free speech, separation of church and state is also not an issue that divides liberals and conservatives the way economic issues do. A prореligion position is illustrated by governments that have a specific state religion or close to it, such as contemporary Iran (Islam), Israel (Judaism), Ireland (Catholicism), and medieval governments.

An antireligion position is illustrated by governments that have sought to substantially decrease the influence of a dominant religion as part of a post-revolution activity such as Turkey in the 1920s (Islam), the Soviet Union from 1920 to 1990 (Eastern Orthodox), and France/Italy after their revolutions (Catholic).

The neutral position attempts to help religion in general but not one religion over another. This includes aid like tax exemption and grants, religious blessings at public ceremonies, and generic religious symbols on money or other government displays.

The super-optimum position allows virtually no aid or interference with religious institutions. The concepts of aid and interference are difficult to deal with in the abstract. It is better to discuss aid in terms of something like organized prayers and Bible reading in the public schools, or to discuss interference in terms of government interference with the refusal of Christian Scientists or Jehovah's Witnesses to allow emergency-room blood transfusions.

Whether the United States fits under conservative or liberal depends on what one means by virtually no aid or interference. The Supreme Court has clearly declared that aiding all religions is unconstitutional. Yet it tolerates lots of aid on the grounds that the aid is to charitable activities rather than religious activities, or the aid is too minor to be objectionable.

Simplified SOS Analysis of School Prayers and Bible Reading

The conservative position is to allow organized prayers and Bible reading in the public schools. The liberal position is no organized prayers or Bible reading in the public schools. A compromise position might be to allow prayers when they are conducted by the students, not faculty or administrators, and then only on special occasions like graduation ceremonies. The Supreme Court has not yet ruled on that position, although lower federal courts have held that if the student-led prayers are during school hours and on school property, then they are unconstitutional.

The conservative goal is to stimulate religiosity and ethical behavior. The liberal goal is to stimulate diversity and creativity and to avoid dogma and divisiveness. A super-optimum solution might be to include in the curriculum (at many levels) modules that emphasize ethical training. Such modules could be based on the Golden Rule and related concepts endorsed by both conservatives and liberals without including the theological aspects.

Due Process: Evaluating Policies Regarding the Right to Counsel

The SOS alternative refers to having a base of salaried government lawyers but with many volunteers, possibly under a mandatory pro bono rule that will someday be adopted by the American Bar Association. In order to use the volunteers more effectively, there is a need for clearinghouse activities to determine their times of availability, their specialties, the clients who need their help, and then to set up appointments at the regular legal aid offices. There is also a need for training the volunteers in the special problems that poor people have as tenants, consumers, family members, welfare recipients, and other roles.

Equal Treatment: School Integration

When it comes to elementary and high school integration, conservatives want a minimum of government-imposed integration. This can be justified on the grounds that it saves taxes and it minimizes disruption.

Liberals advocate government-imposed racial integration, especially by busing black students to white schools, although it may be too politically unpopular to bus white students to black schools. Some black schools can be converted to experimental magnet schools or to nonschools. The remaining black schools can be upgraded through programs of special funding for better facilities and teachers. This can be justified on the grounds that it improves inner-city education for the benefit of the total society.

The neutral position would be some busing and some upgrading, but not as much as is advocated by liberals. An SOS alternative might involve emphasizing economic-class integration, rather than racial integration. This may be especially important in cities where a high percentage of the public school students are black or minority, but they vary in terms of family income and economic class background. This may also be important because the ambition level of poor kids gets raised by contact with middle-class kids, whereas neither black nor white kids especially benefit from contact with each other if they are all from the same economic class.

Economic integration can partly occur by redrawing the lines of the neighborhood schools so as to provide a better economic mix for each school. Housing vouchers that enable poor families to move to more middle-class schools are also relevant. Some busing can also be used, but with more reliance on line drawing.

The results would be to save more tax money and have less disruption than a program that relies more on racial integration and busing. Also the SOS alternative might do more for improving education in terms of changing peer groups across class lines than busing for racial integration.

NEW CONSTITUTIONAL RIGHTS

Economic Growth

Economic growth refers to the annual rate of increase in the gross national product or the gross domestic product. The GNP refers to all income generated in the United States, even if it goes to some foreigners. The GDP refers to all income generated anywhere in the world that goes to Americans.

Economic growth is highly important because it provides the increased income that generates increased spending, taxes, jobs, money for government programs, and appropriations for dealing with schools, crimes, health, transportation, communications, food, housing, defense, new technologies, upgrading skills, and so on.

The conservative approach tends to emphasize taxing and spending that is helpful to investment and business. The increased investment does stimulate economic growth. Conservatives advocate increased investment through lowering taxes on the upper income brackets and lowering the capital gains tax. They also advocate spending for highways, airports, railroads, and other expenditures that will facilitate business profits.

The liberal approach tends to emphasize taxing and spending that is helpful to consumption and workers. The increased consumption does stimulate economic growth. Liberals advocate increased consumption through lowering taxes on the lower income brackets and raising exemptions for dependents and the standard deduction. They also advocate government spending for food stamps, housing vouchers, welfare, teacher salaries, health care, and other government expenditures that result in high consumption.

An SOS package can promote economic growth more directly rather than through private investment and consumption, although it does increase investment and consumption. Such a package might include the government providing (1) long-term, large-scale risk capital; (2) a stimulus to competition by readily granting entry permits into all industries and entry of foreign goods into the United States; (3) a stimulus to business and labor to adopt new technologies and upgrade worker skills; (4) funds for relocating workers displaced by tariff reduction, immigration, new technologies, or conversion from defense produc-

Table 11-3
New Constitutional Rights

ISSUES	CONSERVATIVE	LIBERAL	NEUTRAL	SUPER-OPTIMUM SOLUTIONS
1. ECONOMIC GROWTH	1. Investment - - 1. Trickle down	1. Consumption - - 1. Percolate up	- - Both	1. Package
2. UPGRADING LABOR SKILLS	1. Save tax money - - 1. Leave to individual workers and firms	1. Upgrade skills - - 1. Special government training for unemployed	- - In-between appropriation	1. Everyone in labor force 2. OJT or job-based training 3. Refundable 1% payroll tax

tion; (5) reductions in foreign tariffs to open new markets; (6) immigration policy that brings in innovative, ambitious people with needed skills; (7) free speech to encourage creativity, including suggestions to improve productivity; (8) grants, patents, and purchasing to stimulate inventions but requiring licensing to stimulate diffusion and competition; (9) an educational system that is oriented toward preparation for productive jobs and careers; and (10) conservation of natural resources and a productive, healthful environment. (See Table 11–3 for economic growth and upgrading labor skills categories.)

Other important economic indicators besides economic growth include unemployment, inflation, and measures of income equality. Big economic growth is offset if those other indicators worsen or do not improve.

Upgrading Labor Skills

The Clinton administration is proposing a retraining program for American workers. It involves the same kind of issues of universal coverage, alternative delivery systems, and payment options that the health plan also involves.

Conservatives emphasize leaving training to individual workers and firms rather than having the government adopt large-scale training programs. Their key purposes seem to be to save tax money.

Liberals advocate special government training programs for the unemployed, including the elderly, the disabled, mothers of preschool children, as well as the people in the labor force who are unable to find jobs, including workers who are displaced by new technologies, lowering tariffs, immigration, and conversion to peacetime production.

The neutral position would involve an appropriation that is somewhere between very little (as advocated by conservatives) and very much (as advocated by liberals).

An SOS alternative might include everyone in the labor force in order to increase total productivity, the GNP, national spending, and new jobs that come from new spending. The idea is that unemployed workers will benefit more from an increase in jobs in the economy for which they can apply or be trained, than they will from receiving training for jobs that are not so available.

An SOS alternative would emphasize OJT and training toward specific available jobs. The delivery system would thus be the business firms that are doing the hiring, rather than training by government agencies or by schools separate from the firms that provide jobs.

The financing might come from a 1% payroll tax that is refundable if the business firm uses the money for upgrading skills of its present or incoming workers.

Chapter 12 _____

IMPACT ASSESSMENT

The *Impact Assessment Journal* is one of the best journals on the relevance of natural science and engineering to public policy. The journal called *Technology and Science* published by MIT is better, however, because it deals with substance. The *Impact Assessment Journal (IAJ)* deals with the methodology of assessing the effects of new technologies. Almost every article has the word "assessment" or the word "impact" in its title. There is a lack of concern with substance, but that is the jurisdiction of the journal and it does well within that jurisdiction, which used to be more important in the early development of policy analysis. By now we should know how to assess impact and go onto the next stage of doing so and making some recommendations. The editors of *IAJ* show a concern for developing countries where impact can be studied more easily. This is more like an anthropological approach than one that is concerned with bringing about industry, or modernization to developing countries. We could do an article for *IAJ* entitled something like "Impact Assessment and Super-Optimizing Analysis."

This would involve pulling together the following modules to create an article: some of the general material that is included in the SOS methods handouts; an environmental protection example; an energy policy example; and a patent policy example. All three examples involve a combination of physical science and engineering, but not much of biological science. Part of the article could deal with the pig iron industry as an environmental challenge.

ENVIRONMENT

Improved processes refer to those that cost less and thereby facilitate greater profits, while at the same time being cleaner for environmental protection. This may require a well-placed government subsidy to university engineering departments or other research institutes to develop such processes. (See Table 12-1 for each of the topics discussed in this chapter.)

ENERGY

Support for the nuclear and oil industries has traditionally come more from conservative interests than liberal interests, especially in the United States. The opposite is true of solar energy and synthetic fuels, especially since the Carter administration.

Nuclear and oil do better on present business profits and tax costs because they are currently available, whereas solar energy and synthetic fuels would require substantial implementation costs, probably by both business and government.

In the long run, solar and synthetic fuels might be better for environmental safety and cleanliness than nuclear or oil, and less expensive. They would also be less expensive than oil when oil becomes more scarce.

Safer nuclear energy means safer power plants, and nuclear waste disposal with traditional uranium nuclear energy. Safer nuclear energy may also mean developing hydrogen nuclear energy, which is less likely to involve radioactivity problems.

Massive solar energy means subsidizing the development of such technologies as an economically feasible microwave in the sky to disperse solar energy across the world through concentrated laser beams. It may also mean developing better energy storage batteries and capabilities for storing solar energy for use at night, on cloudy days, and at peak usage periods.

TECHNOLOGY INNOVATION

Preserving the patent system (as it is currently operating) tends to stifle some creativity by providing for a 17-year monopoly renewable once, but frequently renewed repeatedly with slight variations. It also stifles creativity by being the basis for lawsuits designed to obtain injunctions against creative competition.

Abolishing patents can hurt some creativity on the part of people who develop new inventions in order to obtain a monopolistic patent, although as of 1990 those new inventions may be for relatively small matters rather than for new forms of transportation, communication, energy, or health care.

Well-placed subsidies could mean calling a conference of leading scientists and engineers to develop a list of 50–100 important needed inventions. The government could then announce the availability of grants and other monetary rewards to encourage the development of those inventions. The rewards could be worth more than a monopolistic patent while encouraging (rather than stifling) competition.

Changing the system by shortening the patent monopoly, requiring licensing, or having the government as an insurer against product liability can be helpful, but not as much as well-placed subsidies to encourage needed inventions.

Table 12-1
Impact Assessment

ISSUES	CONSERVATIVE	LIBERAL	NEUTRAL	SUPER-OPTIMUM SOLUTIONS
1. ECONOMIC DEVELOPMENT vs CLEAN ENVIRONMENT IN DEVELOPING NATIONS	1. Rapid economic development - - 1. Unregulated economic development	1. Clean enviornment - - 1. Anti-pollution regulations	Compromise regulations	1. Improved manufacturing and agricultural processes
2. EVALUATING ENERGY SOURCES	1. Business profits and tax cost - - 1. Nuclear 2. Oil	1. Consumers and environment - - 1. Solar 2. Synthetic fuels	- - Coal and mixture	1. Safer nuclear 2. Massive solar
3. THE PATENT SYSTEM	1. Profit - - 1. Preserve patents	1. Competition - - 1. Abolish patents	- - Change system	1. Well-placed subsidies to encourage technology

Chapter 13

PUBLIC ADMINISTRATION

There are several win-win public administration examples. There is the SOS analysis that deals with personnel administration, concentrating on the conservative position of a type of social Darwin elitism. The social Darwin idea is kind of name calling. Conservatives defend elitist standards in public administration as if they were inherently right; they reward those who do best. But that is meritocracy. The liberal position is to reward practically everybody. The SOS position is to reward those who do even better than the conservative best, but provide training so that a lot of people can qualify for even higher standards than even the conservative elitists advocate.

A second example would be fiscal management, which relates to budgeting, with an emphasis on economic growth and how to bring it about. We might talk about accountability as a third most important concern of public administrators. Conservatives are concerned about waste, fraud, and abuse, which are generally trivial sins of commission. Liberals are willing to tolerate a lot of waste, fraud, and abuse in welfare programs. And conservatives are willing to tolerate a lot of it in defense programs. One can say that both are concerned with sins of commission, but with regard to different subject matter programs. The SOS approach is to be concerned with sins of omission. The biggest government sin is to fail to adopt a program that could promote much higher prosperity, merit treatment, technological innovation, democracy, world peace, and/or law compliance. Failing to adopt a program that could more effectively achieve these goals is a much worse crime than charging the government for a personal long distance call or stealing some paper clips for use at home. For relevant SOS tables on substantive accountability, see Table 4–1, the universal values table.

ELITISM VERSUS DEMOCRATIC SHARING IN REWARDING PERFORMANCE

The issue here is how to reward performing well in public administration. The conservative approach is mainly to reward those who do especially well, thereby creating a small elite at the top. The liberal approach is to broaden the definition of doing well so there are more winners of the rewards that are available (see Table 13–1). If the conservative approach gives big rewards to the top 10% and the liberal approach gives small rewards to the top 50%, then the neutral approach might give moderate rewards to the top 30%.

The SOS approach might determine that the top 10% operates at a level of 8 on a 1–10 scale. The SOS approach might say that everyone who gets a score higher than 8 will be rewarded, but the SOS approach provides many facilitators to enable a high percentage to score better than an 8, maybe even higher than 50%.

Facilitators especially relate to subsidies to upgrade the skills of public administrators so they can perform better than an 8 on a 1–10 scale. Facilitators might also include introducing new technologies that enable public administrators to be even more productive, especially if they are trained with new skills needed to use the new technologies.

AN SOS APPROACH TO TAX SOURCES

The conservative position on tax sources tends to emphasize consumption taxes, which are roughly equal across the general public. The liberal position tends to emphasize income taxes, which bear more heavily on those with greater ability to pay. A key conservative goal is to stimulate investment. A key liberal goal is to stimulate consumption and to take into consideration the equity goal of ability to pay.

Sales taxes score low on consumption and ability to pay, whereas income taxes score higher. On the matter of stimulating investment, one can argue that relying on sales taxes rather than income taxes frees up more income for investment purposes. Therefore, the scores in the column on stimulating investment should probably be 2, 3, and 4, rather than all 4s. The justification for having a 4 on income tax is that such a tax lends itself well for giving tax credits in order to stimulate investment.

Regardless of how the different taxes are scored on the two goals, there does tend to be a trade-off. Reliance on income taxes generally does better on ability to pay than on stimulating investment. That, however, depends on the extent to which the income tax provides for meaningful credits. Likewise, reliance on sales taxes generally does worse on ability to pay than on facilitating investment.

An SOS alternative would do well on both goals. This kind of alternative might involve a combination of both taxes, but accompanied by well-placed

Table 13–1
Public Administration

ISSUES	CONSERVATIVE	LIBERAL	NEUTRAL	SUPER-OPTIMUM SOLUTIONS
1. ELITISM vs DEMOCRATIC SHARING IN REWARDING PERFORMANCE	1. Elitism - - 1. Reward high performance	1. Democratic sharing - - 1. Winners of lower goals	Reward moderate performance	1. Ask for higher performance 2. Subsidize facilitators
2. TAX SOURCES	1. Stimulating investment - - 2. Sales tax	1. Ability to pay - - 1. Income tax	Other or both	1. Both 2. Decrease tax rates but increase total taxes with well-placed subsidies. 3. Economic growth

subsidies and tax credits to stimulate increased productivity. The tax credits could also include an earned-income payment for those who are regularly working but not earning very much income and thus not having much ability to pay high taxes.

Chapter 14

THE REPUBLICAN CONTRACT AND THE DEMOCRATIC COVENANT

THE REPUBLICAN CONTRACT WITH AMERICA

The contract has 10 big issues (see Table 14–1):

1. Balancing the budget. The conservatives' key goals in this context are national security and investment. They therefore recommend reductions in domestic spending and either no increases in taxes or else an increase in the sales tax. Liberals have as their key goals health, education, welfare, and consumption, leading to cuts in defense spending and increase in income taxes. The win-win solution is economic growth, which brings in more tax revenue and reduces welfare spending. It involves improving skills and technologies.

2. Reducing crime. The conservative position is the goal of deterrence through stiffer penalties. Liberals tend to emphasize education. If we are talking about drug-related crimes, then it's the combination of prevention and treatment. The win-win solution is to deprofitize drug sales, which reduces both property and violent crimes. The deprofitizing comes by way of health care medicalization. On each of these we have the issue stated in terms of a neutral goal.

3. Reducing public aid. The conservative goal is to deter poverty and public aid partly by denying eligibility. The liberal goal is dignity and income of the poor largely by granting eligibility. Job facilitators can reduce public aid with increased dignity and income for the poor. This requires job finders, training, day care, wage subsidies, and economic growth.

4. Raising and educating children. The conservatives advocate parental choice to minimize disruption and taxes. Liberals talk about Head Start and busing directed at improving the quality of education. The win-win solution is preschool socialization in widely accepted values; using facilitators to enable families to move, including housing vouchers and economic redevelopment; and federal equalization money.

5. Raising after-tax family income. Conservatives want to help relatively

Table 14–1
An SOS Analysis of the Contract with America

ISSUES	CONSERVATIVE	LIBERAL	SUPER-OPTIMUM SOLUTIONS
1. BALANCING THE BUDGET	*National security and investment* – – DECREASE DOMESTIC SPENDING AND INCREASE TAXES ON LOWER BRACKETS	*HEW and consumption* – – DECREASE DEFENSE SPENDING AND INCREASE TAXES ON UPPER BRACKETS	A. Economic growth through: 1. Skills 2. Technology B. Economic growth resulting in: 1. - Welfare spending 2. + Tax revenue
2. REDUCING CRIME	*Negative deterrence* – – STIFFER PENALTIES AND CLOSE LOOPHOLES	*Positive incentives* – – EDUCATION-TRAINING AND POLICE PROFESSIONALISM	A. De-profitize drug sales by: 1. Health care coverage 2. Medicalization with phase-out prescriptions B. Resulting in big reduction in: 1. Property crimes 2. Violent crimes
3. REDUCING PUBLIC AID	*Deter poverty and public aid* – – DENYING ELIGIBILITY	*Dignity and income of the poor* – – GRANTING ELIGIBILITY	Job facilitators such as: 1. Job finding 2. Training 3. Daycare 4. Wage subsidies 5. Economic growth
4. RAISING AND EDUCATING CHILDREN	*Reduce disruption and taxes* – – PARENTAL CHOICE	*Quality education, esp. for low-income children* – – HEAD START AND BUSING	1. Pre-school socialization in conservative values 2. Family moving facilitators 3. Federal equalization money
5. RAISING AFTER-TAX INCOME	*Help relatively high-income families* – – TAX CREDIT PER CHILD	*Help relatively low income families* – – CHILDREN'S ALLOWANCE	A. Economic growth by: 1. Skills 2. Technology B. Resulting in increased: 1. National income 2. Per family income

Issue			
6. INCREASING U.S. NATIONAL SECURITY AND WORLD PEACE	*Save U.S. lives and involvement* — — FORTRESS AMERICA WITH MILITARY POWER AND ISOLATION	*Peace* — — INTERVENTION FOR PEACE	1. U.N. volunteer force 2. Relocation of wasteful defense dollars to economic growth
7. INCREASING INCOME OF SENIOR CITIZENS	*Help relatively wealthy elderly* — — NO TAX ON SOCIAL SECURITY AND TAX INCENTIVES FOR LONG-TERM CARE	*Help relatively not-so-wealthy elderly* — — TAX ON WEALTHY RECIPIENTS AND LONG-TERM HEALTH CARE INSURANCE	Job facilitators such as: 1. Job finding 2. Training 3. Subsidies 4. Economic growth
8. INCREASING ECONOMIC GROWTH	*Trickle down* — — TAX CUTS ON INVESTORS	*Percolate up* — — INCREASE EXEMPTIONS OR STANDARD DEDUCTION	Economic growth through productivity: 1. Skills 2. Technology 3. Competition 4. Tariffs 5. Capital
9. REFORMING PRODUCT LIABILITY LAWS	*Reduce business expenses* — — CAPS ON DAMANGES, RESTORING NEGLIGENCE, AND LOSER PAYS	*Compensation and deterrence* — — NO CAPS, STRICT LIABILITY, AND PLAINTIFF PAYS IF FRIVOLOUS	1. Reducing accidents 2. Administrative proceeding 3. Health care insurance
10. ENCOURAGING LEGISLATIVE TURNOVER	*New ideas* — — TERM LIMITS	*Voter choice and experience* — — NO TERM LIMITS	Encouraging retirement with generous pensions

high-income families by giving a tax credit per child. Liberals want to help relatively low-income families by a children's allowance. Both sets of families can be helped through economic growth.

6. Increasing national security and world peace. The conservatives are concerned about involvement and saving U.S. lives and tend to advocate an isolation position. Liberals want intervention for peace. The win-win might be a UN volunteer force with reallocation of wasteful defense dollars to economic growth.

7. Increasing the income of senior citizens. Conservatives want to help the relatively wealthy elderly by not having any tax on social security income and by providing tax incentives for expensive long-term care. Liberals want to help the not-so-wealthy elderly by a tax on wealthy recipients. Long-term care should come under health insurance. The SOS is job facilitators for the elderly who are willing and able to take the right job that might come along.

8. Increasing economic growth. Conservatives endorse trickle-down philosophies, such as tax cuts on investors. Liberals advocate percolate up philosophies, such as exemptions or standard deductions increased or earned income tax credit. The win-win solution is to encourage spending on skills and technology for economic growth.

9. Reforming the product liability laws. Conservatives want to keep down business expenses. This means a cap on damages, restoring negligence defenses, and the loser pays. Liberals want to emphasize compensation and deterrence, meaning no cap on damages, strict liability, and the plaintiff pays only if the plaintiff's lawsuit is frivolous. The win-win solution is to reduce accidents, have administrative proceedings, and provide health care insurance.

10. Encouraging legislative turnover. The conservative goal is to get new ideas through term limits. The liberal goal is to let the voter choose and put some emphasis on experience by not having term limits. The win-win solution is to encourage retirement with generous pensions.

We should note for each of these issues what general subject it comes under. We have three economic issues that relate to the deficit, family income, and economic growth; two social issues that relate to public aid, children, and senior citizens; an international political issue of national security and world peace, and a domestic one of legislative turnover; two legal issues of reducing crime and reforming liability laws; there is no technology issue.

THE DEMOCRATIC NEW COVENANT

President Clinton spoke in February 1995 on ''The New Covenant'' as an answer to the Republican Contract with America. The New Covenant contains twelve parts—reducing the size of government, tax cuts, minimum wage, welfare reform, AmeriCorps, illegal immigration, health-care reform, political reform, unfunded mandates, line-item veto, Mexican financial crisis, and assault gun ban—which will be discussed under economic, social, technology, political, international, and legal policy categories.

Economic Policy

Reducing the Size of Government

This means cutting federal expenditures. The liberal position in the past has been to reduce defense spending, but this now seems too politically sensitive to Clinton. Instead he talks about reducing various miscellaneous projects such as new energy sources or reductions in infrastructure spending and other things that take a while to pay off. He talks about shifting from public housing to vouchers. The Republicans talk mainly about reducing welfare. The neutral position is to reduce a little bit of everything, including both defense and domestic. The SOS is to replace Social Security and welfare with job facilitators; replace Medicare and Medicaid with less expensive HMO insurance vouchers; and eliminate expenditures on cold war weapons systems that have no current applicability. This gets at more meaningful spending reductions.

Tax Cuts

The liberal position has been tax cuts to encourage training by way of college expense deductions, IRA accounts, training vouchers, and $500 credit per child but only for people with incomes under $75,000. The conservatives want tax credits for children in families with income up to $200,000 and also capital gains tax cuts. Neutrals are in between on the size of the cuts. An SOS position on tax cuts would be to give tax cuts in return for doing things that strengthen the economy. This includes training but also stimulating new technologies, stimulating competition, exports, providing capital to business, and tax cuts for displaced workers. Both tax cuts and spending cuts are tied in with the deficit. Spending cuts help lower the deficit but tax cuts hurt the deficit. If economic growth can be stimulated, then both tax cuts and spending cuts can be provided. Tax cuts can occur because growth will increase the national income, which is the tax base. Tax rates can then be lowered and still bring in more money.

Minimum Wage

The liberal Clinton approach is to raise the minimum wage to $5.15 at 45 cents per year for two years. The conservative approach is either to hold the minimum wage constant or abolish it. The neutral approach might be a smaller raise than 90 cents, such as to $4.75. The SOS approach might be to provide for a minimum wage voucher. This would enable the employer to drop down to $4.00 per hour but the workers get paid $5.00 per hour because each voucher is worth $1.00. In return for the extra dollar per hour, the employer agrees to hire unemployed people and the workers agree to do well or they will get fired. The employer also agrees to provide on-the-job training for no more than about six months and then the subsidies stop on the assumption that the workers have now become trained and to be worth the $5.00 per hour minimum wage.

Social Policy

Welfare Reform

The liberal position on welfare reform puts a big emphasis on training as the way to move people from welfare to work. The conservative position puts a lot of emphasis on cutting people off to provide people with incentives to get jobs. The SOS position is a set of effective job facilitators for all people who lack jobs, not just those on welfare, but Social Security, and displaced workers. The facilitators include job placement, wage subsidies, training, day care, economic growth, time limits, and government backup position.

The AmeriCorps National Service Corps

The liberals endorse the program and would like to expand it. It provides opportunities to get and pay off a college education while doing public service. Conservatives dislike the expense and tend to think of AmeriCorps volunteers as some kind of professional liberals. The neutral position would be to keep it as it is rather than to increase it or abolish it. The SOS came up previously as part of defense policy, since national service was originally proposed as an alternative to the draft. In that context conservatives favor the draft, liberals oppose it. The SOS was to have required national service that could include going into the military. This would generate more enlistments and might improve the quality of the armed forces. It would please liberals by having so many people doing national service. We do not have a draft, but we could have compulsory national service. This might cause too many people to go into the military contrary to current personnel cutbacks. We may need a substitute for going into the military that would please conservatives such as taking care of orphanages or working in prisons or as police officers. The object is to make national service broader than just things like Vista and the Peace Corps. For now the liberals want national service because it promotes do-gooder projects and access to college. Conservatives are opposed given the expense and the disruption from what they consider meddlesome people with social work orientations. The SOS is that half the national service people should be going into anticrime work that relates to prisons and police work, and the other half can be going into health care and social work activities. The national service needs to have a set of projects available in both conservative and liberal balances. People who are already doing police work might feel that they should also be entitled to free college tuition. Perhaps they can get it through the training vouchers program, which is good only for two years, however. The justification for just giving it to the AmeriCorps people is that they are getting paid less money than the regular police and some of their salary is in the form of a tuition and fee waiver.

Illegal Immigration

The liberal position is more lenient than the conservative on allowing illegal immigration. More specifically, the conservative approach is to cut off access to public schools, welfare, and emergency health care. The liberal position is to strengthen the borders to prevent illegal immigrants from getting in. The neutral position would do a little of both. The SOS positions are to build up the home country economies so as to decrease illegal immigration; to give priorities to those who are willing to go to states that have few immigrants and to those who have needed skills; to give suspended sentences to illegal immigrants who commit crimes, so they can be threatened with twice the original sentencing if they come back; and to provide transportation money home for illegal immigrants convicted of crimes and for illegal immigrants who apply for welfare.

Technology Policy

Health Care Reform

The liberals were formerly in favor of a system that would involve employer mandates and health care alliances that would direct people into HMOs. Clinton is now proposing an incremental system that involves no preconditions, voluntary group discounts, movable health insurance, and probably vouchers for people who cannot afford the insurance with phasing out of Medicaid and Medicare, and then coverage for people in the same economic category as those who previously received vouchers. The last step of requiring the remainder to get one-bite health insurance is more controversial. The conservative position in the past has been to rely on the marketplace. They are now willing to tolerate Medicaid and Medicare but may not be willing to have a voucher program for covering new people. The new conservative position may be to keep things as they are. Conservatives keep moving to the right on many of these issues, although liberals may be constantly moving to the left. They then arrive at compromises and start over again, frequently with the same issues coming up again every few years.

Political Policy

Political Reform

The liberal position is to place limits on how much individuals, corporations, and labor unions can contribute to candidates and parties and how much politicians can receive. The conservative position is to have no limits. The neutral position is a lot of reporting but no limits. The SOS position is to have public funding as a replacement for private funding. Politicians can voluntarily adopt public funding, which they are likely to do so because it saves on fund-raising efforts and will especially do so if their opposition is doing so. This means they take no PAC money. Political action committees are free to spend their money to try to influence the public. They have a constitutional right to do so.

Unfunded Mandates

The liberal position has been to pass legislation providing for improving the environment and the workplace, for welfare and schools, and for giving money to the states to carry out those programs. The conservatives like legislation for fighting crime, building highways and airports, facilitating business activities, and giving money to the states to carry out these programs. In other words, both sides want funding for programs they favor and would prefer to see no funding for programs they disfavor. If one thinks in terms of requiring funding in the abstract, then conservatives want the requirement because they tend to be more in favor of the states. Liberals want no requirement to buy into the federal government because they are more in favor of the federal government. The neutral position is to have a funded mandate but allow Congress to deviate from it on the 60% vote. The SOS on the abstract requirement is to promote economic growth, which provides money for both the federal government and the states.

Line-Item Veto

This is a tricky issue like the unfunded mandates and there is not a consistent liberal or conservative position. It depends on what is being vetoed and who is the president and which party dominates Congress. In the abstract, liberals normally would like the line-item veto because it does strengthen the president and the president is normally more liberal than the House or the Senate if they are all of the same party. The president would be less liberal if the president were Republican with a Democratic Congress. Members of the House tend to have small rural constituencies that are more conservative than senators, who are sensitive to public opinion in the biggest cities of their states. The president is sensitive to public opinion in the biggest states in the country. Given that reasoning, one would expect conservatives in the abstract to oppose the line-item veto. The neutral position would be to allow it but only for appropriations. The SOS might be to allow it but allow for an override by Congress from the present 67% to 60%. The line-item veto strengthens the president but providing for a 60% override on line-item vetoes or all vetoes strengthens Congress. To have it apply to all vetoes would require a constitutional amendment.

International Policy

The Mexican Financial Crisis

Clinton wants $40 billion to lend to Mexico He is now providing for $20 billion in loan guarantees, using money that was already in the foreign-aid pipeline for encouraging exports or affecting exchange rates. He originally wanted to get a stronger agreement on minimum wages and environmental protection, but the new arrangement involves an executive agreement that is mainly unilateral and thereby bypasses Senate approval. The conservatives want nothing for Mexico in the more extreme version or less than what Clinton is proposing or at least senatorial approval. The SOS arrangement on international trade matters has been to emphasize benefits to business, labor, and other conservative and liberal interests. One thing to emphasize is that without the aid, there may be 700,000 jobs lost in the United States. This means a lot of businesses and workers will be hurt. Another point to emphasize is without the aid there may be 400,000 illegal immigrants from Mexico. This runs contrary to conservatives, who want to keep illegal immigrants out, and contrary to labor, which does not want the job competition. Clinton can also emphasize that letting Mexico fall has a domino effect on other Latin American countries and other countries in the world. This is an example of not changing the administration policies but communicating better to the American people the win-win justification for those policies.

Legal Policy

Assault Gun Ban

The liberals want the ban retained; the conservatives want it repealed; the neutral position is maybe to have it repealed on some assault guns and not on others. The SOS position is to push for crime reduction in order to make society more receptive to gun control. Crime reduction can be best brought about by taking the profits out of drug sales. This can come by putting drug addicts on phase-out cocaine substitutes. The object is to medicalize rather than imprison, with medicalizing taking away customers and the incentives to get new customers. Other crime-reduction methods relate to decreasing violence in the media, economic growth, education and socialization, and gun control (but that needs crime reduction to be politically feasible).

Chapter 15 _____

THE TEN COMMANDMENTS AND WIN-WIN ANALYSIS

ONE COMMANDMENT AT A TIME

The Basic Principle of Monotheism

We could say that the conservative position on the nature of God is that God is an entity that has human personality characteristics. He is rather egotistical and demands a lot of worship or deserves a lot of worship. The liberal position emphasizes that God is omnibenevolent and is more concerned with salvation by deed than by faith.

If we handle this like a multiple issues table, we could say that each of these Ten Commandments represents a different issue. For each one there is a conservative position, a liberal position, and an SOS position (see Table 15–1 for the win-win policy).

First is the issue of monotheism. There are many people who would argue that there are multiple gods. The basic argument is the nature of God. By this we mean the nature of doing good in God's eyes, or what does God consider to be good or goodness? Conservatives would say worship and faith; liberals would say good deeds on an interpersonal level and a societal level; and a neutral position would be a little of both.

On these issues we may have to define more clearly some of the terms. One could say that doing good deeds is a way of showing respect and faith, but showing respect and faith is not a good deed. One can cover the other, but only in one direction. One could also argue that God could not be all good if he rewards people on the basis of worship and faith. The SOS thus recognizes the importance of faith and respect but says that good deeds is the way that it is shown.

Not Having Idols or Graven Images

A conservative position allows for crucifixes and other symbols like the Virgin Mary, which theoretically are not idols but are almost treated as if they are.

Table 15–1
The Ten Commandments and Win-Win Policy

ISSUES	CONSERVATIVE	LIBERAL	SUPER-OPTIMUM SOLUTIONS
1. NATURE OF GOD (What does God consider goodness?)	1. Worship and faith 2. Conflicts with being all good	1. Good deeds on interpersonal and societal level 2. No discrimination on religion	Showing respect ↑ ↓ not necessarily good deeds
2. IMAGES AND AMULETS	Acceptable if not considered supernatural	Unacceptable because inevitably superstitious	Non-divine heroes of the religion
3. AUTHORITARIAN OR DEMOCRATIC	My religion right or wrong	Constructively critical	God's will that people be constructively critical
4. SABBATH	No work on Sabbath	Productive work on other 6 days and good deeds	Justify leisure to fortify or reenergize for doing good deeds
5. ATTITUDE TOWARD PARENTS	1. Authoritarian 2. Extended family	1. Permissive 2. Government services	1. Do well in one's occupation and choose occupation that does good things for others 2. Job facilitators for the elderly
6. KILLING	1. Death penalty OK 2. War OK vs Leftists 3. Prohibit abortions	1. No death penalty 2. War OK vs Rightists 3. Allow abortions	1. Reduce murder via drugs, guns, media, allocation, education 2. Promote UN peacemaking 3. Promote abstinence and birth control
7. SEXUAL WRONGDOING 1. Forced sex 2. Child sex 3. Deceased sex 4. Teen pregnancy	1. Punishment 2. Even consenting adults, in or out of marriage	1. Tolerant 2. Especially consenting adults	1. Merit treatment of women--respect 2. Sex education; abstinence, birth control, and human sexuality 3. Access to skin implant
8. STEALING	Punishment 1. Burglary 2. Mugging 3. Shoplifting	Punishment 1. Consumers 2. Workers	Get at causes 1. Lack of alternative opportunities and job facilitators 2. Increased competition 3. Joint productivity
9. TRUTH SEEKING	Be cautious about new ideas	Welcome new ideas 1. Universe--space 2. Biology--genetics 3. Psychology--consumers and voters	New + profits - prices Ideas + wages
10. JEALOUSY AND COMPETITION	Endorse competition (deregulate monopoly?)	Endorse cooperation (labor-management cooperation?)	Good competition 1. Lease networks 2. Royalties not monopoly patents 3. Seed money

A more liberal interpretation allows no statues in a church or synagogue or mosque. This is the prevailing approach among Jews and Moslems and some Protestant denominations. Even a Jewish star could be treated as a superstitious amulet. It does not have to be an image with a face or statue. One could argue that the Second Commandment was designed to prohibit any kind of superstitious idolatry in the broad sense. It would be hard to say that the First Commandment was designed to promote salvation by faith rather than monotheism, but to say that the first issue is monotheism is rather obsolete. However, Buddhists and Taoists come close to having multiple gods when they claim that they have no gods whatsoever. They claim that Buddha was not a supernatural god but a good human being. Yet they have a whole panoply of gods like the Greeks and Romans did and Hindus still do. I think the Moslems are the strictest on images and charms and allow virtually nothing like that, although they do have a star and crescent as a symbol of Islam. It depends on how it is used. If it is used on a neck chain purely for decoration or to show one is a Moslem, then that would be alright in light of the Second Commandment. But if it is used as a power to ward off evil spirits, then it is a graven image in the broad sense.

In order to arrive at super-optimum solutions we have to clarify the goals of religious conservatives and religious liberals. We may see some underlying goals after going through more of the commandments. On the second one, though, with regard to images and amulets, the conservative position is acceptable if not considered supernatural. The liberal position is unacceptable because almost inevitably the symbols are given supernatural significance. A neutral position would be to allow symbols but not images like wearing a cross or a star, or not anything that looks like a person.

An SOS position might be to fill the church, synagogue, or mosque with secular heroes or at least heroes that are not considered divine. A Catholic Church could put up pictures of the most famous popes, famous Protestants could be pictured from Martin Luther to present important ministers. Likewise, a synagogue could picture former temple presidents, or famous Jews in business, social philosophy, science, politics, world history, or law. This would satisfy the need that people have for images and heroes. It would be nondivine heroes of one's religion. They would be inspiring to liberal concerns for salvation through deeds and at the same time satisfy conservative needs for concrete heroes.

Not Taking the Lord's Name in Vain

This relates to the authoritarian versus democratic nature of religion. The conservative position is sort of "my religion, right or wrong." The liberal position is to be instructively critical. This does not mean swearing, but it does mean raising questions as to whether something in the Bible is ethically correct or scientifically correct. The SOS would be to say it is God's will that people should be constructively critical. God does not want people to be puppets. God wants people to reason and discuss and arrive at tentative conclusions through debate.

Remember the Sabbath Day

Six days shall you labor and do all thy work. The conservative tends to overemphasize no work on the sabbath. The liberal position tends to emphasize productive work, again getting back to good deeds on the other six days, even allowing for productive work on the sabbath. This seems to conflict with the literal wording on the sabbath commandment. One can argue that God is more pleased by people who do good deeds on the sabbath than by people who are couch potatoes on the sabbath. The SOS is to justify some leisure to fortify for doing good deeds on the other days.

Attitude Toward Parents

The Fifth Commandment is attitude toward parents. The conservative position tends to be authoritarian toward God and one's parents. The liberal position tends to be permissive and argue that being bratty is not failing to honor. The SOS position is that the best way to be respectful of one's parents is to do well in one's occupation and choose an occupation that does good things for others. Conservatives would also support the extended family. Liberals tend to support government services. An SOS position would be to support job facilitators for the elderly.

Thou Shall Not Murder

Sometimes it is translated as "thou shall not kill," which is better since it is broader. Thou shall not murder implies that it might be all right to kill under various circumstances. The conservative position is that the death penalty is okay and that war may be okay. Conservatives tend to be generally more supportive of war than liberals, but only in the abstract. Liberals are willing to go to war against fascism, as conservatives are willing to go to war against communism. Conservatives want to prohibit abortions. Liberals want to allow abortions. The neutral position is to consider the trimester. The SOS position is to try to reduce murder by way of drugs, guns, media, allocation, and education—and to promote UN peacemaking and promote abstinence and birth control. This is an example of where we get into secular public policy. The first three or four commandments are very God-oriented rather than society-oriented.

Sexuality Including Adultery

Sexuality (sexual wrongdoing is a better way of putting it) can include rape, child sex abuse, prostitution, spreading AIDS and venereal diseases, and being sexually obsessed. Conservatives tend to emphasize punishment. Liberals tend to be tolerant. An SOS position is to get at the causes of various forms of sexual wrongdoing, even though they have different causes.

Rape is caused by lack of respect for women. As women become more important in society they are less likely to be abused. Sexual harassment is a mild form of rape.

Child sexual abuse has a variety of causes. A key underlying cause is that child sexual abusers are mentally disturbed, although one can say that about almost all forms of sexual wrongdoing. This is definitely not true. Just because a person gets a venereal disease does not mean that they are mentally disturbed. To a considerable extent the people who engage in sexual child abuse are generally the superlosers of society who really need to take advantage of completely defenseless people. There is a need for providing more outlets for these people. The marketplace tries to do that; it would be unseemly for the government to be doing it. The situation may be getting better even though it looks like it is getting worse because of increased reporting.

Another form of sexual wrongdoing is spreading AIDS or venereal disease. This can be helped by public policy that seeks to get rid of venereal disease, which helps to transmit AIDS and which is bad in itself. Also needed is better sex education, including abstinence and as birth control education. There must be research on vaccines, semivaccines, and cures, as well as testing and requiring notification.

Any kind of sexual obsession fits in with child sexual abuse obsession. Thus we are talking about sex against someone's will (nonconsensual sex), which could include rape and child abuse if we are talking about informed consent. We are also talking about transmitting sexual diseases, which is done without people's consent—no one would consent to getting AIDS. A big form of sexual wrongdoing is teenage pregnancy, which may be based on ignorance or on lack of adequate birth control and motivation.

The conservative position is to emphasize punishment. The liberal position tends to be tolerant or overly tolerant. The SOS position on each wrongdoing is to merit treatment of women to generate more respect; provide better sex education including abstinence, birth control, and human sexuality; provide education relevant to child sex, diseased sex, and teen pregnancy; and, for birth control, there must be better education about it as well as access to birth control measures, such as the skin implant.

One might also note that adultery is no longer a crime in more than a handful of states unless it is open and notorious (indecent exposure). It does not involve forced sex, children, or disease. Its original purpose was property rights, not women's rights. It was designed to protect the husband or father from having to support a child that was not his. It always had a double standard in applying to women and not to men. It always required penetration because only then was there a possibility of conception. It was not rape to beat a woman to a pulp with total molestation and no penetration. Adultery was basically a property crime and women were property. It had virtually nothing to do with sex since it only applied to females and it normally takes one male and one female to have sex.

Thou Shall Not Steal

The conservative position on stealing is punishment, with stealing meaning shoplifting, mugging, burglary. The liberal position is also punishment, but with an emphasis on stealing from workers and consumers. The SOS position is to get at the causes. The causes of traditional crime are lack of alternative opportunities, which relates to job facilitators. Stealing from consumers can be reduced by increased competition and joint productivity with workers.

No False Witnesses

This is an endorsement for telling the truth. It would be a bit broad to say that it is an endorsement for the idea that the truth shall make us free in the sense of intellectual innovation. It does seem too narrow to say it just applies to telling the truth on the witness stand. In a broad, positive sense, rather than a "thou shalt not" it means to seek truth. In that sense, conservatives have not been so supportive of the development of new ideas concerning the nature of the physical universe, biological evolution, anthropology, or group interaction. We can say the Ninth Commandment is truth seeking. The SOS answer is that new ideas benefit conservative interests, like new technologies. Marxism is more a philosophy of what ought to be rather than what is. Truth refers to what is. The SOS on truth seeking is how new ideas can benefit all by way of greater profits, greater wages, lower prices, including ideas about the universe that relate to space, genetics, consumer psychology, and voters.

Thou Shalt Not Covet Thy Neighbor's House or Wife

Coveting thy neighbor's house, ox, or donkey sounds like thou shall not steal. Coveting one's neighbor's wife is akin to thou shall not commit adultery. These are redundant to Commandments Seven and Eight. What could the Tenth Commandment mean that is not redundant? It could mean that one should not be jealous to the point where one tries to sabotage others. Coveting has a sound of jealousy. We could say that Ten deals with jealousy and competition. Conservatives endorse competition—at least they pay lip service to it. Liberals endorse cooperation. Some conservatives are reluctant to deregulate monopolies. Liberals who talk about endorsing cooperation may be reluctant to endorse labor-management cooperation. The SOS is that competition is a good thing in the form of leasing networks (we call it good competition), royalties rather than monopoly patents, or seed money to develop competition.

Table 15–2
The Ten Commandments and the Six Universal Values

COMMANDMENT	VALUES
1. God	2--Merit Treatment
2. Images	3--Technological Innovation
3. Name in vain	4--Democracy and free speech
4. Sabbatch	1--Prosperity
5. Parents	4--Democracy 1--Prosperity
6. Killing	5--World Peace 6--Law Compliance
7. Sexual wrongdoing	2--Merit Treatment
8. Stealing	6--Law Compliance
9. Truth seeking	3--Technological Innovation 6--Law Compliance
10. Jealousy	1--Prosperity

VALUE	COMMANDMENTS
1. Prosperity	4--Sabbath 10--Jealousy 5--Parents
2. Merit Treatment	7--Sexual wrongdoing
3. Technological Innovation	2--Images 9--Truth seeking
4. Democracy	3--Name in vain 5--Parents
5. World Peace	6--Killing
6. Law Compliance	9--Truth seeking 6--Killing 8--Stealing 1-10--All

RELATION TO THE UNIVERSAL VALUES

We do not have an explicit conservative goal or liberal goal on each of these six values (see Table 15–2). We are just talking about a conservative position.

Prosperity is clearly involved in talking about competition, truth seeking, consumers, workers. Prosperity is also promoted by talking about doing productive work at least six days per week.

Merit treatment is involved in talking about women under sexual wrongdoing. We could say that God does not discriminate on the basis of religion as long as people do good deeds.

On technological innovation, it is truth seeking. Also belief in images and amulets is designed to get away from superstitious versus scientific truth seeking.

On the matter of democracy, the authoritarian bit comes in talking about no other gods or graven images or not being insulting to God or one's parents. All this is consistent with the idea of being constructively critical.

On the matter of world peace, this is where not killing is relevant.

Complying with the law is all Ten Commandments, because these are God's laws. It comes out in talking about being a witness. This implies judicial process. Not stealing or killing gets at crimes against property and persons. Thus the commandments do tie in with the six universal values. If God is responsible for these commandments, then it shows that He is a foresightful being for having foreseen the six universal values and what is good for the mutual quality of people and God.

Chapter 16 ———————————————

LOSE-LOSE AND WIN-WIN POLICIES

LOSE-LOSE ITEMS

Lose-lose includes Democrats and Republicans competing to see who can do the most cutting of spending, including spending that is relevant to long-term economic growth like developing new technologies, such as energy; or cutting spending in ways that actually increase spending, such as cutting off people from foster care or orphanages. (See Table 16–1 for lose-lose policies.)

Retaliatory tariffs with China cause China to lose out on a billion dollars worth of American goods they would like to buy, and the United States to lose out on a billion dollars worth of Chinese products that Americans would like to buy. The United States also loses out on influencing Chinese political attitudes, and on decreasing tariff barriers in the world by setting a bad precedent that other countries may resort to, claiming that they have rights to monopolize the production of certain products. This is the worst kind of tariff barrier.

Subsidizing farmers to cut back on production hurts food consumers and may also hurt farmers by limiting their access to foreign markets. Nonproductivity subsidies are the equivalent of a tariff because they enable farmers to be able to compete unfairly with foreign food, not because they are more productive, but because they are getting a subsidy for being less productive. This encourages other countries to do the same thing, thereby hurting the main way of helping the farm income problem.

Raising interest rates hurts business profits, jobs, and wages, and does not necessarily gain anything with regard to inflation, which seems to be under control and better dealt with through economic growth than through raising interest rates.

Allowing sweatshops in the United States is contrary to good workplace conditions, and they are contrary to business profits, except in the short run. Even compared with developed countries, where they make more use of automation

Table 16-1
Lose-Lose Policies in American Politics

LOSE-LOSE POLICIES	CONSERVATIVE GOALS THAT ARE HURT	LIBERAL GOALS THAT ARE HURT	IMPROVED POLICIES
I. ECONOMIC: Increased Interest Rates	Decreased business profits	Increased consumer prices and decreased jobs	Economic growth
II. SOCIAL: Welfare Cutoffs	Increased taxes and decreased welfare	Decreased dignity	Job facilitators
III. TECHNOLOGY: Decreasing New Energy Sources	Decreased business profits and decreased GNP	Decreased clean environment	Dollars for research, with such rewards as royalties, government purchases, and Edison prizes
IV. POLITICAL: Drastic Budget Cuts	Increased recession	Increased recession	Economic growth amendment
V. FOREIGN: Retaliatory Tariffs for Piracy	Increased free market	More jobs and lower prices to consumers	Use tariffs to obtain rights and to open trade, with royalties to inventors
VI. LEGAL: No Prison Dollars unless 85% Sentences	Increased taxes and preserve state rights	Decreased rehabilitation	Decrease drugs profits to reduce prison costs

than a sweatshop does, the cost of labor in the United States may really be higher than the cost of using machines, but short-sighted businesspeople are unwilling to invest in machines because it means up-front money. They are acting contrary to their own best interests and those of labor and the economy. Public policy is partly responsible by not cracking down on sweatshops and providing alternative jobs for the displaced labor and the displaced entrepreneurs. Sweatshop industries should especially be wiped out by lowering textile tariffs and other relevant tariffs in order to enable other countries that have cheaper labor and maybe even use more automation to service the American market.

The continuation of the war in Cambodia is an example of a lose-lose war in which the communists seem to be greatly antagonizing the people, contrary to Maoist principles about winning over the peasants. Some of the irrationality is the responsibility of the United States for having supported the Khmer Rouge in the 1980s when Vietnam was trying to bring some peace to Cambodia. The United States supported the communists because we disliked Vietnam even more, but for reasons that had to do with being a bad loser, not because Vietnam was acting more contrary to American interests. We now are trading with Vietnam. We are not trading with Cambodia, which has an economy that is largely in ruins, just slightly above Rwanda or what Haiti was during the embargo.

A seventh lose-lose situation is the heavy emphasis on prisons as the answer to the crime problem. The crime rate has not gone down even though the prison population has tripled since about 1980. A lose-lose situation is one in which costs go up and benefits go down, or remain about constant.

Newt Gingrich is taking a stand against NASA, even though it now has some significant potential to develop space platforms that could be used for manufacture and mining, and could bring in far more money than the future cost of NASA. The past cost is irrelevant to whether to proceed. It will be a while before space manufacturing, solar energy, and moon mining will pay off. The Republican opposition to NASA and the Democratic opposition to Department of Energy research both represent lose-lose shortsightedness, whereby we miss out on a lot of potential benefits that would well exceed the incremental costs.

Rejecting a potential surgeon general because he has performed some abortions seems irrational when he has such a good track record on reducing teenage pregnancy through a combination of motivation, abstinence, and birth control. It is irrational policy when one characteristic is given so much importance, especially when that characteristic involves doing nothing illegal. The candidate was not a back-alley abortionist, he is an obstetrician-gynecologist, and performing certain abortions is a legitimate part of that medical specialty.

A tenth item that illustrates public policy that is more harmful than helpful to the goals of both Democrats and Republicans might be the way immigration is being handled. The emphasis on the part of the Democrats is to push for more border guards, which is more a symbolic gesture than anything that really cuts down on immigration. One bizarre aspect of the increase in guards is that the number of apprehensions and telling people to walk back has increased greatly in recent months. This is taken as a sign that the guards are doing a much better job. In reality it indicates that a lot more people are getting through because virtually everyone who is sent back eventually gets through if they keep trying. It is like the drug enforcement people arguing that they are doing a good job because they confiscated $1 billion dollars worth of drugs last year and only confiscated $1,000 worth of drugs 20 years ago. If one recognizes that they are only confiscating at most 50% of the drugs, and maybe 10%, then that means that anywhere from $5 billion to $9 billion have gotten through. One does not judge how well crime is being kept down by how many arrests are being made. One judges by how many people are being victimized. The police are not doing a better job if they have made a million arrests last year and only made 100,000 the year before.

We can easily come up with ten lose-lose situations, just on the basis of yesterday's news. It is not clear that we can come up with ten win-win situations.

WIN-WIN ITEMS

The line-item veto does strengthen the president's bargaining power by threatening to veto certain items in return for favorable legislation, whereas before he had to veto the whole bill, including clauses that he favored. The line-item veto strengthens Congress by way of enabling the leadership to get rid of pork-barrel items after the leadership has obtained the favorable votes of legislators who will not vote favorably unless they get pork-barrel items. The president could then veto those items and the rest of the bill passes. One could also say that the Democrats come out ahead because there is a Democratic president and a Republican Congress. The Republicans come out ahead because the reverse situation may be more likely to be true in the future, because it was true for so many presidential administrations since the end of World War II, including every Republican president: Eisenhower, Nixon, Ford, Reagan, and Bush all had some Democratic Congresses. This is likely to happen in the future, since a majority of the American people still identify with the Democratic party, but Republicans can get elected president as individuals. Eisenhower had a more attractive personality in public opinion than Stevenson. Nixon looked more attractive in 1968 than Humphrey and the disorganized Democrats. And then Nixon was more attractive than McGovern in 1972. Reagan was more attractive than Carter; and Bush more than Dukakis. (See Table 16–2 for win-win policies.)

A second upturn item is China offering to pay royalties on U.S. videotapes, books, and other products but not willing to recognize any monopoly rights. That seems a very reasonable solution. They would be paying royalties on all reproductions and government factories. They do not have much control over amateur reproducing, but neither does the United States. There is a lot of amateur Xeroxing of books and reproducing of software, which the U.S. government does not crack down on in the United States, so why should China be

Table 16-2
Win-Win Policies in American Politics

WIN-WIN POLICIES	CONSERVATIVE GOALS THAT ARE HELPED	LIBERAL GOALS THAT ARE HELPED	IMPROVED POLICIES
I. ECONOMIC: Increased HMOs	Decreased taxes and increased quality	Decreased consumer costs and increased access	Vouchers, discount groups, and no pre-conditions
II. SOCIAL: Increased Training	Increased workfare and increased GNP	Increased individual income	Training vouchers, deductions, IRAs, on-the-job training
III. TECHNOLOGY: Space Rendezvous	Increased business income and decreased business expense	Increased jobs	Drugs, metals, solar power, helium fusion, satellites
IV. POLITICAL: Line-Item Veto	Republican president in the future. Clinton cannot veto whole bill. Preserve congressional power.	Democratic president at present. Delete pork and preserve good parts. Increase presidential power.	Line-item veto, but 60% override
V. FOREIGN: Russian Withdrawal from Former Republics	Decreased taxes for defense	Increased lives saved from peace	Allow geographical ethnic secession and independence for former colonies
VI. LEGAL: Tort Reform without Litigation or Lawyers	Increased business profits and decreased taxes	Compensation to injured person	Accidence reduction and insurance processing

expected to crack down on the amateur stuff in China? This could be a win-win solution where the publishers and videotape makers get big royalties and China profits on selling duplicate copies. The United States benefits from spreading its culture. China benefits from whatever they learn from American books and videotapes, although the videotapes might be more corrupting than enlightening. For now the United States is demanding royalties that are close to being prohibitive, which is the same thing as demanding an exclusive monopoly. China has at least offered a win-win solution. Clinton and Gore have proposed a win-win solution with regard to revising the American patent system.

After Gingrich had recommended wiping out NASA, there was a big rendezvous between Russian and U.S. spaceships. This represented a new breakthrough on building commercially valuable space platforms, as contrasted to some relatively useless military star wars weapons or a not-as-useful telescope. Both the United States and Russia could benefit from a space platform idea. So can the rest of the world.

The Russians are moving back to Russia from the former republics (although not yet to Chechnya). Granting independence to those nations is a win-win solution. Russia saves a lot of money, not fighting to retain them as colonies. They feel better about themselves being independent, sovereign nations. England and France have not regretted granting independence to their colonies, from about 1945 until 1970. The last major French colony to get its independence was Vietnam. The last major British colony before Hong Kong was British Guyana. Before that it was India and Pakistan for Britain; Algeria and Northern Africa for France. Russia is about 25 years behind. They were way behind Western Europe in adopting democracy, and they are now trying to catch up on dropping imperialism and colonialism. It is ironic that Russia is the last major imperialistic country of the world, yet it did so much screaming about capitalist imperialism. Current capitalist imperialism seems to be a highly welcomed thing in much of the world, although the word "imperialism" is not the right term. The right term is "international trade and investment."

A win-win solution to reduce terrorism is to get at the causes. Much of the current terrorism has some anticolonial resistance elements. The leading terrorists tend to be Arab. Here, one can make the point that Russia is not the last imperialist country. There has been a lot of imperialism in the Middle East on the part of the United States, Britain, France, and Israel. It is not so much legalistic imperialism in the sense of converting countries over to official colonies, but instead manipulating their governments in order to get more favorable concessions concerning oil. This has been happening since the end of World War II with regard to Iraq, Iran, Saudi Arabia, and Lybia.

The United States in particular has sought to keep friendly but reactionary governments in power and to overthrow unfriendly socialistic governments. This is not just due to the Cold War, although that accentuated the problem. The United States is interested in oil—the Persian Gulf War is an example. It had nothing to do with the United States versus Russia. It is the United States versus

Middle Eastern countries that want more independence to just do what they want to do, even if it means being run by fundamentalist Moslems, as in Iran, or somewhat weird Arab socialists, as in Iraq or Syria or Libya. The terrorists involved with the bombing of the World Trade Center building in New York City are supportive of Hamas, Hezbollah, Iran, and fundamentalists in Algeria. Some of the causes are being removed, such as independence for Palestine. This has largely wiped out Palestine Liberation Organization (PLO) terrorism, but there is still fundamentalist Moslem terrorism directed against Israel, the PLO, and the United States in the World Trade Center building bombing incident in New York City. If independence is granted, the countries that have been the victims of terrorism, and the United States with regard to the World Trade bombing, will be less victimized and the Palestinians will be better off running their own government, even if in the short run there are a lot of transition problems. That is the usual situation after a revolution or independence, including the United States. In time these countries will develop more viable economies and political states capable of exporting, importing, and being meaningful members of the United Nations.

LOSE-LOSE, WIN-WIN, AND THE SIX POLICY FIELDS

For economic issues, an example of lose-lose is raising interest rates. An example of win-win is the HMO arrangement as replacement of Medicare and Medicaid.

For social issues, the Republican welfare reform of emphasizing cut-offs without job facilitators may be an example of lose-lose. A win-win policy might be training, including national service, vouchers, and going to college.

On technology policy, a lose-lose would be failure to develop alternative energy sources. A win-win might be the spaceship rendezvous.

On domestic politics, the balanced budget could be a lose-lose in comparison to economic growth, if it hurts economic growth. A win-win might be the line-item veto in which both the Republicans and Democrats find benefits.

On foreign policy, retaliatory tariffs with China is a lose-lose. A win-win is Russian withdrawal from the former republics.

On legal policy, a lose-lose is an emphasis on prison, including the 85% rule and the three strikes rule. A win-win could be the ideal of SOS tort reform, which emphasizes accident reduction and insurance processing.

Part V _____

CASE STUDIES OF WIN-WIN ANALYSIS

———————————————

Chapter 17

THE OKLAHOMA BOMBING: CRIMINAL WRONGDOING

CAUSES OF THE BOMBING

The causes are not isolated psychotic individuals. None of the men who killed John F. Kennedy, Robert F. Kennedy, and Martin Luther King were isolated individuals. They all represented group thinking, even if they were not representing a specific group as an official representative. The assassin of Martin Luther King represented Southern racist hate. The assassin of Robert F. Kennedy represented the kind of Moslem fundamentalism that has been killing people for the last 30 or so years. The assassin in the John F. Kennedy case, according to Oliver Stone, represents a right-wing ideology that hated Kennedy because he was a liberal. The more prevailing explanation is that the John F. Kennedy assassin was egged on by left-wing extremists who did not like Kennedy's policy toward Cuba, Vietnam, and the Soviet Union. Lee Harvey Oswald was assassinated by Jack Ruby before Oswald's motives could be determined.

Conservatives like to blame the bombing on isolated individuals. Liberals like to talk about a sick society. This holds them open for conservatives to say that liberals hate America and hate society. The SOS is that the defendants are a product of very rapid social change that has been occurring since the Renaissance, but especially since about 1980. From the year zero until about the year 1500 society was relatively stagnant. There was little new development of technology. Women and blacks were virtual property. Daughters did what their mothers and grandmothers did, and sons did what their fathers and grandfathers did. Since the Renaissance, we have seen big technology changes from agriculture to commerce and industry. We have also seen big political changes in the move from monarchy to nationalism and democracy, big economic changes in the move from feudalism to capitalism and modified socialism, and big international changes in terms of international trade in goods and ideas. Big legal changes include constitutional and consumer rights as well as worker rights. (See Table 17–1 for the win-win policies.)

Since about 1960, big changes in the rights of women and minorities have taken place. Also the computer revolution has wiped out factory jobs in favor of office jobs. Defense conversion, tariff reduction, new immigration, productivity downsizing, and competition have also affected women and minorities. All of this causes a lot of frustration, especially on the part of white males who were formerly so much more dominant.

EFFECTS OF THE BOMBING

The conservative position is no effects at all. It is an isolated incident. It has no political effects. Although if it had been some immigrant Moslems, as in the New York World Trade Center building, that might have been recognized as very politically relevant by the right to stir up more foreign bashing. Liberals might think that is going to hurt Republicans directly, such as arguing that Gingrich and Rush Limbaugh have stirred up these people.

The SOS perspective is that these people have some legitimate complaints that would have stirred them up without Limbaugh and Gingrich. There may be a recognition on the part of public opinion that a lot of hate bashing has been a factor and it needs to be toned down. It may change some of the rhetoric without changing the voting behavior, unless Clinton does something to make him into a statesman rather than just a passive observer of what is going on. Clinton could come out with a win-win program.

IDEOLOGICAL LOCATION OF THE MILITANT RIGHTISTS

A third issue is how do these "kooks" differ from Nazis and right-wing Republicans? The conservative position is that they are just a bunch of neo-Nazis and nothing like right-wing Republicans. The liberal position is they are like right-wing Republicans who are basically closet Nazis. The SOS is that they do differ from Nazis on the six public policy issues. In that sense, they are more like right-wing Republicans, but right-wing Republicans are not closet Nazis.

We can talk about what the Nazis represented in terms of the six policy fields: (1) capitalism and anticommunism, (2) genocidal racism, (3) war technology, (4) dictatorship, (5) imperialism, and (6) police state repression.

As for the contemporary right wing on those six issues: (1) The current right wing is antitax, antiwelfare, antigovernment regulation; there are (2) instances of bashing immigrants, foreigners, gays, non-Christians, and affirmative action including outreach; there is an (3) antitechnology feeling with regard to productivity downsizing; there is a (4) restricted electorate or alienation and religious fundamentalism bordering on theocracy (a better phrase is state-imposed religion or government-imposed religion); (5) guns and a big defense budget are important "safeguards"; and there is (6) advocacy for the death penalty, long

Table 17-1
The Bombing and Win-Win Policy

ISSUES	CONSERVATIVE	LIBERAL	SUPER-OPTIMUM SOLUTIONS
1. CAUSES OF BOMBING	Isolated individuals	Sick society	A. Changes: 1. Technology change in re factories 2. Social change in re women and blacks B. Resulting in: Anger by white male workers
2. POLITICAL EFFECTS OF BOMBING	No effect	Will hurt Republicans	1. May change rhetoric 2. But not voting 3. Unless Clinton has a program
3. IDEOLOGICAL LOCATION OF MILITANT RIGHTISTS ON: 1. Prosperity 2. Merit Treatment 3. Technological Innovation 4. Democracy 5. World Peace 6. Law Compliance	Like Nazis, not like conservatives: 1. Capitalism and anti-communism 2. Genocidal racism 3. War technology 4. Dictatorship 5. Imperialism 6. Police state repression	Like right-wing Republicans who are closet Nazis	Militant rightists are like right-wing 1. Anti-tax, anti-welfare, anti-government regulation 2. Bashing of immigrants, foreigners, gays, non-Christians, and affirmative action 3. Anti-technology in productivity downsizing 4. Restricted electorate or alienation: religious fundamentalism, government-imposed religion 5. Guns and big defense budget 6. Death penalty, long prison sentences, less due process, e.g. search, appeal
4. POLICY IMPLICATIONS	Execute the individuals	Crackdown on militant rightists like KKK	1. Economic growth and job facilitators for displaced workers 2. Merit treatment for rural whites 3. New technologies in depressed areas like upper Michigan, Oregon, Appalachia 4. Voting participation with no advance registration, job precinct, election holiday 5. Tariff reduction and transplants to create jobs 6. Medicalization of drug-related crimes

prison sentences, and less due process (e.g., search and seizure and right to appeal).

POLICY IMPLICATIONS

The next issue is what to do about the problem. The conservative position is that these are isolated psychotic individuals who do not represent any fundamental defects in society. Some liberals would like to have a crackdown on militant rightists like the Ku Klux Klan.

The SOS position is to recognize that a lot of working-class males have some legitimate grievances that relate to the six policy fields:

1. Economic growth needs to take into consideration displaced workers. This means job facilitators.
2. There should be merit treatment for people who speak with rural or unusual accents who may be assumed to be not as bright as they really are.
3. There should be new technologies in depressed areas like upper Michigan, Oregon, and Appalachia, as is being done in China and other places.
4. There should be more public participation in politics, which means no voter registration, or registration at multiple places and times.
5. There should be demonstration that tariff reduction means jobs and especially foreign corporations in the United States who employ United States workers.
6. There should be medicalization of drug-related crimes.

Chapter 18

A UNION-MANAGEMENT DISPUTE

The concept of a super-optimum solution refers to resolving a dispute in such a way that all sides simultaneously come out ahead of their best expectations, not just ahead of their worst expectations.

An example is the product liability case of Traveler's Insurance versus Sanyo, in which the author of this book was a special master with a mandate to try to develop a computer-aided resolution. The plaintiff demanded a minimum of $900,000; the defendant offered a maximum of $300,000. A traditional compromise would be $600,000 where everybody comes out ahead of their worst expectations but not their best expectations. (This case is also discussed in Chapter 20.)

A super-optimum solution in that case might involve Sanyo Electronics supplying the agents of Traveler's Insurance computers for processing transactions and large-size TV sets as bonuses for the agents. That kind of settlement could be worth more than $900,000 to Traveler's Insurance, but it could involve a variable cost worth less than $300,000 to Sanyo Electronics. Such a settlement would thus be better than the plaintiff's best expectation of getting $900,000, and better than the defendant's best expectation of paying only $300,000.

The final result in the case represented a mixture of (1) super-optimizing whereby the defendant agreed to give things of considerable value to the plaintiff but of relatively small variable cost to the defendant, plus (2) a traditional cash outlay. The cash outlay was largely prompted by the lawyers for the plaintiff wanting their 33% contingency fee in cash, rather than in computers or TV sets. The author as the special master should have conducted a separate SOS mediation conference between the plaintiff company and the plaintiff lawyers to arrange for a side payment that would be less disruptive to the main SOS settlement.

The approach to arriving at super-optimum solutions of having big benefits on one side and low costs on the other can apply to resolving disputes between labor and management. The illustrative example that follows involves a leading grower in the Peoria, Illinois, area (who employs approximately 7,000 farm-workers a year) being sued by the Migrant Legal Counsel, which is a legal services agency that specializes in the legal problems of migratory farm workers.

The workers as a large class action (the plaintiff) were suing to recover approximately $3 million in wages that had been deducted to pay for loans, rents, and other expenses without proper legal authorization. The money had actually been loaned or advanced to the workers, but the procedures designed to prevent illegal exploitation had not been followed. The growers (the defendant) insisted they should pay nothing since the money they deducted was for loans actually made, regardless of the paperwork that followed. The best expectations of the workers in terms of net gain would be rather low, since whatever they collected they would have to repay, with the exception of about $50,000 in compensation to some of the named plaintiffs who were fired or quit their jobs, unless unlikely punitive damages could be obtained. The best expectations of the growers would be to spend $50,000 or more going to trial and win with no liability. Thus, the object for an SOS court mediator would be to come up with a settlement that would be worth more than $50,000 to the farm workers and would simultaneously save more than $50,000 in litigation costs for the growers.

What follows is a two-part description of the super-optimum solution in this specific case. The first part is mainly verbal, the second is mainly computer-based. The essence of the solution is that the growers agree to deposit $100,000 to begin an employee credit union. Depositing $100,000 costs nothing to the growers since it is insured by the federal government and can be withdrawn after an agreed-upon time period, possibly even with interest. The $100,000, however, serves as the basis for the beginning of an economic development fund that enables the workers through real estate leveraging to obtain a mortgage for building more than $500,000 worth of housing for the workers as a big improvement over their current housing. The existence of the credit union also enables them to avoid having to get advances from the growers, which generates a lot of friction as a result of alleged favoritism in giving and collecting the advances. There are other elements involved, too, such as new grievance procedures and reports regarding compliance with other rules governing the working conditions of migratory labor. The essence of the solution, though, is that both sides come out ahead of their original best expectations.

THE SUPER-OPTIMUM SOLUTION

The *preliminary elements* of the SOS solution are: the establishment of a kind of bill of rights for the workers and an institutionalized grievance procedure with a grievance committee and provision for mediation and arbitration of grievances; the submitting of a nine-part report by the lawyers for the growers as to exactly how the growers are now in compliance with the nine sets of violations listed on pages 7 and 8 of the complaint; and compensation for the named plaintiffs for the special out-of-pocket expenses that they incurred as contrasted to the other 2,000 members of the class who were not listed by name in the complaint. There are seven named plaintiffs. Only one of the seven was present at the hearing, Fidel Boyso. Three of the named defendants were present— Michael Rousonelos, Sr., Michael Rousonelos, Jr., and Gus (Butch) Rousonelos. It is definitely desirable right from the start to have the clients and not just the lawyers present. Otherwise, for this kind of solution the lawyers would logically say they have to go back and consult with their clients.

The *main element* of the SOS solution is an economic development credit union. It will be partly funded as a result of deposits made by the grower. The deposits need to be determined as to the amount, the length of time, and the interest. The amount is about $100,000 for the first year, with subsequent amounts to be determined. The length of time that the money will be kept on deposit needs to be fairly substantial, maybe as long as five years in order for the money to be available for loans. The interest rate would be the normal rate given under credit union provisions. A board of directors will be established, which will include mainly representatives of the workers and at least one representative of the growers. There will also be expertise supplied by professors of business administration or economics.

The money should be especially loans for economic development projects, not consumer goods. These projects will include housing for workers, education programs and business investments that will benefit the community. Help is available in establishing the credit union from the Illinois Finance Agency. Help is also available for training workers. The Illinois Credit Union League puts out a useful set of materials.

The features that are *attractive to the plaintiff* are: being able to borrow money without begging for it or being discriminated against; being able to pay back the money under reasonable repayment arrangements rather than in such large payments; the economic development projects will benefit the workers, such as housing, education, and businesses; the solution can apply to former workers who are eligible to borrow; it involves money from the defendant, possibly other farmers, and possibly grant money from the federal government, especially the Departments of Agriculture and Commerce; a benefit to the workers is that by the farm not going bankrupt, jobs will continue to be available; and the plaintiff's side also get psychological rewards from having originated the idea rather than having it imposed from the outside.

The features *attractive to the defendant* are: a release from being sued, which runs the risk of substantial judgment concerning the deductions and possible penalties; a release from expensive litigation costs; better relations with the workers; being relieved of being in the lending business, of giving advances to forthcoming workers and present workers; the possibility of the prestige that goes with inviting other farmers to participate in this credit union in order to have a lending institution that would relieve them of lending burdens; avoidance of what could be a revenge-oriented lawsuit or one designated to make an example of the grower; avoidance of possible bankruptcy; some psychological rewards from having improved upon the idea, especially with the funds on deposit, the other farms, and the federal grants; and both sides may take considerable pleasure in the idea being adopted elsewhere in the country or even in other countries that have problems between farmworkers and growers.

THE COMPUTER ANALYSIS

Table 18–1 shows the spreadsheet that was used to analyze the case of *Ramirez v. Rousonelos* in order to arrive at a super-optimum solution whereby all sides come out ahead of their best initial expectations simultaneously.

The columns show four relevant items of value over which the plaintiff and defendant are in dispute or are considering as part of an exchange or a package settlement. The rows show the six alternative settlements that might be possible. The cells show how each alternative scores on each item of value, criterion, or goal for resolving the dispute. At the far right are totals for each alternative adding across the six rows.

Focusing more specifically on the alternatives, the plaintiff's best expectation is to get 1,000 monetary units out of the defendant, which is $1 million. The defendant's best expectation is to pay nothing as a result of the plaintiff failing to establish liability if the case goes to court. The likely compromise settlement under these circumstances is approximately $500, which splits the difference between $1,000 and $0. The object of the SOS analysis is to enable the plaintiff to obtain more than $1,000 and to enable the defendant to pay less than $0. This means the defendant should in effect receive income as a result of the settlement.

Table 18–1 helps clarify the basic alternatives available to the opposite sides in this labor-management case. In summary terms, the alternatives are as follows: going to court where the plaintiff might win as much as 1,000 monetary units or as little as nothing, with considerable litigation expense to the plaintiff either way; going to court where the defendant might lose as much as 1,000 monetary units or win by paying nothing, with considerable litigation expense to the defendant either way; a compromise at about 500 monetary units—this would mean the plaintiff would not receive the additional 500 units which the plaintiff feels entitled to. It would also mean the defendant pays 500 units more than the defendant feels it should be paying; a super-optimum solution whereby the plaintiff receives items of value totaling more than 1,000 units and the defendant also receives items of value totaling more than nothing; and other broader super-optimum solutions discussed later that involve seed money or investment money from the federal government for upgrading the skills of the workers and the technology of the farm. This kind of SOS solution (involving a third-party benefactor) could mean substantially greater income for both the farmworkers and the growers. It is an SOS solution emphasizing public policy or legislation rather than an individual case or adjudication.

Focusing on the items of value, or criteria, the key item is establishing an economic development credit union. This is not an ordinary consumer credit union that provides loans for buying TV sets or cars. Instead, it is a credit union mainly to provide capital for obtaining a mortgage to buy rental housing that generates income or to invest in business opportunities. The second item is establishing a grievance procedure to handle the complaints of the workers about working conditions, promotion matters, alleged discrimination, and other labor-management disputes. The third item is cash money to the named plaintiffs partly as compensation for their time and effort in pursuing the case. The fourth item is compliance information that has been sought by the lawyers representing the workers in order to determine the extent to which wrongful immigration practices are occurring and also accounting information that can be helpful in developing a reasonable monetary settlement.

Looking at the relations between the alternatives and the items of value, the credit union is especially important. It could conceivably provide approximately $2,000 in benefits, since the credit union is capable of lending a down payment for a mortgage that would buy $2 million worth of housing. It only takes approximately 10% for a down payment, especially in buying housing that is federally subsidized for farmworkers. The housing could also be used as collateral for obtaining further capital for business opportunities. Those businesses could provide services to the workers at more reasonable prices than businesses operated for profit. Looking down that first column, the credit union provides nothing with regard to a cash settlement either in terms of the plaintiff receiving something or the defendant giving something. Looking further down the column, the credit union is shown as costing the defendant less than nothing. The defendant deposits $100,000 in the credit union for the first year to get it started, with subsequent amounts to be determined. The money deposited receives interest and can be withdrawn in five years. The interest is reasonable income.

The grievance procedure is difficult to monetize. It has substantial value to the workers psychologically to be able to have an objective procedure to resolve their grievances. It is not a loss to the defendant farm owner. He might even welcome a more orderly grievance procedure that leads to less friction. An important part of the grievance procedure would be some kind of mediation or arbitration that would relieve the farm owner of the headaches of trying to resolve disputes between two different workers or a worker and a supervisor. Paying money to the named plaintiffs is a cash gain to the plaintiff and a cash loss to the defendant. It was a factor complicating this SOS settlement, but the amount of money was kept small in the eyes of the wealthy defendant, but large in the eyes of the relatively poor workers. The compliance information is also difficult to monetize. It is psychologically valuable to the workers so that they do not feel they are being treated illegally. It is no loss, though, to the defendant if no illegal behavior is revealed. It is shown at the bottom of column 4 as being approximately $0 in monetary value to the defendant because nothing illegal was revealed, and the only cost was having to pull together various records.

Table 18–1
Super-Optimizing Litigation Analysis (Using *Ramirez v. Rousonelos* as an Illustrative Example)

ALTERNATIVES	CRITERIA / RELEVANT ITEMS OF VALUE				RELEVANT TOTALS
	Credit Union, Housing, and Business Opportunities	Grievance Procedure	Payment to Named Plaintiffs	Compliance Information	
Plaintiff's SOS Settlement (Big Benefits)	$2,000	> $0	$50	> $0	> $1,000
Plaintiff's Best Expectation = $1,000	0	0	0	0	$1,000
Likely Compromise Settlement = $500	0	0	0	0	$500
Defendant's Best Expectation = $0	0	0	0	0	$0
Defendant's SOS Settlement (Low Costs)	< $0	< $0	$50	~ $0	< $0

NOTES:

1. All the above items are in $1,000s.

2. The plaintiff's wildest initial expectation is to be repaid approximately $1 million in wages. This is a wild expectation since the money was deducted for goods, services, and advances that had been provided to the workers by the grower, but not in accordance with the proper paperwork procedures.

142

3. The defendant's wildest initial expectation is to have to pay nothing. It is a wild expectation since the defendant admittedly failed to comply with the proper deduction procedures with no good defense other than that the money was owed. The defendant would thus be likely to lose on the issue of whether they complied with the proper procedures. A penalty is likely to be assessed to deter such improprieties on the part of the specific defendant and other potential defendants. The penalty is likely to be substantial in order to have deterrent value. There is also likely to be compensation to the named defendants for their efforts plus considerable litigation costs if the case goes to trial.

4. The object is thus to arrive at a super-optimum solution whereby the workers in a sense receive more than $1 million and the defendant pays less than nothing.

5. The key element in the super-optimum solution is the establishment of a credit union mainly consisting of $100,000 from the defendant to be deposited with interest for five years.

6. That $100,000 can quickly generate $2 million worth of housing by serving as a 10% down payment on a mortgage for existing or new housing units for the workers. The housing might be used as collateral for additional capital. It is also possible that a federal or state government agency will match the $100,000 as part of an economic development plan, thereby further increasing the lending opportunities.

7. The workers thereby obtain multiple family housing and a lending source for business opportunities that may be worth at least $2 million plus the benefits of improved grievance procedures, payments to named plaintiffs, and compliance information. The total value is worth more than their wildest best expectations.

8. The growers thereby obtain the benefits of not having to provide housing for the workers. They also get interest on their savings and a subsequent return of the principal if requested. The grievance procedure can decrease friction. The compliance information can increase credibility. Payment to the named plaintiffs is a cost rather than a benefit, but it is more than offset by the benefits from the other relevant items of value. Therefore the growers are making a net gain as a result of this SOS settlement, which is the same as paying less than nothing.

143

Looking at the last column of relevant totals, the top cell is shown as being worth more than 1,000 units. It could be shown as being worth more than 2,000 units if the monetary value of the grievance procedure and the compliance information is worth more than $50. It is not necessary to determine how much the total value is of the plaintiff's SOS settlement. The important thing is that it is an SOS settlement if it is worth more than the plaintiff's best expectation, which was 1,000 monetary units.

Likewise, down at the bottom of the totals column, the defendant's SOS settlement is shown as involving paying out less than $0. We cannot tell how much less than $0. We can say that it is less than $0 if the monetary value of the credit union and the grievance procedure exceed the $50 paid to the named plaintiffs. We should also point out that the credit union is income-producing not just in terms of the interest paid, but also in terms of saving the farm owner money that is otherwise wasted in making loans to the workers that are not paid off, provided that the credit union can issue some emergency loans. The farm owner also saves money that would otherwise be spent providing the workers with housing, which can now be obtained through a mortgage loan with a down payment from the credit union. The farm owner may also save money by encouraging the business opportunities to replace aggravating services that the farm owner otherwise provides to the workers. This is a farm owner who is legitimately in the business of making big money selling farm products, not a plantation owner who makes money renting shanties to workers and overcharging them at a company store.

Between the plaintiff's SOS settlement of more than 1,000 monetary units and the defendant's SOS settlement of less than $0 are the three traditional litigation-negotiation figures. The first is the plaintiff's initial demand of $1 million. The third is the defendant's initial offer of nothing, accompanied by an accurate or exaggerated prediction of victory if the case goes to trial. The plaintiff would possibly faint if the defendant were to respond to the $1 million demand by saying, "Why only a million dollars when I would be pleased to offer you more than that?" Those words were not spoken, but that is in effect what happened. The defendant would possibly faint if the plaintiff were to respond to the offer of nothing by saying, "Why are you so generous in offering me nothing when I would be pleased to pay you for your inconvenience in being subjected to this lawsuit?" Those words were not spoken, but that is in effect what happened.

This kind of SOS settlement can be facilitated through the kind of spreadsheet perspective that is shown in Table 18–1. It lends itself to thinking in terms of exceeding the plaintiff's best expectation and the defendant's best expectation by getting away from a straight exchange of dollars. It also lends itself well to various kinds of what-if analysis whereby one can add additional columns or change the amounts in the present columns. More important than the decision-aiding software or the spreadsheet base is the idea of thinking in terms of super-optimum solutions to real-world cases. This is in contrast to traditional compromises where everybody comes out compromising their principles and exceeding only their worst expectations, rather than their best expectations.

An important point is that the above settlement actually occurred in the dispute between a huge farm near Peoria, Illinois, and a large quantity of farmworkers. This is an actual, rather than a hypothetical, case. Both sides were more satisfied with this type of solution than they would have been with a traditional money compromise. Such a compromise solution would have meant paying out more by the growers than the super-optimum or win-win solution. It would have also meant receiving less by the farmworkers than the more imaginative and mutually beneficial solution that emphasizes big benefits to one side and low costs to the other side.

BROADENING THE DISPUTE RESOLUTION IN THE RAMIREZ CASE

Going to Trial

A lawyer for the Migrant Labor Council or the AFL-CIO or the National Labor Relations Board (NLRB) goes to court or initiates an administrative proceeding to sue for the dollars owed to the workers that were not covered by previous loans. The amount of money may amount to $10,000 for which there is documentation showing that money was deducted by mistake or deliberately, and for which there is nothing to show that it was owed. The lawyer succeeds in winning the case fully, meaning getting the whole $10,000 without any compromising. He or she is considered as having done a great job. In reality, the case probably cost $20,000 to collect the $10,000. The Migrant Labor Council, AFL-CIO, or NLRB could have saved money by just paying $10,000 out of its own treasury to the workers. This would thus not waste any time, and especially not waste an extra $10,000 in litigation costs.

Settling Out of Court

The alternative approach would be to settle out of court, possibly through mediation. This is a newer approach, although there have been out-of-court settlements ever since there were courts. The idea of a mediator (a third-party facilitating the settlement) is relatively new. The agreement is to split the difference and the growers pay $5,000 to the workers. Everybody comes out ahead of their worst expectations because the plaintiffs save $20,000 in litigation costs and so do the growers. This is maybe even worse than the first way of resolving the matter because one can say that the growers are allowed to steal the $5,000 difference from the workers, and the growers suffer no penalty whatsoever. There is no disincentive for them to not do it again. They came out ahead. The workers should feel demoralized since they have been cheated out of $5,000. The lawyers representing the workers should feel they have betrayed them. This settlement, however, would probably be considered a victory because it saved the litigation costs, meaning that things could have been worse. Going to trial at least has the advantage of making the growers suffer $20,000 of litigation costs as a disincentive. It may, however, cost the plaintiffs $20,000 in their litigation costs to make the other side suffer $20,000. This does seem like a rather strange way to provide disincentives to wrongdoers. What it amounts to is arranging for both the plaintiff and the defendant to each cut off one arm so that the defendant will thereby suffer, or to each cut off $20,000 worth of their assets.

Establishing a Mutually Beneficial Credit Union

The super-optimum solution that was worked out in the case of setting up a credit union looks good. The workers are able to borrow money in the future without being subjected to discriminatory favoritism as to who borrows, what the terms are, and what the collection procedures are. The workers especially benefit from the real estate leveraging, which provides better housing. The growers benefit by virtue of the fact that the whole thing costs them virtually nothing. They can withdraw the money they have put on deposit in the credit union after a certain time, maybe even with interest. If one is oriented toward revenge or deterrence, that settlement would be undesirable.

The big problem here is not that the growers have gone unpunished. A more adequate way of preventing a recurrence is not to punish them, but rather to put into the agreement the lending procedures that are to be followed. The credit union, however, does that even better. There is no need to specify how the growers are supposed to make loans to workers in the future. The growers would no longer be making loans, just the credit union would. One could still specify the proper procedures in case somebody cannot qualify for a loan from the credit union, but to whom the growers want to make a loan anyhow. The rules are clear in the Illinois state law and the federal law governing payroll procedures for farmworkers. It is unlikely that the growers are going to violate those rules again, especially since it is not profitable for them to do so. It was more just a kind of arrogance of ignoring what the legal rules are. It was not the sort of thing that one finds in business firms that violate environmental standards in order to save money. No substantial amount of money is saved by not having the workers sign proper forms authorizing the payroll deduction.

The big problem with regard to thinking on a higher level of problem solving is that after the solution is adopted, the industry is still the same. It is still the worst or one of the worst industries in the United States with regard to labor-management relations.

Obtaining Union Recognition

A labor lawyer viewing the situation who thinks more broadly than the exchange of dollars (even including the credit union innovation) might say that the Migrant Legal Council should be devoting more effort to getting legislation passed that provides for secret ballot elections among farmworkers so they can form unions. The unions would then protect the workers from abuses like illegal wage deductions or bad housing. This is a higher level solution that would affect all farmworkers and affect a lot more than just illegal wage deductions. It is a solution from out of the 1930s. Unionizing the farmworkers would not make much difference, as is illustrated by the unionized farmworkers in the grape fields of California, who continue boycotts after many on and off years.

The basic problem is that farmworkers are generally desperate Chicanos, poor whites, poor blacks, sometimes Puerto Ricans, occasionally Cubans, or other kinds of Latin Americans. Any Chicanos who go on strike can easily be replaced by other unskilled laborers who will cross picket lines because they are hard up for jobs and need no special training. It is rare that there will even be a picket line or a union. The workers will not readily join unions given their fear of losing their jobs or maybe being deported, even if there are secret-ballot elections. It may be difficult to get 30% to sign a petition calling for secret-ballot elections. If 30% sign, it may be quite difficult to get 51% to say they want a union. They can be so easily made to think it is not secret and that the union is worse for them than the allegedly paternalistic employer.

Legislation to Facilitate Credit Unions for Farmworkers

Another broad (but really relatively narrow) way of dealing with the problem is to think in terms of pushing for legislation that facilitates credit unions for farmworkers. Growers can be expected to make contributions just as employers make matching contributions for Social Security, unemployment compensation, workmen's compensation, and other kinds of social insurance. That sounds like an improvement, but might be undesirable if it worked well, as would any kind of legislation that perpetuates a career of stoop labor. The basic problem is how to enable the farmworkers to cease to be farmworkers. They need to move into something that requires more intelligence as contrasted to stoop labor, which could be done so easily by machines if the cheap labor were not available.

Upgrading Labor Skills and Job Opportunities

This means pushing for legislation outside the labor law field, the credit union field, or the housing field. It means pushing for legislation that provides for testing the people involved to see what abilities and interests they have. The legislation should then provide them with programs designed to get the kind of training that can put their interests and abilities to good use. The program also needs to get them into jobs as quickly as possible so the training becomes on-the-job training. This kind of legislation may require the cooperation of people who are experts in the training of semiliterate rural people in modern urban skills. It means bringing in some experts who are not likely to be labor lawyers.

Upgrading Farm Technology and Profitability

As part of this activity, we need to think even more broadly from a societal perspective, rather than just from the perspective of the workers' interests. Thus society or the government should be helping the growers to develop more efficient mechanization. Any farmer who needs cheap labor to make a profit is coming close to saying that he or she or at least the industry is run by not-so-competent people who are operating under near-medieval or even prehistoric conditions. The object is not to insult them for not adopting modern methods or for being exploitative of cheap labor. The object is to provide incentives for developing and using machines that can pick grapes, peaches, or whatever it is that is being picked by the migrant workers.

Even Broader Societal Implications

The result of all this is the farms become much more productive in producing more at lower cost. They are better able to compete in the world market, and this helps reduce the international trade deficit. It also adds to the GNP and the tax base, thereby helping reduce the domestic budget deficit. The workers with their new skills become more productive, and they do not need so many government services, if any. They add to improving the foreign trade balance and the domestic deficit. Both the growers and the workers contribute more to other people's incomes, creating multiplier effects regarding other people's prosperity. Those other people can thereby improve their productivity and then pay more taxes. This in turn provides for more spending on well-placed subsidies and tax breaks, especially those designed to improve workers' skills and management technology. This is a super-optimum solution.

Even if the credit union were an SOS in the sense that both sides came out ahead of their best expectations, the solution of improving farming technology and worker skills is a much better SOS. It enables both sides to be even better off, and society as a whole is better off. This example is a good illustration of vertical broadening to cover more problems in the same field of dispute resolution, as contrasted to horizontal broadening to cover more fields. It is also a good illustration of improving on super-optimum solutions, since the definition of an SOS does not mean that it is a perfect solution. It just means that it is capable of exceeding the best expectations of both liberals and conservatives. The above solution is not necessarily perfect. It is, however, better than the initial super-optimum solution of the mutually beneficial credit union.

SOME CONCLUSIONS

Several characteristics make this case especially challenging. There is a big element of racism by virtue of the growers being white anglos and the workers almost 100% Hispanic. The company-town idea of the workers living in housing provided by the employer and buying from the company store reeks of the old "16 tons." There also is a big divide-and-conquer kind of element with the old mansion slaves and fieldhand slaves pitted against each other. The Hispanics from Texas who are generally native-born Americans or close to it are given considerable favoritism over the Hispanics from Mexico.

There is an interesting conflict, especially on the side of the workers, between their crusading lawyer and what they themselves are seeking. There is some of the opposite kind of conflict on the other side, where the lawyers are very business-like and the growers are more emotional. By bringing out the differences between the lawyers and the clients, we have four sides to the case. Or maybe we really have a lot more than four sides if we divide the Hispanics into Texans and Mexicans, and also divide the growers into young and old.

This intergenerational conflict where the son of the growers is college trained in modern business administration and has a very different attitude about how things should be run from his father, who has been trained in the equivalent of grower-farmworker streetfighting. Even his overseers almost come to the point of saying that the way to resolve the problem is to kick a lot of ass, as contrasted to the young son who talks in terms of setting up grievance procedures.

The computer-aided mediation adds an interesting element by virtue of how it helps to convert what otherwise would be a much more emotional divisive argument into something that at least on the surface sounds like a matter of relatively simple calculations. This is especially illustrated in statements from people associated with the Community Relations Service of the Department of Justice. They say that the argument boils down to: (1) The lawyer for the farmworkers says it is an insult to the named plaintiffs to receive only 10% of the settlement if there is going to be a $500,000 settlement and they are only going to get about $50,000, when they constitute 100% of the named plaintiffs. (2) The lawyer for the growers says the named plaintiffs are getting way too much when one takes into consideration that they are only about 1% of all the plaintiffs. The calculations are a little more complicated than this, but it partly illustrates the desire of both sides to reduce the problem to some simple calculations rather than make it a more emotional problem.

The receptiveness to super-optimizing is interesting in the sense of both sides treating it almost as a challenging game to try to come up with ideas that each side will consider better than their original best expectations.

There are also several sequencing principles in finding an SOS solution. It is important to talk on the telephone in advance in order to get some basic understanding of each side's position before meeting in person. All parties also should have exchanged some papers, including the plaintiff's complaint and the defendant's response. It is possible in one day to develop a super-optimum solution without having to have multiple meetings.

It makes sense to provide an introduction to super-optimum solution-finding in the beginning. The computer serves as a good visual aid. The Sanyo elec-

Table 18–2
Resolving Litigation Disputes Through Super-Optimum Solutions

CRITERIA / ALTERNATIVES	C GOAL Benefits to Defendant C=3 L=1	L GOAL Benefits to Plaintiff C=1 L=3	N GOAL -Costs to Defendant C=2 L=2	N GOAL -Costs to Plaintiff C=2 L=2	N TOTAL (Neutral Weights)	L TOTAL (Liberal Weights)	C TOTAL (Conservative Weights)
C ALTERNATIVE Defendant Wins on Trial	5	1	2	2	20	16	24*
L ALTERNATIVE Plaintiff Wins on Trial	1	5	2	2	20	24*	16
N ALTERNATIVE Settle	2.5	2.5	3	3	22	22	22
SOS ALTERNATIVE Insurance, Products, Credit Unions, etc.	5	5	3	3	32	32**	32**

Table 18–2 (continued)

NOTES:

1. The relation between each alternative and each goal is expressed on a 1-5 scale where a 5 indicates the alternative is highly conducive to the goal, a 4 indicates mildly conducive, a 3 indicates neither conducive nor adverse, a 2 indicates mildly adverse, and a 1 indicates the alternative is highly adverse to the goal.

2. The relative weights of each goal are expressed on a 1-3 scale where a 3 indicates the goal is highly important, a 2 indicates middling importance, and a 1 indicates relatively low importance. Conservative goals by definition are highly important to conservatives, but of relatively low importance to liberals. Liberal goals, on the other hand, are highly important to liberals, but of relatively low importance to conservatives.

* = The winning alternative before considering the SOS alternative.

** = The alternative that simultaneously does better than the conservative alternative on the conservative totals, and better than the liberal alternative on the liberal totals.

151

tronics case mentioned at the beginning of this chapter is a good example. It makes sense for each side to briefly state its position with everybody present.

The negotiators/mediators then meet with the defendant. The defendant normally has to do the offering, which is a more difficult position to be in, and the plaintiff does the receiving. Thus one should expect to spend more time with the defendant. The plaintiff may be difficult to convince to accept the defendant's offer. There is nothing inherent in being the plaintiff or the defendant as to how difficult obtaining an agreement may be. It does make sense to start with the defendant as to what he is willing to offer the plaintiff in the way of a mutually beneficial solution.

Then there is a meeting with the plaintiff to see what he thinks could be offered that would be mutually beneficial. The plaintiff's ideas are taken back to the defendant instead of meeting jointly, and the plaintiff's reactions are presented to the defendant. The two sides meet jointly when everyone is sure that doing so will emphasize a handshaking atmosphere.

Table 18–2 provides a more general table that goes beyond the Ramirez case with regard to resolving litigation disputes through super-optimum solutions. The conservative alternative in most damages disputes is for the defendant to win. This usually means victory on trial for an insurance company, a manufacturer, a landlord, or an employer. The liberal alternative is for the plaintiff to win on trial, since that usually means victory for an injured person, a consumer, a tenant, or an employee. The neutral or compromise position is to develop a settlement to avoid going to trial. The super-optimum solution is for the defendant to give the plaintiff insurance, manufactured products, a rent-free apartment, a better job, or something that has high value to the plaintiff but not much variable net cost to the defendant.

There are four goals or criteria involved in deciding among the alternatives: benefits to the defendant, benefits to the plaintiff, costs to the defendant, and costs to the plaintiff. The defendant winning on trial scores well in terms of benefits to the defendant, and that alternative wins on the conservative column using the conservative weights. The plaintiff winning on trial scores well on benefits to the plaintiff and that alternative wins on the liberal column using the liberal weights. The out-of-court settlement wins on the neutral column and comes in second on both the liberal and conservative columns. It is the alternative most likely to be chosen in the absence of the super-optimum solution because it is everybody's second choice and has acceptability for both sides.

The super-optimum solution provides benefits to the defendant by enabling him to pay the plaintiff an amount of variable cost that is likely to be even less than the defendant's low starting position for bargaining purposes. The SOS also provides benefits to the plaintiff by enabling him to receive from the defendant an amount that is likely to be even more valuable than the plaintiff's high starting position for bargaining purposes. At the same time, the SOS alternative represents only moderate costs to the defendant and only moderate or no costs to the plaintiff. With those scores, the SOS alternative is able to easily win on both the liberal and the conservative totals using either liberal or conservative weights. There are three general principles of SOS analysis derived from this case study. (1) The arrangement in the Ramirez case was really more super-optimum than in the Sanyo electronics case. The big feature in the electronics case was a seller or a manufacturer giving the plaintiff products that are valuable to the plaintiff but cost relatively little to the defendant. (2) The big feature in the Ramirez case was developing a set of institutions that could benefit both sides, such as the grievance procedures and economic development credit union. This comes more under the heading of a package arrangement than a solution that involves high benefits to one side at low cost to the other side. (3) It is important to get people in a super-optimum solution frame of mind by emphasizing that we are looking for mutually beneficial solutions and not compromises and not determinations that one side is in the right and another is in the wrong.[1]

NOTE

1. On traditional dispute resolution in labor-management disputes, see Nolan (1979), and Oberer et al. (1986). On super-optimum solutions in general and in dispute resolution, see Susskind and Cruikshank (1987), Nagel (1989), and Nagel and Mills (1990).

REFERENCES

Gass, S. et al., eds. *Impacts of Microcomputers on Operations Research.* Amsterdam: North-Holland, 1986.

Goldberg, S., E. Green, and F. Sander, eds. *Dispute Resolution.* Boston: Little, Brown, 1984.

Humphreys, P. and A. Wisudha. *Methods and Tools for Structuring and Analyzing Decision Problems.* London: London School of Economics and Political Science, 1987.

Magaziner I. and R. Reich, *Minding America's Business: The Decline and Rise of the American Economy.* New York: Harcourt, Brace, 1982.

Nagel, S. *Evaluation Analysis with Microcomputers.* Greenwich, Conn.: JAI Press, 1989.

Nagel, S. "Super-Optimum Solutions in Public Controversies," *Futures Research Quarterly,* Vol. 5. No. 4 (1989), pp. 57–75.

Nagel, S. and M. Mills, "Microcomputers, P/G%, and Dispute Resolution:" *Ohio State Journal on Dispute Resolution,* Vol. 2 (1987), pp. 187–223.

Nagel, S. and M. Mills, *Multi-Criteria Methods in Alternative Dispute Resolution: With Microcomputer Applications.* Westport, Conn. Quorum Books, 1990.

Nolan, D. *Labor Arbitration Law and Practice in a Nutshell.* St. Paul: West, 1979.

Oberer, W. et al., eds. *Cases and Materials on Labor Law: Collective Bargaining in a Free Society.* St. Paul: West, 1986.

Roberts, P. *The Supply Side Revolution.* Cambridge, Mass.: Harvard University Press, 1984.

Susskind, L. and J. Cruikshank, *Breaking the Impasse: Consensual Approaches to Resolving Public Disputes.* New York: Basic Books, 1987.

Chapter 19 ──────────────────────

THE INVENTORY PROBLEM: BUSINESS POLICY

The subject of super-optimizing solutions was presented at the annual meeting of the Institute of Management Science and the Operations Research Society of America in Nashville in May 1991. The main illustrative example was the subject of optimum jury size, which had been analyzed by a number of operations research and management science people in the 1970s. Some of the results were used in the Supreme Court decision of *Ballew v. Georgia* to decide whether it was constitutional to allow juries to be smaller than 6 people. The Court said that juries could be smaller than 12, but not smaller than 6. Within the range of 6 to 12, conservatives or prosecution-oriented people like 6-person juries because it is easier to convince 6 people unanimously of the guilt of a defendant than any number greater than 6. Liberals or defense-oriented people like 12-person juries because it is more difficult to convince 12 people of the guilt of an innocent defendant than any lesser number. The compromise position is a quantity between 6 and 12, or to have 12-person juries deciding less than unanimously.

The key conservative goal is to convict the guilty, as compared to liberals who tend to emphasize acquitting the innocent. The 6-person jury does well on the conservative goal, but the 12-person jury does relatively well on the liberal goal. This is a classic trade-off situation where moving toward bigger juries decreases Type I errors but increases Type II errors, and moving toward smaller juries does the opposite. In one sense, the SOS object is to find a jury size that is both bigger than 12 and smaller than 6. In another sense, the SOS object is to develop one or more legal rules that simultaneously increase the probability of convicting the guilty and increase the probability of acquitting the innocent. Such legal rules include videotaping trials, allowing note-taking, or having training sessions for potential jurors. All these rules improve both kinds of accuracy. They are capable of achieving the set of conservative goals and weights better than 6-person juries, and more capable of achieving the set of liberal goals and weights better than 12-person juries.

After the presentation, the issue was raised that the same kind of analysis could be applied to reorienting a key aspect of OR/MS thinking—namely, the modeling of inventories and other problems that involve thinking in terms of trade-offs or Type I versus Type II errors. More specifically, one business policy tends to emphasize having larger inventories in order to avoid outage or opportunity costs. Another policy emphasizes having smaller inventories to avoid spoilage and storage costs. It is commonly thought that the basic choice is moving in one direction or the other and thereby suffering more of one kind of cost while lessening the other kind of cost. The typical solution is a compromise somewhere in the middle based on calculus-oriented formulas.

In recent years, new thinking has emphasized the possibility of being able to have small inventories and not suffer outage costs. Such systems are referred to as inventory on demand, and the systems are associated with innovative Japanese firms. They still result in possibly unnecessary outage costs, but they represent a form of SOS thinking whereby one seeks to lower both costs simultaneously. A better SOS solution may be the rolling inventories that are associated with computerized trucking. Under such a system a business firm could theoretically have no inventory whatsoever, and never miss being able to meet incoming orders even faster than with traditional warehouse inventories. In its most developed form, the complete inventory is in trucks moving across the nation in a predetermined pattern in light of where orders have come from in the past. A truck traveling from Phoenix to Tallahassee at 1:05 P.M. may be informed by computer that an order has been received at 1:00 P.M. from New Orleans. The truck is then directed to turn south and deliver so many units to the New Orleans buyer by 2:30 P.M. If the system is operating correctly, there are virtually no storage or spoilage costs, only the delivery costs that would otherwise be incurred. This is an example of American SOS thinking that is better than the Japanese approach, although it reflects the geographical differences of the United States versus Japan.

The SOS approach to the inventory modeling problem is shown in Table 19-1. The conservative or cautious alternative is to have a big inventory. The liberal or risk-taking alternative is to have a small inventory. The neutral alternative is something in between based on inventory-modeling assumptions and calculations. The cautious alternative does well on the goal of reducing outage costs. The risk-taking alternative does well in reducing spoilage and storage costs. The SOS alternative of computerized trucking does well in reducing both kinds of costs simultaneously. In quantitative terms, the SOS alternative receives a higher total score than the liberal alternative using the liberal weights of a 3 for reducing spoilage-storage costs and a 1 for reducing outage costs. The SOS alternative simultaneously receives a higher total score than the conservative

Table 19–1
Deciding on Inventory Size

CRITERIA ⟍ ALTERNATIVES	C GOAL Outage Down C=3 L=1	L GOAL Spoilage & Storage Down C=1 L=3	N TOTAL (Neutral Weights)	L TOTAL (Liberal Weights)	C TOTAL (Conservativa Weights)
C ALTERNATIVE Big Inventory	4	2	12	10	14*
L ALTERNATIVE Small Inventory	2	4	12	14*	10
N ALTERNATIVE Medium Inventory	3	3	12	12	12
S ALTERNATIVE Computerized Trucking	≥ 3.5	≥ 3.5	> 12	> 14**	> 14**

NOTES:

1. Having a relatively big inventory does well on keeping down outage costs that relate to losing customers because orders cannot be quickly filled.

2. Having a relatively small inventory does well on keeping down spoilage and storage costs.

3. A compromise is likely to be reached which may unnecessarily incur more outage costs than a big inventory and more spoilage-storage costs than a small inventory.

4. The object is to develop an inventory system that may do better on quickly meeting orders than a big inventory and simultaneously better on spoilage-storage costs than a small inventory.

5. Computerized trucking may be such a super-optimum solution. Most or all of the inventory is carried in moving trucks that can be quickly dispatched to the place of the orders. The trucks serve the purpose of both storage and transportation. If the system is working well, it can reduce both kinds of costs simultaneously.

* = The winning alternative before considering the SOS alternative.

** = The alternative that simultaneously does better than the conservative alternative on the conservative totals, and better than the liberal alternative on the liberal totals.

alternative using the conservative weights which reverse the 3 and the 1 on a 1–3 scale of importance.

This approach for arriving at an SOS solution is referred to as redefining the problem. The traditional problem definition is how big should the inventory be. The redefinition emphasizes the goals to be achieved, and asks how can we simultaneously achieve or improve upon both the conservative and liberal goals. On a higher level of generality, what alternative will simultaneously receive the highest total score using the liberal weights and the highest total score using the conservative weights, or the weights of whatever the conflicting viewpoints are? This general definition is the essence of super-optimizing analysis that builds on MCDM, decision-aiding software, spreadsheet analysis, and other tools in the broadening toolkit of management science and operations research.

Chapter 20

A PRODUCT LIABILITY CASE: CIVIL DAMAGES

Computer-aided mediation can be considered to have officially begun in November 1987, because that is when the first court case was known to have been settled as a result of computer-aided mediation. The case involved an American insurance company suing a foreign electronics company in the Federal Court of the Northern District of Illinois. The purpose of this chapter is to describe briefly what the case involved, as a good example of computer-aided mediation in general.

THE CASE

The subject matter of the case was product liability. The plaintiff was Traveler's Insurance Company, seeking reimbursement, and the defendant was Sanyo Electronics, seeking to avoid liability. Some of the facts have been simplified or made more general for methodological purposes, including exact amounts. The case can be used especially to indicate how computer-aided mediation can facilitate super-optimum settlements or at least ordinary settlements.

Figures 20–1 and 20–2 illustrate what is involved in a super-optimum settlement. The plaintiff demands $700,000 as a minimum in order to settle. The defendant offers $350,000 as a maximum in order to settle. The object of a super-optimum settlement is to provide the plaintiff with more than $700,000 while simultaneously not having the defendant pay more than $350,000. In other words, the problem is to find a number that is simultaneously bigger than $700,000 and smaller than $350,000, which are roughly the best expectations of the plaintiff and defendant respectively.

THE SETTLEMENT

Such a settlement can be arrived at by considering additional settlement criteria beyond the exchange of money. In almost every damages case, the defen-

Figure 20–1
Settle Versus Trial from the Plaintiff's Perspective

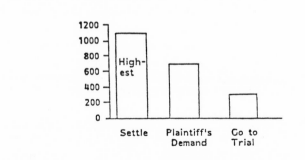

NOTES:

1. The expected value of settling from the plaintiff's perspective is $1,099,000, as described in the text (first bar).

2. The middle bar shows that the plaintiff's first demand or best expectation was $700,000.

3. The expected value of going to trial from the plaintiff's perspective is only $290,000, as described in the text (the third bar).

Figure 20–2
Settle Versus Trial from the Defendant's Perspective

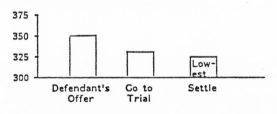

NOTES:

1. The defendant's first offer or best expectation is $350,000 (the first bar).

2. The expected value of going to trial from the defendant's perspective is $330,000 (the second bar).

3. The value of settling from the defendant's perspective is only $326,000 (the third bar).

4. Note that the settlement is lower and thus better than the defendant's best expectation from the defendant's perspective.

5. The $326,000 settlement figure could be substantially lower and still bring the plaintiff to a settlement in view of the big gap in Table 20-1 between the settlement value and the trial value form the plaintiff's perspective.

dant is an insurance company, a manufacturer, a transportation company, or some other kind of company that can offer something of considerable value to the plaintiff, but having relatively low cost to the defendant. In this case, it was possible for the defendant to consider offering electronic equipment, insurance claims, and insurance annuities to the plaintiffs and their insurance companies. That combination of equipment, claims, and annuities had an estimated cost value of only $326,000 to the defendants as indicated by Figure 20–2. That combination, however, had an estimated purchase value of $1,099,000 to the plaintiffs.

Such a solution could conceivably be developed without computer-aided mediation. Computer-aided mediation, however, greatly facilitates being able to deal with four or more criteria simultaneously from both the defendant's perspective and the plaintiff's perspective. It also facilitates making calculations concerning the expected value of going to trial. From the plaintiff's perspective, the expected value of going to trial is only $290,000 as shown in Figure 20–1 which is far less than the special settlement value of $1,099,000, or the traditional settlement value of something between $350,000 and $700,000. Likewise from the defendant's perspective, the expected value of going to trial is $330,000 which would cost the defendant more than the $326,000 settlement.

Table 20–1
Super-Optimizing Litigation Analysis (Using *Traveler's Insurance v. Sanyo Electronics* as an Illustrative Example)

ALTERNATIVES	CRITERIA — Relevant Items of Value Other than Money				Transacting for All Sides to Come Out Positively Ahead	Relevant Totals
	Computers from D to P	Big Screen TVs from D to P	Insurance Claims from D to P	Annuities from D to P	P as D's Sales Agent for Marine Insurance	
Plaintiff's SOS Settlement (Big Benefits)	$800	$500	$200	$100	$5,000 gross	+$1,600 or +$5,000
Plaintiff's Initial Demand = $900	0	0	0	0	0	$900
Likely Compromise Settlement = $600	0	0	0	0	0	$600
Defendant's Initial Offer = $300	0	0	0	0	0	$300
Defendant's SOS Settlement (Low Costs)	$150	$100	0	$20	$5,000 gross	-$270 or +$5,000

NOTE: This table illustrates one approach to generating super-optimum solutions. It is called big benefits for one side and low costs for the other. SOS solutions enable plaintiffs, defendants, conservatives, liberals, and other major viewpoints to all come out ahead of their best initial expectations simultaneously. Such solutions are facilitated by spreadsheet-based decision-aiding software.

Chapter 21

JURY PROCEDURES: CONSTITUTIONAL POLICY

Quite often a highly emotional controversy between liberals and conservatives may be capable of being resolved beyond the best expectations of each side through the approach of redefining the problem. They may be arguing over how to deal with a problem that is really relatively unimportant in terms of achieving their goals, as contrasted to a more important problem on which they might be likely to get a mutually satisfying agreement. This involves seeing beyond a relatively superficial argument to the higher level goals that are endorsed by both liberals and conservatives although possibly not to the same relative degree.

THE CASE

A concrete example is the controversy over the size of juries in criminal cases, as was shown in Table 8.1. Liberals argue in favor of preserving the traditional 12-person jury, as contrasted to allowing juries as small as only 6 people. Liberals view the larger jury as being important for protecting the innocent, since it is more difficult for a prosecutor to convince 12 jurors unanimously of the defendant's guilt than it is to convince 6 jurors. Liberals may also argue that 12-person juries allow for more public participation, but this seems less important than decreasing convictions, although public participation may sound more acceptable.

Conservatives argue in favor of allowing 6-person juries. They view smaller juries as being important for convicting the guilty, since it is easier for a prosecutor to convince 6 jurors unanimously of the defendant's guilt than it is to convince 12 jurors. Conservatives may also argue that 6-person juries reduce delay, but that seems less important than increasing convictions, although delay reduction may sound more acceptable.

Liberals in this context are thus especially sensitive to avoiding errors of convicting the innocent, although they also want to avoid errors of not convicting the guilty. Conservatives are especially sensitive to avoiding errors of not convicting the guilty, although they also want to avoid errors of convicting the innocent. So long as the problem is defined in terms of optimum jury size, there is an inherent trade-off between those two goals. Liberals see any reduction in jury size as sacrificing protection of the innocent, in favor of convicting the guilty. Conservatives see a retention of the 12-person jury as sacrificing the need to convict the guilty, in favor of an undue sensitivity to protecting the innocent, whom they tend to see as not being a significant percentage of the defendants who are tried.

THE RESOLUTION

What may be needed in this policy controversy is to redefine the problem away from "How many people should be present on a jury in criminal cases?" A more appropriate definition of the problem in light of what the liberals and conservatives are actually arguing over is "How can we simultaneously increase the probability of convicting guilty defendants and increase the probability of acquitting innocent defendants?" There is no inherent trade-off between those two goals. In fact, there may be no inherent trade-off between any two goals. By so restating the problem, one's attention is directed toward thinking about which procedural changes could achieve increases on both goals simultaneously, rather than thinking what is the ideal compromise, middling position, or equilibrium between 12-person and 6-person juries.

There are some procedural changes that could simultaneously increase goal achievement on both the liberal and conservative goals. They all involve increasing the general accuracy of juries and decreasing the general inaccuracy. One such procedural change would be allowing jurors to take notes. In most states, they are prohibited from doing so. It is unclear as to why that prohibition began. One plausible explanation is that when the jury system was started in about the 1500s in England, few people could read or write. It may have been felt that if those few jurors who could take notes were allowed to do so, then they would dominate jury decision making. A 12-person jury could then in effect become a jury of one or two people who have been making a written record of what those jurors perceived as having occurred. As of 1990, virtually all jurors are capable of taking notes and should be allowed to do so. It would improve their accuracy in both convicting the guilty and acquitting the innocent.

Along related lines, an especially useful innovation would be to provide for automatic videotaping of jury trials and bench trials. This is a possible double SOS. It is super-optimum in the sense that it increases the accuracy of convicting the guilty and acquitting the innocent simultaneously. Quite often in jury deliberations, there is disagreement among the jurors as to what was said by a certain witness, lawyer, or the judge. One juror who is especially domineering may say that the witness said the defendant was seen at the scene of the crime at 8:00 A.M. Other jurors may think it was 8:00 P.M. The disagreement can be quickly and accurately resolved with a videotape made by a camcorder that can be played back on any TV set with a video playback capability. Otherwise the winning perception is the one held by whichever jurors may have the most aggressive personalities. This could result in either an error of acquitting a guilty person, or an error of convicting an innocent person.

The second sense in which the camcorder videotaping is super-optimum is that it decreases costs and increases benefits simultaneously. It is substantially less expensive to videotape a jury trial than it is to pay a stenotypist to try to record verbatim what was said at the trial. The camcorder can be operated by someone who can easily be taught what little is involved. The cost of each tape is nominal and can be reused. The benefits are substantially increased because (1) one gets instant replay as contrasted to transcribing stenotyping months later, (2) one gets accurate replay as contrasted to the extensively ad-libbed record that is made by court reporters, (3) one can see facial expressions, (4) one can hear voice connotations, and (5) one can hear two or more people talking at the same time, which tends to become gibberish or missing information in steno-typing notes.

In addition to note-taking and videotaping, there are a number of other ways of increasing general jury accuracy. They include allowing jurors to have access to a written copy of the judge's instructions. This helps improve the interpretation of the law by juries just as note-taking and videotaping improve their understanding of the facts. Most states do not provide for written judicial instructions. This also goes back to medieval times when relatively few people could read. It was felt that those few who could read the judge's instructions would dominate jury decision making, just as those few who could write notes would also dominate. The contemporary reason for the inertia in allowing juries to have written instructions may relate to the fact that the instructions tend to favor safeguards for the innocent. Legal decision makers may be reluctant to do anything that will further increase acquittals and decrease convictions.

Other approaches to improving general juror accuracy that have been adopted in only a minority of states, if any, include: Jurors should be allowed to submit questions to the judge, the lawyers, or even the witnesses indirectly through the lawyers. This could clarify factual and legal ambiguities that lead to wrong decisions.

A training course should be provided for each juror that would last a full day before being eligible to decide cases. The course could clarify what is involved in conducting a trial, jury deliberating, judicial instructions, various kinds of evidence, and other matters. The course could allow jurors to ask questions during the course. The course could also have a test at the end to determine whether each juror has a minimum level of understanding of what is involved.

The ability to read and write or other educational qualifications could improve the general accuracy of jurors. Such requirements, though, can be subject to abuse, like southern literacy tests for voting. Even if the tests are objective, they could bias the composition of juries in favor of middle-class attitudes that favor the prosecution in criminal cases and the defendant in civil cases. Any measure designed to improve accuracy should not unthinkingly change the direction or bias of jury outcomes.

Jury accuracy can be improved by having counsel on both sides. We now tend to guarantee counsel to indigent defendants in criminal cases, but we do not adequately guarantee counsel to indigent litigants in civil cases where there is no contingency fee involved. The Legal Services Corporation is not sufficiently funded to guarantee counsel to indigent civil litigants, although the result is they do not litigate or go to trial, rather than go to trial without a lawyer.

FACTORS INTERFERING WITH ADOPTION

One might ask why such procedures as taking notes and using videotaping have not been adopted already. The key answer with regard to videotaping is that it is a relatively new technology, although audiotaping has been around for some time. The potential for taking meaningful jury notes has been around for at least a hundred years. An important answer may be the overemphasis on trade-off controversies in discussing jury decision-making such as jury size, the percentage needed to convict, the admissibility of various kinds of evidence, and other controversies in which going one way protects the innocent but facilitates convicting the guilty, and going the other way does the opposite.

Asking why note-taking has not been adopted or why it may be a long time before videotaping will be adopted raises a separate set of SOS problems that have to do with getting super-optimum solutions adopted after they have been generated. A key problem is simply inertia, especially in the legal system where there is possibly an overemphasis on preserving the past regardless of the present consequences. There is no system of evaluation that places so much emphasis on prior precedent, rather than present and future benefits and costs.

In any SOS adoption, there may also be problems of vested interests, property and jobs. Changing procedural rules may often change substantive results contrary to powerful interest groups. For example, having a trial for liability separate from the trial for damages is likely to lead to a much higher percentage of victories for the defendant. The jury under such split trials cannot adjust the damages to take the plaintiff's contributory negligence into consideration. That kind of change in substantive results does not seem to be a factor in allowing note-taking or videotaping. Vested property can complicate the adoption of SOS solutions with regard to replacing public housing with rent supplements or moving unemployed workers to better jobs. These kinds of considerations do not seem to be present here. Vested jobs can be a problem in mutually beneficial international tariff reductions. Videotaping would greatly reduce the need for court reporters, but they may not be a strong enough interest group to block videotaping, and they probably would not object to jurors taking notes.

Table 21–1
Justice and Criminal Procedure

CRITERIA / ALTERNATIVES	C GOAL	L GOAL	N TOTAL	L TOTAL	C TOTAL
	Convict the Guilty	Acquit the Innocent	(Neutral Weights)	(Liberal Weights)	(Conservative Weights)
C ALTERNATIVE Easier to Convict the Guilty	4	2	12	10	14*
L ALTERNATIVE Easier to Acquit the Innocent	2	4	12	14*	10
N ALTERNATIVE Between <C and <L	3	3	12	12	12
SOS ALTERNATIVE Between >C and >L	>3.5	>3.5	>14	>14**	>14**

THE IMPORTANCE OF PROBLEM DEFINITION AND SOS AWARENESS

Looking over the points that relate to the adoption of either note-taking or videotaping as a super-optimum solution to the problem of increasing both convicting the guilty and acquitting the innocent, one can draw at least two conclusions. First is that redefining the problem to emphasize simultaneous goal achievement can greatly facilitate generating super-optimum solutions. Perhaps as a general matter, one could even start with that approach in seeking to arrive at an SOS. It works even with alternatives that are inherently incapable of being combined, such as liberals wanting juries that consist of 12 or more people, and conservatives wanting juries that consist of 6 or less people.

Second is the important point that the battle for achieving super-optimum solutions is not won by merely generating policy alternatives that satisfy the definition of an SOS. There may be problems of technology, inertia, vested interests, property, and jobs that need to be taken into consideration. The main reason for lack of adoption, however, may be a lack of awareness as to what there is to adopt. Thus, a key conclusion may be the importance of communicating basic ideas as to what is meant by a super-optimum solution, and how one or more super-optimum solutions may be possible in any policy controversy.[1]

BROADENING THE CRIMINAL PROCEDURE EXAMPLE

In Table 21–1 the conservative alternative is broadened to include any public policy that makes it easier to convict the guilty, not just 6-person juries. The liberal alternative is broadened to include any public policy that makes it easier to acquit the innocent, not just 12-person juries.

The neutral alternative is broadened to include any public policy that is less conservative than the conservative alternative and is less liberal than the liberal alternative. The super-optimum alternative is broadened to include any public policy that is more conservative than the conservative alternative (or at least does better on conservative goal achievement), and is more liberal than the liberal alternative (or at least does better on liberal goal achievement).

Given the reasonable numbers in the cells, the super-optimum alternative only needs to score better than nothing on both the conservative and liberal goals in order to be the leading alternative on both the conservative and liberal totals using conservative and liberal weights.

NOTE

1. For literature on the criminal justice aspects of super-optimizing, see S. Nagel, "What's New and Useful in Legal Analysis Technology?" 5 *Ratio Juris* (1992), 172–190; and S. Nagel, *Legal Process Controversies and Super-Optimum Solutions* (Westport, Conn.: Quorum Books, 1993).

Chapter 22

RIGHT TO COUNSEL: LEGISLATIVE POLICY

The purpose of this chapter is to discuss two especially exciting and related professional developments in policy studies: dispute resolution or, more frequently, "alternative dispute resolution," and sensitivity analysis, or often "what-if analysis."

BASIC CONCEPTS

Alternative dispute resolution refers to deciding among alternative policy positions through mechanisms that involve third parties like arbitrators, mediators, or conciliators, as contrasted to traditional dispute resolution which involves courts, legislatures, or administrative agencies. Arbitrators tend to decide who is right and who is wrong, whereas mediators tend to emphasize bringing the sides together in compromises that do not assess blame. Conciliators tend to passively provide facilities for facilitating compromises.

In the policy studies context, sensitivity analysis refers to changing policy evaluation inputs to see what effect the changes would have on which decision should or would be reached. The inputs refer to the goals to be achieved, the alternatives available for achieving them, the relations between goals and alternatives, and any other inputs such as weights of the goals or constraints on the alternatives. The outputs may relate to determining the best alternative, combination, allocation, or predictive decision rule. Sensitivity analysis is also referred to as what-if analysis, threshold analysis, or other terms that vary slightly in their definitions.

The kind of dispute resolution with which this chapter is especially concerned is disputes over how to provide legal services for the poor. Liberals and Congress advocated salaried government lawyers by way of the Legal Services Corporation. Conservatives (and the Reagan White House) advocated a program of volunteer lawyers serving the poor. Both sides agree that the key criteria for deciding among the alternative delivery systems are inexpensiveness, accessibility, political feasibility, and competence. There is also rough agreement that volunteers are better on inexpensiveness and political feasibility, whereas salaried government lawyers are better on accessibility and competence. The big dispute as to the inputs for arriving at a conclusion is over the relative weights of the goals. The liberals place a higher weight on accessibility and competence, whereas the conservatives place a higher weight on inexpensiveness and political feasibility.

Disputes can often be resolved by changing the alternatives being considered, changing the criteria for evaluating the alternatives, or changing the relations between alternatives and criteria. Microcomputer software can be helpful in determining the effects of any of those changes.

This kind of dispute resolution is facilitated by spreadsheet-based software that makes use of multi-criteria decision-making. Such software can process a set of goals to be achieved, alternatives available for achieving them, and relations between goals and alternatives in order to choose or explain the best alternative, combination, allocation, or predictive decision rule. This kind of software is referred to as decision-aiding or information-processing software. It can be contrasted with information-retrieval software. Retrieval of information can sometimes be relevant to resolving disputes. More important, however, is the need to systematically process information that has already been obtained, including information in one's head.

The most useful aspect of such software is its ability to indicate what it would take to bring a second-place or other-place alternative up to first place. Such software can also do other kinds of what-if analysis whereby the goals, alternatives, relations, and other inputs can be quickly changed in order to see what effect the changes have on the willingness of each side to agree to a settlement. Spreadsheet software is especially relevant, partly because it allows for so many criteria or goals to be considered simultaneously. This enables each side to make concessions on some criteria that are not so important to it, but are important to the other side, and vice versa. This kind of interaction can lead to super-optimum solutions, whereby each side comes out ahead of its original best expectations.

CHANGING THE ALTERNATIVES, GOALS, AND RELATIONS

Alternatives

Perhaps the best way to resolve disputes over the relative weights of the goals (or for that matter over any disputed policy problem) is to try to find a new alternative that will please both sides in light of their differing weights, goals, perceptions, constraints, or other inputs. An example is working with the existing Legal Services Corporation, but requiring all Legal Services Agencies to use 10% of their budgets to improve the accessibility and competence of vol-

Table 22–1
An Example of Computer-Aided Mediation

	Inexpensiveness	Accessibility	Political feasibility	Competence
A. With unweighted criteria				
Volunteer	2.00	1.00	2.00	1.00
Salaried	1.00	2.00	1.00	2.00
Compromise	1.50	2.00	2.00	2.00
B. With conservative values				
Volunteer	4.00	1.00	4.00	1.00
Salaried	2.00	2.00	2.00	2.00
Compromise	3.00	2.00	4.00	2.00
C. With liberal values				
Volunteer	2.00	2.00	2.00	2.00
Salaried	1.00	4.00	1.00	4.00
Compromise	1.50	4.00	2.00	4.00

NOTES:

1. The alternative ways of providing legal counsel to the poor include:
    (1) Volunteer attorneys, favored by the White House.
    (2) Salaried government attorneys, favored by the Congress.
    (3) A compromise that involves continuing the salaried system, but requiring that 10% of its funding to making volunteers more accessible and competent.

2. Conservative values involve giving a weight of 2 to inexpensiveness and political feasibility when the other criteria receive a weight of 1. Liberal values involve giving a weight of 2 to accessibility and competence when the other criteria receive a weight of 1.

3. With conservative values, the volunteer system wins over the salaried system 10 points to 8. The compromise is an overall winner with 11-1/2 points.

4. With liberal values, the salaried system wins over the volunteer system 10 points to 8. The compromise is an overall winner with 11-1/2 points.

5. The "10% compromise" is thus a super winner in being better than the original best solution of both the conservatives and the liberals.

unteer lawyers. Accessibility can be improved by bringing the volunteer lawyers to the agency offices to meet with relevant clients. Competence can be improved through training manuals, training workshops, and matching specialist lawyers with clients who relate to their specialties. Such a 10% system may be better than a pure Legal Services Corporation, even for those with liberal weights, because it provides a better benefit/cost ratio and greater political feasibility without decreasing accessibility or competence. Such a system is also better than the existing Legal Services Corporation from a perspective with conservative weights, because it represents an improvement on all four goals over the existing system. Also if volunteering becomes mandatory for license renewal, then the volunteers are likely to dominate the system.

Computer output for the legal service example is given in Table 22–1. The first part of the table shows how the two original alternatives and the new alternative score on the four criteria on a scale of 1–2, corresponding to "relatively no" and "relatively yes." The second part of the table shows the same data, but with the scores on inexpensiveness and political feasibility doubled to reflect conservative values. The third part shows the same data as the first part, but with the scores doubled on accessibility and competence to reflect the liberal emphasis. The key item to note is that the optimizing compromise scores better than the favored alternative of either side using each side's own value system. Finding such optimizing compromises is facilitated by this kind of analysis.

Instead of adding an alternative, subtracting one might be helpful where more than two alternatives are involved. For example, by reducing three alternatives to two, we may have a clear-cut runoff where one of the two alternatives in effect gets an especially large portion of the votes or points that would otherwise go to the third alternative. Related to adding an alternative is the idea of consolidating two or more alternatives. Doing so in effect creates a new alternative, which may be a good compromise if there were only two alternatives at the time of the consolidation. If there were more than two alternatives, then consolidating can have the beneficial effect of reducing the number of alternatives. Related to consolidating (although in the opposite direction) is subdividing one alternative into two or more alternatives. Perhaps one of those newly created alternatives may be a compromise alternative on which the disputants can agree. If not, some of the newly created alternatives might be quickly eliminated as clearly inferior, thereby clarifying the situation although not reducing the number of alternatives. Each time there is an addition, subtraction, consolidation, or subdivision, the policy/goals percentaging (P/G%) program can quickly show how the new alternatives compare in terms of their overall or summation scores on the criteria, with regard to either raw scores or percentaging scores.

Criteria

All of the above approaches to making changes in the alternatives can also apply to making changes in the criteria. For example, a dispute might be more capable of being resolved by adding a criterion that brings out that alternative B is clearly the winner, even though the two alternatives were originally tied. Likewise, subtracting a criterion could make alternative B clearly the winner. The same effect in terms of clarifying the winner can also occur as a result of consolidating two or more criteria or as a result of subdividing a criterion.

Unlike the alternatives, the criteria are subject to different weights to indicate their relative importance, although the alternatives are subject to different overall scores to indicate their relative importance. The overall scores of the alternatives, however, are outputs of the analysis, whereas the weights of the criteria are inputs of the analysis. By changing those criterion weights, alternative B may become the clear winner. Working with different weights when all the weights were originally the same can help resolve many disputes. Along related lines, one can work with the weights and criteria of just the first disputant, and then just the second disputant. Doing so generates two sets of overall or summation scores for the alternatives. One can average those overall scores in order to see which alternative might be the winner, or one can average the weights that the disputants assign to the criteria. The averaging can be a weighted average if one side of the dispute is considered to have more weight or to be entitled to more votes than the other sides or other disputants.

Working with minimum and maximum constraints is another approach that especially applies to the criteria, although it could apply to the alternatives. For example, the subject matter of a given dispute may cause the disputants to agree that a certain criterion is desirable, such as the age of the person to be hired, but only up to 70 years because of a relevant retirement rule. That could estimate some alternatives as could a minimum requirement of age 21. Likewise, the subject matter of a given dispute may make it meaningful to have a maximum and/or a minimum constraint on an alternative. Perhaps, for example, the original alternatives are spending $100 on activity P and $10 on activity Q versus spending $90 on activity P and $30 on activity Q. The alternatives under consideration may be reduced if there is a maximum budget of no more than $115, a maximum expenditure on an activity of no more than $95, or a minimum expenditure on an activity of no less than $20. The P/G% program allows one to determine quickly the effects of changing minimum and maximum constraints on criteria and alternatives, as well as changing the criteria and the alternatives themselves.

Relations

In resolving disputes, the third big area of change involves the relations between the alternatives and the criteria. What begins as a tie could possibly be resolved by changing the scores for some of the relations. One could also show the overall summation scores for the alternatives when all the relations are scored from a conservative or liberal or other perspective. One can then average those two or more sets of overall scores in order to arrive at a super-overall winner as was discussed in talking about conservative and liberal weights and criteria.

Along related lines, one can change the relations by providing for more refined measurement as when one goes from a 1–2 scale to a 1–5 scale, or a less refined but clearer measurement as when one goes from a 1–5 scale to a 1–2 scale. One could change the measurement units from a 1–5 scale to a scale measured in dollars, years, miles, or another dimension. Changing the measurement scale may require shifting from a raw-score approach to a percentaging approach if multidimensionality is introduced. For example, although one can add the raw scores on two criteria, both of which are measured on 1.5 scales, one cannot so meaningfully add the raw scores from a 1.5 scale to the scores from a scale measured in miles. It may, however, be meaningful to indicate how each alternative scores on each criterion in terms of the percentage relation of each raw score to the maximum raw score possible or to the total of the raw scores on a criterion. The P/G% program works especially well with such multidimensionality in view of the program's emphasis on working with part/whole percentages or raw scores converted into percentages of the total points on a criterion.

CONCLUSIONS

In light of the above general principles and specific examples, one can conclude that microcomputers and the P/G% program can help facilitate negotiation and mediation leading to dispute resolution by proceeding in accordance with the following *steps or options*: Determine the initial alternatives, the criteria, and the relations between the alternatives and the criteria in light of each side's values and perceptions. The P/G% input-format facilitates clarification of those dispute parameters.

Determine what it would take each side to convince the other side. The threshold, breakeven, or tie-causing analysis of the P/G% program facilitates that determination. If each side could at least partly convince the other side, encourage them to do so, since the result may be a mutually acceptable alternative or compromise.

Experiment with a variety of additional alternatives, as contrasted to the original deadlocked alternatives. Use the P/G% program to determine quickly the overall or summation score for each alternative using the criterion weights of each side to the dispute. Look especially for new alternatives that could be endorsed by both sides more strongly than their original first choices. At least find an alternative that could be each side's second choice and thus serve as a compromise winner in a series of paired comparisons.

Try changing the alternatives by subtracting some, by consolidating two or more, or by subdividing some. Try doing the same things with the criteria. Use the P/G% program to determine the overall or summation scores of the new set of alternatives.

Try changing the criterion weights, or try averaging the alternatives in light of the different sets of weights which the conflicting disputants have.

Try working with reasonable minimum and/or maximum constraints on the criteria and/or the alternatives to see what difference that makes.

Try changing some of the relation scores and maybe the measurement units on which the scores are based. This may mean experimenting with the procedures of the P/G% program for dealing with criteria measured on multiple dimensions.

Some of the *implications of these procedures* are as follows:

By thinking in terms of super-optimum solutions with the disputants coming out ahead of their original best expectations, there should be a lessening of problems between groups based on economic class, race, sex, religion, ancestral nationality, geography, age, and other demographic characteristics that tend to be divisive.

This kind of dispute resolution can result in a higher percentage of disputes being resolved. They should also be resolved at a faster speed and with more satisfaction for the disputants.

Super-optimum dispute resolution does not require a mediating third party, although such people can be helpful, especially where the disputants are emotionally involved. Instead of a third party, the disputants themselves can adopt a mediating frame of mind so they can both or all come out ahead, rather than have winners and losers.

This kind of alternative dispute resolution does not require going outside the regular court system. There is no reason why regular judges cannot under appropriate circumstances seek to bring about super-optimum solutions between plaintiffs and defendants in civil cases.

Microcomputers and spreadsheet-based software can be helpful in resolving disputes, but more important than either the hardware or the software is having the disputants think in terms of multiple alternatives and multiple criteria so each side can give a little on criteria that are not so important to it but that may be important to the other side.

The idea of super-optimum solutions can apply to both rule-making disputes and rule-applying disputes. It can apply in the administrative, legislative, and judicial processes. It can also apply in business, family, and other social institutions.

It is hoped that this chapter will stimulate more use of computer-aided negotiation and mediation for resolving disputes. These uses should help build a literature of experiences from which other disputants, mediators, and arbitrators can benefit. In no way does a computer take the place of a negotiator, mediator, or arbitrator. Computers can, however, be substantial aids in clarifying the effects of new alternatives, criteria, and relations in resolving legal and other disputes.

REFERENCES FOR FURTHER READING

The following references are designed to provide further relevant reading for those who wish to follow up on the topic of super-optimum mediation in rulemaking and other disputes.

Fisher, Roger and William Ury. *Getting to Yes: Negotiating Agreement Without Giving In* (Houghton Mifflin, 1981).

Folberg, Jay and Alison Taylor. *Mediation: A Comprehensive Guide to Resolving Conflicts without Litigation* (Jossey-Bass, 1984).

Goldberg, Stephen, Eric Green, and Frank Sander (eds.). *Dispute Resolution* (Little, Brown, 1985).

Moore, Christopher. *The Mediation Process: Practical Strategies for Resolving Conflict* (Jossey-Bass, 1986).

Nagel, S. *Higher Goals for America: Doing Better Than the Best* (University Press of America, 1988).

Nagel, S. and M. Mills. *Multi-Criteria Methods for Alternative Dispute Resolution: With Microcomputer Software Applications* (Quorum Books, 1990).

Nagel, S. and M. Mills. *Systematic Analysis in Dispute Resolution* (Quorum Books, 1991).

Nyhart, Daniel (ed.). *Computer Models and Modeling for Negotiation Management* (Massachusetts Institute of Technology, 1987).

Susskind, Lawrence, and Jeffrey Cruikshank. *Breaking the Impasse: Consensual Approaches to Resolving Public Disputes* (Basic Books, 1987).

Ury, William, Jeanne Brett, and Stephen Goldberg. *Getting Disputes Resolved: Designing Systems to Cut the Costs of Conflict* (Jossey-Bass, 1988).

For further reading that relates to sensitivity analysis, see the following:

Carroll, Owen. *Decision Power with Supersheets* (Dow Jones-Irwin, 1986).

Dawes, Robyn. *Rational Choice in an Uncertain World* (Harcourt Brace Jovanovich, 1988).

Harris, Clifford. *The Break-Even Handbook* (Prentice-Hall, 1978).

Hendrick, Rebecca. "The Role of Heuristic Thinking in Policy Analysis," in S. Nagel (ed.), *Public Policy Analysis and Management* (JAI Press, 1992).

Kmietowicz, Z. and A. Pearman. *Decision Theory and Incomplete Knowledge* (Gower, 1981).

Kotz, Samuel and Donna Stroup. *Educated Guessing: How to Cope in an Uncertain World* (Marcel Dekker, 1983).

Mack, Ruth. *Planning on Uncertainty: Decision Making in Business and Government Administration* (Wiley, 1971).

Moore, Carl. *Profitable Applications of the Break-Even Systems* (Prentice-Hall, 1971).

Nagel, S. "Changing the Goals, Means, or Methods." In his *Policy Studies: Integration and Evaluation* (Greenwood, 1988), 145–162.

Nagel, S. "Multiple Missing Information." In his *Evaluation Analysis with Microcomputers* (JAI Press, 1989), 129–180.

Part VI _____

GENERALIZED WIN-WIN
POLICY ANALYSIS

Chapter 23

PUBLIC POLICY

GENERAL BACKGROUND

Economic Policy

In the context of reducing inflation and unemployment simultaneously, economic growth through increased productivity can be a win-win solution. Productive economic growth can come about through training, new technologies, competition, exports, and government capital where private enterprise is reluctant to get involved.

This five-part program can promote an increase in productivity which in turn results in an increase in the gross domestic product. If there is a productivity growth in the GNP, then that means more goods are available. Inflation means too many dollars chasing too few goods. Thus when more goods are competitively available, prices tend to go down. Increased production can reduce inflation better than increasing interest rates, because increasing interest rates has the effect of reducing the GNP and increasing unemployment.

Likewise, if there is a productivity growth in the GNP, then that means the population has more money available to spend. Increased national income means increased national expenditure. If the population does have more to spend, then the increased spending helps to create new jobs, thereby more than offsetting the previous unemployment, or the unemployment that is caused by worker displacement as a result of productivity downsizing.

Technology Issues

On health care, the conservative position has been charity or local aid; more recently, Medicare for the aged and Medicaid for the poor. The liberal position is government-salaried doctors or an expansion of Medicare to cover everyone.

The SOS is variations on subsidized HMOs including seed money, vouchers, and employer contributions.

The conservative position on technological innovation is basically to preserve the patent system. The liberal position is to abolish patents or restrict the monopolistic aspects, such as requiring licensing. The SOS position is to develop well-placed subsidies or incentives to encourage needed inventions.

The environmental protection SOS involves technological problems in developing new technologies that are both more profitable and cleaner. The development of work (meaning resources and development) may be also quite expensive in terms of government appropriation.

On the matter of toxic waste, there are administrative problems involved in trying to determine when there is no substantial health danger. There may also be administrative problems in allowing liability to be determined by negotiation. This could lead to some corruption where the business firms are able to work out a settlement, possibly by offering some kind of bribe to the negotiators to accept a lesser settlement.

The licensing of patents involves a lot of political opposition from those who do not want any licensing. There may also be administrative problems in determining what constitutes a reasonable royalty.

The energy sources matter involves technological feasibility with regard to the microwave in the sky for massive solar energy. The large-scale storage batteries also represent technological problems. There may be psychological problems in getting acceptance on the safer second-generation reactors, given the lack of believability in previous claims from the nuclear industry.

Social Issues

On the matter of poverty, the conservative position has been no public aid or Aid to Dependent Children without reform. The liberal position has been aid with dignity such as Negative Income Tax, Old Age and Survivors Insurance, or children's allowance. The SOS is incentives to welfare recipients to take training and jobs and to employers to give training and jobs.

On leisure the key discussion has to do with casinos. One conservative position favors business profits and another is opposed to gambling. One liberal position favors increased jobs while another proposes taking advantage of the poor. The SOS might be funds for education, inner-city jobs, and facilitating suburban customers. Conservatives on integrated education are willing to prohibit segregation but not take affirmative government action to bring about integrated education. Liberals tend to endorse busing. The SOS that we came up with involved housing vouchers to get integrated schools, teacher pay incentives, and supplements for low-income districts.

The key family issue is abortion. The conservative position is opposed to virtually all abortion. The liberal position is willing to allow virtually all abortions. Again the neutral position is in between. The SOS position is more effective birth control and adoption.

Political Issues

On the matter of reforming government structures, conservatives tend to emphasize chief executives over legislatures and states over the national government. Liberals tend to emphasize legislatures over chief executives or the national government over the states. The SOS position emphasizes continuous growth rather than the more static kind of stability that is associated with presidential government. The SOS position also emphasizes responsiveness to training needs rather than to new elections. Both are directed toward increasing international competitiveness so that both conservatives and liberals can come out ahead.

On electoral reform, conservatives in general tend to like few political parties and a limited franchise for voting. Liberals like more political parties for greater responsiveness and expanded voting rights. The SOS might be a two-party system that allows third-party candidates, direct primaries, nonpartisan redistricting, registration, and campaign funding.

International Issues

On foreign policy, conservatives tend to be strong on defense and to favor right-wing governments; liberals tend to be strong on domestic matters and to favor left-wing governments. The SOS is to favor Democratic governments regardless of whether they are left-wing or right-wing and to favor free trade as leading to world peace and prosperity.

On international trade, the conservative group wants to preserve monopoly profits and to facilitate selling overseas. The liberal group wants to preserve wages of noncompetitive workers and emphasizes buying abroad for consumer benefit. The SOS encourages free trade but provides well for displaced workers, and agressively seeks to have other countries participate in free trade unions and international economic commissions.

ECONOMIC POLICY: UNEMPLOYMENT AND INFLATION

Conservative and Liberal Positions

The goals of conservatives with regard to unemployment and inflation tend to emphasize a reduction in inflation. Conservatives also want to reduce unemployment, but relative to liberals, conservatives tend to place more emphasis on inflation. Liberals have as their goal in this policy problem the reduction of unemployment, but liberals recognize that inflation also is important to reduce. Inflation means higher prices to consumers, and consumers make up a key liberal constituency. Conservatives recognize that unemployment is undesirable from the perspective of business, because it means that wage earners will not be earning wages. They will be buying less goods, which will cut into business profits. Reducing inflation and reducing unemployment are goals desired by both conservatives and liberals, but they vary regarding the relative emphasis they place on each of those goals. This will be the case with regard to virtually all policy problems; mainstream conservatives and mainstream liberals do tend to agree on the overall goals, but they disagree on their relative importance. (See Table 23–1 for all economic policy issues.)

With regard to alternatives, conservatives traditionally seek to reduce inflation by manipulating the money supply, which means changing interest rates. During a time of inflation, which is too many dollars chasing too few goods, you raise interest rates in order to reduce the money supply. By increasing interest rates, the quantity of dollars or at least the quantity of credit is reduced. If people have less consumer credit and less business credit, then there is less buying. In times of recession or high unemployment, the conservative alternative tends to emphasize decreasing interest rates so that more money is available to stimulate businesses to expand, and thereby reduce unemployment. Liberals, on the other hand, have traditionally emphasized manipulating the budget, rather than interest rates. Manipulating the budget means manipulating taxing and spending. More specifically, in times of inflation, liberals advocate raising taxes and decreasing government spending to take money out of circulation. In times of recession, liberals advocate lowering taxes and increasing government spending to put money into circulation.

The trouble with these alternatives is they tend to involve trade-offs that are not desirable. Raising interest rates may decrease inflation, but it is also likely to increase unemployment. Likewise, if you have tax reductions and increased government spending, you may decrease unemployment but cause inflation. What is needed is a win-win alternative that can simultaneously reduce inflation and reduce unemployment, as contrasted to this traditional trade-off thinking.

A Win-Win Alternative

The SOS or win-win solution in this context may be economic growth, which means production that will increase the gross national product. How do you increase economic growth? One way is through public policy. Public policy should stimulate the adoption and innovation of new technologies through government subsidies and incentives, and also should stimulate training of the workforce so it will be able to handle these new technologies. These new technologies and training will have a positive effect on productivity, which then has a positive effect on economic growth. True economic growth means more goods, and that helps to defeat inflation. In other words, economic growth produces enough goods so you do not have too few for the amount of dollars in circulation. Economic growth has a negative effect on inflation, within reasonable limits.

Table 23-1
Economic Policy

ISSUES	CONSERVATIVE	LIBERAL	NEUTRAL	SUPER-OPTIMUM SOLUTIONS	FEASIBILITY
1. INFLATION AND UNEMPLOYMENT	1. *Reduce inflation* -- 1. CHANGE INTEREST RATES	1. *Reduce unemployment* -- 1. CHANGE TAXING AND SPENDING	1. A LITTLE OF BOTH	1. *Increase technology and skills* 2. *Increase GNP*	1. Economic 2. Displaced workers
2. ECONOMIC GROWTH	1. *Increase investment* -- 1. TAX BREAKS TO INVESTORS AND HIGH INCOME 2. CAPITAL GAINS	1. *Increase consumption* -- 1. TAX BREAKS TO CONSUMERS AND LOW INCOME 2. EXEMPTIONS AND STANDARD DEDUCTIONS	1. TAX BREAKS IN GENERAL	1. *Energy* 2. *Immigration* 3. *Free speech* 4. *Education* 5. *Equal opportunity* 6. *Health* 7. *Low crime rate*	1. Economic 2. Displaced workers
3. SPENDING, TAXING, AND DEFICIT	1. *Increase defense and investments* -- 1. CUT DOMESTIC SPENDING 2. RAISE SALES TAXES	1. *Increase domestic consumption* -- 1. CUT DEFENSE SPENDING 2. RAISE INCOME TAXES		1. *Economic growth* 2. *Increase goods* 3. *Increase spending* 4. *Decrease public aid* 5. *Increase taxes*	1. Displaced workers
4. ORGANIZING THE ECONOMY	1. *Increase productivity* -- 1. CAPITALISM 2. PRIVATE OWNERSHIP	1. *Increase equity* -- 1. SOCIALISM 2. GOVT. OWNERSHIP		1. *Contracting out* 2. *Competition* 3. *Partial subsidies, e.g., HMOs*	1. Political 2. Administrative
5. LAND USE AND AGRICULTURE	1. *Increase farm profits* -- 1. RESTRICT SUPPLY 2. GOVT. PURCHASE	1. *Lower food prices* -- 1. DIRECT PAYMENT 2. FOOD STAMPS 3. RELOCATE 4. DECREASE EXPENSES		1. *International sales by way of (1) lowering tariffs and (2) improving exchange rates*	1. Political
6. LABOR AND MANAGEMENT	1. *Lower business expenses* -- 1. DECREASE UNIONS 2. DECREASE WORKPLACE REGULATIONS	1. *Increase wages* -- 1. INCREASE UNIONS 2. INCREASE WORKPLACE REGULATIONS		1. *Productivity councils to (1) increase total revenue and (2) ease relocation of workers*	1. Displaced workers
7. BUSINESS AND CONSUMERS	1. *Increase business income* -- 1. MARKETPLACE	1. *Lower consumer prices* -- 1. REGULATIONS		*Competition through:* 1. *Free entry* 2. *Licensing and patents* 3. *Leasing networks* 4. *Lowering tariffs* 5. *Seed money*	1. Political

Economic growth also has a negative effect on unemployment, because economic growth means that you have increased the number of available jobs for the unemployed through increased production, increased income, and increased spending.

The feasibility problem is keeping these ideas from being adopted, because economic growth comes from increased productivity, which in turn comes from new technologies and from better training of the workforce. Increased productivity means that one worker can now produce what formerly took a greater number, resulting in a number of displaced workers. Public policy has to find some place to put the displaced workers. It cannot give them boondoggle jobs, but rather real jobs that get created as a result of increased gross national product and increased spending. Finding real jobs for displaced workers may mean retraining them. It may also mean subsidizing employers to take them on, or commissioning employment agencies to find new jobs. But the displaced workers themselves represent the difficult feasibility problem with regard to the kind of productivity increases associated with economic growth.

TECHNOLOGY POLICY

Energy

On energy sources the conservative approach emphasizes oil and nuclear energy sources. The liberal approach emphasizes solar and synthetic fuels. The conservative goal tends to be oriented toward business profits—meaning the least expensive energy. Liberals are concerned with protecting the environment. A neutral position would be to think in terms of a combination or coal as a fallback position. But coal is less clean than oil. The combination is typical of a neutral approach. The SOS seeks to develop safe nuclear and massive solar energy and also competition in the sale of electricity. Liberals are also interested in safety. Trying for safe nuclear power can give cheap and safe fuel. Massive solar power also gives cheap and safe fuel. Increasing competition helps bring down the price and brings up the quality. The feasibility problem is that it may not be possible to develop safe nuclear and massive solar energy within a short time frame. The competition runs into political opposition.

We are also concerned with new energy sources that involve safer nuclear energy and massive solar energy, with government-stimulated competition in the electricity business regardless of the sources of energy. It is necessary to add a neutral goal that relates to business consumers of energy who especially welcome competition on the part of business suppliers. (See Table 23–2 for all technology policy issues.)

Medical Care

Medical care involves conservative reliance on the marketplace and liberal reliance on socialized medicine. The marketplace has been modified by Medi-

Table 23-2
Technology Policy

ISSUES	CONSERVATIVE	LIBERAL	NEUTRAL	SUPER-OPTIMUM SOLUTIONS	FEASIBILITY
1. ENVIRONMENTAL PROTECTION	*1. Profits and business expansion* - - 1. MARKETPLACE, STATES, AND COURTS	*1. Clean environment* - - 1. REGULATION, FEDERAL GOVT., AND ADMINISTRATIVE AGENCIES	- - 1. POLLUTION TAXES OR MARKETABLE RIGHTS TO POLLUTE	*1. New processes that are less expensive and cleaner*	1. Technological 2. Economic
2. TOXIC WASTE	*1. Business profits* - - 1. LOW COST COVERUP OR GOVT. PAYMENT	*1. Clean up with cost on wrongdoing* - - 1. TOTAL CLEAN UP WITH JOINT SEVERAL LIABILITY	- - 1. BIG TALK AND LITTLE ENFORCEMENT	*1. Remove health danger* *2. Negotiate proportionate liability*	1. Administrative 2. Economic
3. ENCOURAGING INVENTIONS	*1. Business profits* - - 1. PRESERVE PATENTS	*1. Clean and safe fuel* - - 1. REPLACE PATENTS WITH GRANTS	- - 1. SHORTEN PATENTS	*1. Require licensing of patents*	1. Political 2. Administrative 3. Legal
4. ENERGY SOURCES	*1. Low tax costs* - - 1. HELP ENERGY INDUSTRY 2. OIL AND CONVENTIONAL NUCLEAR	*1. Clean and safe fuel* - - 1. SOLAR AND SYNTHETIC FUELS	- - 1. COAL TO REPLACE OIL	*1. Safe nuclear* *2. Massive solar* *3. Competition*	1. Technological 2. Economic 3. Psychological
5. HOUSING	*1. Landlord profits and lower taxes* - - 1. MARKETPLACE	*1. Minimum quality housing for the poor* - - 1. PUBLIC HOUSING		*1. Housing vouchers, especially economic integration*	1. Economic
6. TRANSPORTA-TION	*1. Decrease taxes* - - 1. MARKETPLACE	*1. Decrease time* - - 1. MASS TRANSIT		*1. Stimulate suburbs to provide (1) jobs for suburbanites and (2) housing for low income people* *2. Stimulate inner-cities to provide (1) jobs for inner-city residents and (2) housing to attract suburbanites*	1. Economic
7. HEALTH CARE	*1. Quality* *2. At low cost to taxpayer* - - 1. MARKETPLACE 2. MEDICAID AND MEDICARE	*1. Access* *2. At low HMOs* *3. No pre-conditions cost to consumer* - - 1. SOCIALIZED MEDICINE 2. SINGLE PAYER		*1. Health insurance, especially* *2. Group discounts* *3. Vouchers*	

caid and Medicare. A substitute for socialized medicine is the single payer system. The conservative goal is quality medicine. The liberal goal is access at low costs to the consumer; conservatives are concerned about costs to the taxpayer. The SOS is health insurance with no preconditions, group discounts, and vouchers. Such a system can provide quality and access simultaneously. The health insurance by way of health maintenance organizations provides quality. Three rules help provide access: (1) no preconditions, (2) group discounts, and (3) vouchers for those who cannot afford the full premium. The feasibility problems are that it is not politically feasible if there is an employer mandate or if there is an HMO requirement.

Regarding alternative health care delivery systems, we are talking about a package of items. One item is removing preconditions as a justification for higher rates. A second is allowing people to join artificial groups in order to get big discounts. A third is vouchers for middle-class people who cannot afford the full insurance premiums. A fourth aspect is phasing in Medicare and Medicaid. A fifth aspect would be to cover with vouchers people from the same economic class as those who had no insurance and received vouchers. A final provision might be to require the remainder to have health insurance just as people are required to have liability insurance in order to drive. The penalty is that if they need emergency care then they are provided with the care but billed for the cost plus a 10% fine. This is too much detail. It could be called facilitated health insurance, with the key facilitation being the vouchers, but also joining artificial groups, removing preconditions, changing Medicaid and Medicare, and requiring what is usually referred to as first bite insurance, meaning no penalty is imposed or even billing until there is a use of emergency facilities.

SOCIAL POLICY

Poverty and Welfare

On the welfare to work idea, the conservative approach emphasizes cutoffs to get people to work. Job finding is left up to the individual. The liberal approach tends to leave it up to the government, especially training. Conservatives are trying to save tax money; liberals are trying to find jobs for the poor—one might say jobs, dignity, and income for the poor. The SOS position is to have job facilitators that rely on the private sector. This includes placement, training, day care, wage subsidies, and economic growth, especially job-based day care and training. The feasibility problem here is money. It does require a willingness to spend in order to find jobs for the poor. (See Table 23-3 for all social policy issues.)

The subject of finding jobs for people on public aid may need to be changed, since it was a lot of separate issues. If we lump all the job-finding issues together, we could say that the conservative approach is to leave it up to the individual and the marketplace. This is the current Gingrich idea. It saves on

Table 23-3
Social Policy

ISSUES	CONSERVATIVE	LIBERAL	NEUTRAL	SUPER-OPTIMUM SOLUTIONS	FEASIBILITY
1. PUBLIC AID RULES	*Deter poverty and public aid* 1. DEPENDENT CHILD 2. NO NATIONAL MINIMUMS 3. DEDUCTED EARNINGS 4. PRIVILEGE VS RIGHT	*Dignity of the poor* 1. WORKING PARENTS 2. NATIONAL MINIMUMS 3. RETAINED EARNINGS 4. DUE PROCESS	1. LEAVE IT TO THE STATES	*Job opportunities*	1. Economic 2. Psychological
2. JOBS FOR AID RECIPIENTS	*Minimize tax costs* 1. TWO-YEAR CUTOFF WITH MINIMUM HELP	*Maximize good jobs* 1. TWO-YEAR CUTOFF WITH GOVT. AS POTENTIAL EMPLOYER	1. MIDDLING APPROPRIATION	*Privatized* 1. Commissioned job finders 2. Job-based private sector day care 3. Training 4. Wage subsidies 5. Economic growth 6. Job facilitators	1. Economic 2. Psychological (motivation)
3. ABORTION	*No killing of fetuses* 1. PROHIBIT ABORTIONS	*No killing of pregnant mothers in illegal abortions* 1. ALLOW ABORTIONS	1. ALLOW IN FIRST TRIMESTER; PROHIBIT IN THIRD TRIMESTER	1. More effective birth control and subsidized adoptions	1. Economic 2. Political 3. Legal
4. SEX EDUCATION	*Reduce or eliminate teen sexuality* 1. ABSTINENCE	*Reduce or eliminate pregnancy and AIDS* 1. BIRTH CONTROL, ESPECIALLY CONDOM DISTRIBUTION	1. BOTH WITH PARENTAL CONSENT	1. Abstinence and skin implants and condoms if voluntary, decreasing sexuality and pregnancy, along with parental involvement	1. Economic 2. Psychological 3. Technological
5. INNER-CITY SCHOOLS	*Reduce taxes and disruption* 1. PROHIBIT LEGAL SEGREGATION AND PROVIDE CHOICE	*Improve education, esp. of poor* 1. BUSING FOR INTEGRATION	1. LIMITED BUSING	1. Integration without busing 2. Economic integration 3. Housing vouchers 4. Line drawing 5. Combat pay 6. Equalization 7. Contracting out 8. Redevelopment	1. Economic 2. Psychological 3. Political
6. STUDENT AID	*Reduce tax costs* 2. ENFORCE COLLECTIONS	*Increase education and GNP* 1. POSSIBLE AMNESTY	1. EFFICIENT ENFORCEMENT	1. Serve in place of collection and payment	1. Political 2. Administrative
7. STANDARD WORK WEEK	*Reduce labor expense* 40 HOUR WEEK	*Spread work* 2. *More leisure* 35 HOUR WEEK WITH 40 HOUR WAGE		1. Staggered; reduce 1 hour when productivity goes up 3% 2. More constructive leisure	

taxes, at least in the short run. The liberal approach is for the government to undertake the finding, training, day care, subsidies, and backup. The SOS position is variations on contracting out to employment agencies, on-the-job training, and job-based day care.

Leisure and the Work Week

The conservative position on the standard work week is to retain the present 40-hour week. Liberals would like to shorten the week. This relates to when time-and-a-half gets paid. The conservative goal is to reduce labor expense. The liberal goal is to spread work and have more leisure. The SOS is to reduce by one hour whenever the productivity goes up by 3%. The effect is to not hurt the GNP, which would otherwise be hurt if the work week were reduced. If the work week drops by one-eighth, then so would the GNP. Liberals want a 35-hour week with a 40-hour wage. This is not possible unless productivity has gone up. Reducing the workweek and retaining the same wage will leave no money left over for hiring additional people. The feasibility problem is partly technological but also psychological whether people will feel that they are only working part time.

The SOS for a standard work week for overtime purposes involves a staggered reduction based on national productivity increases. This has the effect of simultaneously raising total GNP while providing for more leisure. A second aspect is that it is up to each individual company in bargaining with the union or the individual employees as to how their productivity changes are going to be translated into wage increases or overtime labor. All the law does is change the starting point for time-and-a-half.

Education

The conservative position on economic integration in education is school choice. The liberal position tends to be busing. Conservatives want to preserve neighborhood schools. Liberals want to improve the quality of education for low-income kids. The SOS involves housing vouchers to move to better neighborhoods; redevelopment of inner cities for condominium communities with 25% low-income people; and upgrading the schools that are not integrated. This may mean federal equalization money, performance money, and subsidies for contracting out. The feasibility problem is economic, because housing vouchers cost money. The federal funding is also expensive, but may be well worth it in terms of reducing welfare, crime, and lack of productivity.

School choice versus busing are traditional alternatives, but adding housing vouchers to move low-income kids to better neighborhoods and doing economic redevelopment of inner-city areas to create integrated condominium communities could also help economic integration in education.

Abortion

The conservative position is to prohibit all abortions. Liberals want to allow them. Conservatives are concerned with saving the lives of the unborn. Liberals are concerned with saving lives of pregnant mothers whose lives might be jeopardized by illegal abortions or self-induced abortions. The SOS is to get at unwanted pregnancies through better abstinence programs and better birth control and to provide subsidized adoptions for unwanted pregnancies that still occur. Providing subsidized abortions and better birth control may run into some economic problems. But the bigger opposition is political to the birth control part and psychological to the abstinence part.

Abortion policy should have an emphasis on better birth control to reduce unwanted pregnancies, including abstinence and voluntary skin implants, which may actually be more acceptable to conservatives who object to condom distribution. The distribution systems are highly visible and obtrusive. They may involve replenishing one's supply every week or few weeks. The skin implant involves a one-hour visit to the doctor's office once every five years. It would be even more voluntary than condom distribution or participation in a required sex education course. No such course is required, but fundamentalist kids might suffer some stigma from not participating, just as libertarian kids or those from minority religions might suffer stigma from not participating in organized prayers. The skin implant would be like having one big prayer that lasts five years, as contrasted to every morning. Liberals might be able to tolerate a prayer every five years, and maybe conservatives might be willing to tolerate one long-lasting birth control pill every five years. The sex education classes could then put more emphasis on abstinence if birth control is largely covered by skin implants. This does not cover AIDS protection, which is a separate issue. The problem of teenage pregnancy is a worse problem than that of teenage AIDS. They are not mutually exclusive, but they do not have to be tied together. Abstinence does cover both. Condoms in an ineffective way applies to both, but they are especially ineffective in birth control compared to the skin implant.

POLITICAL POLICY

Legislative Procedures

The conservative position on the filibuster issue has been to allow it. The liberal position has been to abolish it. The conservative goal is to block populist legislation. The liberals want to abolish it to promote majority rule with minority rights being protected by the courts. The SOS position might be to expand guaranteed time to the minority in return for allowing a majority vote. This might mean a guarantee of 200 hours for a 51% vote and 100 hours for a 55% vote. As of now a 60% vote is required to cut off debate and discussion, which could go on for long enough to keep the issue from ever coming to a vote because Congress adjourns before it gets a chance for a vote. The feasibility problem is political adoption. It is possible that the Supreme Court could declare the filibuster unconstitutional. This raises issues about judicial feasibility. The filibuster is definitely a big problem in Congress.

The filibuster SOS involves a rule that specifies that if 200 hours of debate are allowed, then the legislation should need only 55% of the Senate to pass. If 300 hours of debate are allowed, then the legislation should need only 51% to pass. This seems a bit much or a bit contrary to majority rule but acceptable. A filibuster of 200 hours could be about eight days at 24 hours per day; 300 hours is then more than 12 days at 24 hours per day, which is a lot of time; and 24 hours per day of the Senate being in session would be a burden depending on how much attendance is required. If very little attendance or no attendance is required, then it is just a delaying tactic. The provision might have to specify that it is 100 hours and 200 hours, but every hour must involve a quorum. This forces the majority party to show up at least to fill the quorum. The minority party could stay away, since they do not want to see the legislation passed anyhow. Requiring a quorum means nothing if there is no one there to listen.

There is a political feasibility problem. The minority party would prefer to have things remain as they are, which gives them a veto power, especially toward the end of the session. It is a good time for reforming a filibuster rule, since both the Democrats and Republicans have taken turns being the majority party and the minority party. As long as they both think they have about an equal chance of being in the majority, they may support restricting the filibuster rule. The Republicans may support it now (mid-1990s) since they are in the majority. The Democrats may support it in anticipation that they will be in the majority in the future. The counterargument is that both sides also anticipate they will be in the minority in the future.

One could appeal to some sense of democracy in the public interest. This may be naive in comparison to partisan advantage, especially since the general public does not understand the filibuster so well. It is a matter of procedure rather than substance. It has been changed in the past only because one party was overwhelmingly in the majority, with more than 60% of the Senate, and they had the foresight to make changes in anticipation that they would be still in the majority in the future, but not more than 60%. If there is going to be a change and the argument is going to be based on the need to change the mind of the majority, then there has to be a time guarantee, as contrasted to arguing that the filibuster is needed in order to block majority rule. It would be hard to defend that, although it depends on what spin is done.

We do have restrictions on majority rule, such as free speech under the First Amendment. A counter to this is that the proposed reform guarantees free speech. It even guarantees an audience of influential senators who have to listen or at least be there. The First Amendment does not guarantee that minority viewpoints must win. It just guarantees that they be given an opportunity to speak. The counter is that there are other clauses like Equal Protection that cannot be infringed upon regardless of which procedures are used. Thus, no matter how much free speech is allowed to blacks or their supporters, they cannot be subjected to slavery or disenfranchisement. The counter to this is that reducing the filibuster is not going to result in legislation being passed that provides for slavery or disenfranchisement. We do have Constitutional clauses to prevent these without meeting a filibuster rule.

This kind of reform has serious political feasibility problems unless the courts step in and tell the U.S. Senate that the filibuster is the equivalent of giving 40% of the Senate 1.5 votes apiece and the other 60% get only 1 vote apiece. This also conflicts with one senator one vote, which is part of the body of the Constitution without even having to go to the Equal Protection Clause. This has some judicial feasibility problems as to whether the Court would be willing to take the case. If they took redistricting cases, they should be willing to take a filibuster case. (See Table 23–4 for all of the political policy issues.)

Voter Participation

The conservative position on voter turnout is to keep things as they are. The liberals are in favor of tinkering with the system, such as motor-voter registration. The conservative goal is to prevent double voting. Liberals are concerned with the increase in turnout. The object is to develop a system that can increase turnout while decreasing double voting. A four-part program seems relevant, with on-site registration, multiple-day voting, multiple-place voting, and using invisible ink to prevent double voting. Or maybe the Supreme Court might declare the present system unconstitutional since it gives more votes to some people than others, namely those who register. There are feasibility problems, possibly overcome if the Democrats could ever get enough votes to cut off a Republican filibuster or if Republicans ever recognize that they can also benefit from increased turnout if they broaden their appeal.

INTERNATIONAL POLICY

World Peace

The conservative position on United Nations peacekeeping is low cooperation with the United Nations. Liberals advocate high cooperation. Conservatives are concerned about saving U.S. lives and dollars. Liberals are more concerned about increasing peace. The SOS might involve a volunteer United Nations force. It would probably be English-speaking with maximum numbers from any one country. The force could promote peace better than the present system of national units and at the same time only involve volunteers. The feasibility

Table 23-4
Political Policy

ISSUES	CONSERVATIVE	LIBERAL	NEUTRAL	SUPER-OPTIMUM SOLUTIONS	FEASIBILITY
1. FILIBUSTER	Block populist majoritarian laws - - ALLOW	Majority rule (one senator, one vote) - - ABOLISH		1. 200 hours 51% vote, 100 hours 55% vote, or 2. Supreme Court case	
2. VOTER TURNOUT	Prevent double voting - - AS IS	Increase turnout - - TINKER, E.G., MOTOR-VOTER		1. a. On-site registration b. Multiple day c. Multiple place d. Invisible ink or 2. Supreme Court	
3. U.N. PEACEKEEPING	Save U.S. lives and $ - - LOW COOPERATION	Increase peace - - HIGH COOPERATION		1. Volunteer U.N. force 2. English speaking and diverse countries MAX 3. Mercenary and idealistic 4. Army, Navy, and Air Force with aid	
4. TARIFFS	1. Protect U.S. firms 2. Labor unions - - #1 HIGH TARIFFS	1. Exporters 2. Investors 3. Consumers - - #2 LOW TARIFFS		1. Low tariffs 2. Job facilitators	
5. CAMPAIGN FUNDING	Free speech -- 1. No restrictions 2. No reporting	Equity -- 1. Restrictions 2. Reporting	- - REPORTING BUT NO RESTRICTIONS	1. Voluntary contributions public funding 2. Voluntary restrictions 3. Voluntary spending by business	Political

problems in the past have been partly political, involving distrust of the United Nations. Now it is more a matter of how to administer the force and funding, which would come from the regular United Nations treasury and contributions. It would be partly a mercenary and idealistic army. It could call upon member countries to supply additional aid.

International Trade

The traditional conservative position on tariffs has been high tariffs in order to protect U.S. companies. Labor unions are now also generally in favor of high tariffs. Liberals want low tariffs, since they benefit exporters, investors, and consumers. The SOS position is low tariffs but with job facilitators for those who are displaced. The facilitators cost money. Getting low tariffs in the past has been a political problem, but recent tariff reductions passed easily.

Russia and China as Trouble Spots

The conservative position is especially concerned with opening up trade and investment opportunities in both places, and keeping down inflation. The liberals are interested in promoting democracy in both places. This affects the type of aid that might be given. If democracy is the big concern, then maybe aid should be given to potential opposition parties in China. This is risky; it would certainly antagonize the dominant Communist party. Also, there are no organized opposition parties, or even an organized faction within the Communist party. One of the main ways the National Endowment for Democracy operates is to give money to the opposition party, like the Contras in Nicaragua, or give money to the party in power to conduct fairer elections, as was done in El Salvador. Neither approach is applicable to China or Russia. There are no opposition political parties in China. There are in Russia, but we are not going to aid them. They mainly include right-wing nationalists and left-wing communists. What this amounts to in Russia is to help the democratic middle by helping the economy, which is the same thing that conservatives are advocating although for a different reason. They want to help the economy so that it will be a better market, supplier, and investment outlet. In the case of China, aid is not the issue. It is more trade. These two issues are too much unlike to treat as if they were similar problems. China wants trade, not aid, although they would welcome some aid too. Russia especially wants aid, not trade, although they would welcome some trade. China is doing well enough in economic growth to be able to buy American products. Russia is not doing so well. Russia has democratic elections; China doesn't.

If we talk just about policy toward Russia, it does simplify matters, but if the only meaningful policy is the same for achieving both the conservative and liberal goals, then we really don't have much of a controversy. This is not true because there are still some holdovers from the cold war. The number of conservatives who view Russia as a cold war threat has diminished to the point where it is not a serious matter. And the number of liberals who consider Russia as some kind of cold war helper or liberal revolutionary forces has disappeared. The United States may be doing more to try to help liberal forces than the Soviet Union ever did, given its lack of funding as compared to the United States. An example might be Jean-Betrand Aristide of Haiti, who represents the left wing of Haiti but has received no help from Castro or Eastern Europe, although he hasn't received much help from the United States either.

Some of these post-cold war issues are in such a state of flux in transition that it is hard to say what the clear-cut positions are. The left and right positions were very clear during the cold war. One could argue that Yeltsin represents the conservative side of the middle, and that American conservatives would be expected to be more supportive of him, just as Reagan supported Thatcher rather than people from the Labour party, and American Democrats felt more at home with the Labour party leadership. Russia has no serious equivalent of a labor party. They basically have three parties—communist, fascist, and republican—and no democrats or social democrats, or at least not big enough to provide a mainstream left opposition. If there were such a party, the liberals would probably be supportive of it, and the conservatives supportive of Yeltsin. The SOS would then be to support the economy, which will benefit both mainstream parties.

The best clarification of the conservative and liberal positions on Russia involves noting that conservatives are in favor of a different kind of string attached to old money. The key string is raise interest rates in order to reduce inflation. The key democratic or liberal string is do not suppress opposition free speech or other nonviolent methods used to convert voters to either the communist or fascist point of view. For a while it looked like Yeltsin was coming close to establishing at least a temporary dictatorship rather than tolerate vigorous opposition. The situation may revert back to some repression when he runs again for president, although he has talked about retiring. He may lose if the opposition can unite behind a popular candidate, although that depends on the state of the economy as of about 1996. The conservative aid is thus oriented toward reducing inflation, allowing investment, and allowing American factories to open up in the Soviet Union, or at least have access to Russian consumers without tariffs or other barriers. The liberal aid requires tolerance of opposition. In that sense we can say that liberals and conservatives are divided toward China pretty much the way they are toward Russia, except China has further to go on democracy and Russia has further to go on economic growth. The SOS is that it is quite possible to have both kinds of strings attached to either aid or trade. The aid-trade distinction is not important. The important distinction is over what kind of strings are to be attached.

SUMMARY

Economic

The example given for economic growth policy is more one of reducing inflation and unemployment simultaneously. The traditional conservative position is to emphasize investment. This means tax breaks for higher brackets and capital gains. The liberal position emphasizes consumption, which means tax breaks for the lower brackets, larger exemptions, standard deduction, and now the earned income tax credit. The SOS has a 10–15 part package. The short run involves new technologies and skills. The intermediate run involves licensing patents and networks to promote competition, tariff reduction, and government capital. The long run involves doing better in every public policy field, which includes education, health, discrimination, immigration, labor-management relations, transportation, communication, free speech, and world peace. We are lumping technological innovation and diffusion together. We've covered the main technologies, although we haven't mentioned specifically energy sources, which is very important. Crime reduction is important, too. Competition is important as an intermediate economic issue, and so is tariff reduction and government capital. Economic growth is what all of these economic issues are directed toward.

Technology

Conservatives emphasize oil and nuclear energy sources, liberals solar power and synthetic fuels. The SOS is safer nuclear and massive solar energy. Conservatives are oriented toward profits of oil producers and business users. The business users tend to endorse oil and nuclear over solar and synthetic because oil and nuclear are available now. The liberals are more oriented toward the environment and the long term. Conservatives are more oriented toward profits, short-term considerations, and tax savings, which might go way up if a lot of money is put into massive solar power.

For health care, conservatives advocate the marketplace, liberals socialized medicine or at least the single payer system. Conservatives are now willing to concede Medicare and Medicaid. The SOS is managed competition by way of HMOs as the main delivery system, and an employer mandate as the main payer system. The HMOs are capable of dealing with cost containment, access, and quality. Conservatives are especially concerned with quality in this context, liberals with access. And both are concerned with cost, although for liberals it is more costs to the consumer; for conservatives, it is costs to the taxpayer.

The conservative alternative to toxic waste dumps is leave things as they are or provide some kind of cover-up, the goal being to reduce business expense. Liberals want a total cleanup, the goal being to reduce public health risks. The neutral position is a partial cleanup until incremental costs exceed incremental benefits. The SOS involves the standard of no substantial danger and government participation in the cost sharing, as contrasted to a single firm being sought to pay 100% of the total cleanup, and then nothing gets done.

Social

The key issue on public aid jobs is who has the responsibility for finding jobs for public aid recipients. The conservative position is that it should be largely up to the recipients themselves. The liberal position is to leave it up to the relevant government agency. Conservatives want to reduce the tax costs of the government doing the job finding. Liberals want to increase the benefits in terms of finding jobs. A neutral position would be to give the work to not-for-profit organizations. The SOS is contracting out under a commission arrangement, with half payment after two months and the other half after four months. This kind of contracting out provides good incentives and know-how for finding jobs.

Conservatives are in favor of retaining the 40-hour week. Liberals want to decrease it to as low as 30 hours. A compromise would be 35 hours. Conservatives want a high GNP. Liberals also want a high GNP, but they want to spread the work and they would like to see more leisure. The SOS might be to go to 35 hours, but with new technologies and skills in order to retain the high GNP.

Improving inner-city schools should not be referred to as the integration problem, which overemphasizes one part of the solution. Conservatives are in favor of choice; with vouchers to make choice more meaningful. Liberals have been in favor of busing. A key conservative goal is to keep taxes down and not disrupt neighborhood schools. The key liberal goal is to provide improved education, especially for the poor. Integration is not a goal in itself. A neutral position would involve trying to improve the inner-city schools, partly to avoid integration with the outlying schools, although most improvements would be quite expensive. Liberals are interested in equalization, mainly between urban versus rural schools, not inner-city versus outlying schools. The SOS partly involves providing integration without busing, such as emphasizing housing vouchers to move the whole family, and emphasizing economic integration, which is easier to bring about because it doesn't necessarily involve such long distances. A third integration feature in addition to housing vouchers and socioeconomic situations is the redrawing of district lines to provide for more integrated districts. Also there should be economic development of inner-city territories to provide better elementary and high schools for the people who come from the suburbs to live in the redeveloped housing, with 25% set aside for low-income families.

The conservative position on abortion is no abortion, with few possible exceptions. The goal is to eliminate the killing of preborn babies. The liberal position is abortion on demand to eliminate the killing of pregnant women in back-alley abortions. The neutral position is to have the Supreme Court allow abortions in the first trimester, but to uphold prohibitions in the third trimester, and reasonable regulations in the middle. The SOS is better birth control and subsidized adoptions, when unwanted pregnancies still occur, with better birth control, especially use of the skin implant.

Political

The conservative position on registration and turnout is to leave the system as it is, with the express goal to prevent noneligibles from voting. Liberals want to introduce facilitators like postcard registration or motor-voter registration. The goal is to facilitate eligibles voting. The neutral position is to have registration in the precincts about one day a year, and not require reregistering every ten years. The SOS as expressed here emphasizes the facilitating side, with on-site registration, vote anywhere, and weekend voting. The punched picture ID is designed to prevent noneligibles from voting. The dipping of one's hand into invisible ink is even better. As with any SOS solution, the object is to achieve goals of both conservatives and liberals, even though they may appear to be conflicting.

The conservative emphasis on political action committees is on unrestricted and unreported spending, partly to increase business influence but also to maintain free speech. The liberal approach is to require restrictions in the reporting in order to provide more electoral equal opportunity. The neutral position is reporting, but no restrictions. The SOS involves voluntary restrictions, but making them so attractive that they are hard to refuse by way of government funding, and also to lessen the stigma that is associated with not accepting the government funding but instead accepting funding from special interest groups. The free speech element is especially preserved by allowing PACs to use the mass media with the money they otherwise would have used for campaign contributions.

International

The conservative position on UN peacekeeping forces is minimum U.S. involvement. The liberal position is substantial U.S. involvement. Conservatives are looking to save taxes and U.S. lives. Liberals are especially interested in promoting peace. The SOS is a volunteer UN force consisting of experienced people from all over the world who could constitute officers and enlisted men and women for a navy, air force, and army, or at least an army. This should satisfy conservatives with no direct U.S. lives or taxes at stake, although there would be indirect contributions by way of the dues the United States pays to the United Nations and some of the volunteers would be Americans. The volunteer force can probably promote peace better than calling upon member nations to provide troops.

The traditional conservative position on removal of trade barriers has opposed repealing tariffs, because that would mean increased competition for the U.S.

domestic market, with a loss of profits and jobs for some businesses. The traditional liberal position is to favor tariff reduction, since it helps consumers with lower prices but also helps exporters, importers, and people who want to invest or build factories overseas. The neutral position is partial tariff reduction or delayed reduction. The SOS is free trade, but with retraining of dislocated workers and noncompetitive business firms. There should also be an expanding economy, partly from foreign trade, to provide replacement jobs and business opportunities; and there should be side agreements on fair labor standards and the environment.

FEASIBILITY PROBLEMS RAISED BY THE SOS PROPOSALS

Economic Policy

The economic policy of new technology and skills to increase the GNP does involve a willingness to spend for those technologies and skills. It may be that the technology is not there, at least for a while, as in talking about safe nuclear energy. Here we are talking about new technology in any sector of the economy. There is some resistance based partly on shortsightedness, especially on the part of workers who have traditionally resisted new technologies that disrupt the way one is accustomed to doing things and may displace workers.

On inflation and unemployment and on all of these we want to get to the more important problems, such as what is to happen to the workers who are dislocated? Also important, though, is where is the money going to come from in order to pay for all the training and technology? How are the programs going to be administered?

On the matter of economic growth, if we are thinking in terms of about a dozen social institutions that need improving, including the education system, criminal justice, health, free speech, immigration, and energy conservation, then we are talking about putting a lot of money into investment purposes, more so than just technology and skills.

Technology Policy

On the matter of energy resources we have technology problems in developing safer nuclear energy and massive solar energy. The energy sources matter is a combination of a technological feasibility with regard to the microwave in the sky for massive solar energy. Large-scale storage batteries also represent technological problems. There may be psychological problems in getting acceptance on the safer second-generation nuclear reactors given the lack of believability in previous claims from the nuclear industry.

Health care is a problem in political feasibility that will require compromising. The Clinton health plan failed largely because it antagonized such strong political groups as (1) businesses, by financing the program through a business tax, and (2) industries that do not want to compete with HMOs such as fee-for-service doctors, private insurance companies, and pharmaceutical companies that can charge more to drugstores that have less bargaining power than HMOs. The financing problem could have been handled through a six-year phased-in plan involving:

1. Prohibiting preconditions for insurance coverage and allowing alliances for group discounts, both of which have bipartisan support.
2. Covering those who cannot afford HMO premiums by way of a subsidy supported from cigarette taxes. Such taxes have bipartisan support much more so than business taxes. This would cover half of the 40 million Americans who lack health insurance.
3. Phasing out Medicaid in favor of HMO coverage. This would save a lot of money that is wasted under Medicaid which is a fee-for-service system. Medicaid covers poor people who are not so politically resistant.
4. Phasing out Medicare in favor of HMO coverage. This would also save a lot of money because Medicare is also a fee-for-service system. The phasing out would probably have to allow more options for the elderly to choose their doctors in order to be politically feasible.
5. Using the savings from phasing out Medicaid and Medicare to provide voucher subsidies for those who are paying for health insurance but who are in the same income brackets as those who would be getting subsidies under Step 2 above. It would be inequitable not to also help those with similar incomes who have managed to better budget their incomes in order to be able to buy health insurance.
6. Dealing with the remaining uncovered group who are those who can afford health insurance but refuse to buy it. They are a burden on society since society provides them with expensive emergency health care. A politically feasible solution might be to allow these people one such visit to the emergency room. Then they have to buy health insurance or they lose their driver's license or other occupational license until they do so. This is being used to encourage the buying of auto liability insurance and the payment of child support.
7. Handling the political opposition of those who do not like HMO competition. The fee-for-service doctors are decreasing in number and political power. The percentage of people covered by HMOs has risen from about 5% in 1990 to 55% in 1996. The private insurance companies like Prudential are increasingly working with HMOs to do their health insurance work. Likewise the pharmaceutical companies are increasingly working with HMOs to provide medicines that are sold in HMO pharmacies.

The environmental protection SOS involves technological problems in developing new technologies that are both more profitable and cleaner. The development of work (meaning resources and development) may also be quite expensive in terms of government appropriation.

On the matter of toxic waste, there are administrative problems involved in trying to determine when there is no substantial health danger. There may also be administrative problems in allowing liability to be determined by negotiation. This could lead to some corruption where the business firms are able to work out a settlement, possibly by offering some kind of bribe to the negotiators to accept a lesser settlement.

The licensing of patents involves a lot of political opposition from those who do not want any licensing. There may be administrative problems too in determining what constitutes a reasonable royalty.

Social Policy

Public aid is mainly economic feasibility as to where the money is going to come from with regard to the cost of training, day care, wage supplements, and the like. These are the three key items. They involve more expenditure than can probably be provided by reallocating present spending.

The job opportunities that are associated with dealing with public aid also require money. In addition, there are monitoring problems and motivation problems. The monitoring problems relate to how to make sure that the person has a job. That is no problem—if they have no job they are likely to come back seeking public aid. Monitoring the work of the job finders involves paying on a commission basis after the jobs have been found. The problem is mainly economic. It costs money for training and for wage subsidies.

On the work week, we could add psychological feasibility in the sense of workers feeling that they are partly unemployed if they only have a 30-hour work week. It is possible with improved technology for workers to be able to produce more in a 30-hour week than they now do in 40 hours. At the turn of the century the work week was more like 50 hours and workers produced far less in 50 hours than they do now in 40 hours. It is possible that in another generation they will be able to produce more in 30 hours than they now do in 40 hours. This assumes that technological improvements will be so good that we will wind up with too much leisure. The opposite could be true—namely, that technology does not improve so fast and workers demand a shorter work week, say down to 30 hours, but they are producing only slightly more than what they were formerly producing in 35 hours. This means that the total GNP will go down, although it could remain approximately constant if more people are working. The ideal arrangement would be to work less and produce more through better technology rather than through working harder.

It would be undesirable to work less and not produce more since then the GNP would go down if everything else is held constant. It would also be undesirable to either work more or produce less, but neither of these possibilities is likely to occur. All the trends are toward shortening the work week. Likewise, all the trends are toward producing more. A key question is will working less run rampant more than production increases? If so, then the GNP falls. Or will working less run rampant (even if the GNP does not fall or rise) so much that people feel partially unemployed and thus unhappy?

There are thus two possible bad effects: a lowered GNP, and lowered happiness as a result of not being constructively busy. The first one is a technological problem, the second is psychology problem. I am noting that the psychology of unemployment is a possible defect as well as the technology problem with regard to reducing production if there is a substantially shorter work week.

The idea of integration-oriented housing vouchers raises an economic problem. There is some political and administrative opposition, although less so with economic class integration than racial integration. There is also the problem of the people being left behind, maybe worse off than ever, unless there is also some compensatory education.

The object is to provide quality education for everybody. This requires having good fellow students to interact with, not just good physical facilities and teachers. Busing is designed to provide good fellow students, but it wastes too much time and money. It does have the advantage that one could bus every poor kid into the middle-class schools, at least in a small city. In a big city like Chicago one cannot bus every poor kid. Some public school systems in the big cities now have a black percentage and a poor white percentage that is way higher than the population. The Chicago population is 40% black, about 25% of the whites are poor, making a total of almost 65% that is either black, poor, or both. But that 65% may generate 90% of the K-12 school kids. This means that if all 90% were bused to other places in both directions, the best one could do would be to have 90–10 schools (90% black and/or poor and 10% middle class). This is contrasted to having lots of schools that are 100% black and/or poor and a few schools that are less than 90%.

The housing voucher system moves kids out of the district into a lower-middle-class district elsewhere. As mentioned, this requires money for the vouchers, but it is a good investment. It also requires acceptance by the receiving district, which can be done if it is intraracial but across economic classes. The third problem is that the more ambitious students or parents will take advantage of the integration-oriented housing vouchers and leave behind students who will be in even worse shape.

One thing about this kind of analysis is that we come up with an SOS, then come up with defects in the SOS, then try to remedy the defects. This type of approach may lead to improved public policy, but it does cause some headaches thinking about the problems. It also needs to recognize that no matter what is done, there will always be some room for improvement, meaning there will always be defects from perfection even though the defects in the second cycle may be not as bad as in the first cycle.

The answer to leaving behind highly disadvantaged students is partly that this is a program in which those who move are chosen purely out of ambition. The more ambitious students and parents will move anyhow without housing vouchers. The housing vouchers go only to the very poor—that is, the people who are most likely to be left behind if the rule were simply if anybody could afford the time and money to pay their own transportation to go to an outlying school or suburban school would be allowed to do so. This was the scheme in Chicago for a while in the 1960s. The richest black kids chose to go to the better white schools. What is being proposed now is different in at least two ways. First, those rich black kids have moved out. They now live in black suburbs of Chicago, like Rich township, rather than on the south side of Chicago. Second, this kind of program is specifically directed toward the poorest kids, not the rich kids, since only the poorest can qualify for the housing vouchers.

This could mean that if the poorest kids move out then the kids that are left behind may have a higher average family income and actually be better off in terms of middle-class values than they were before the poor kids moved out with the housing vouchers. Thus the idea of making things worse for those who are left behind is not such a problem in this kind of integration. It does satisfy many objections to other forms of integration. On the economic matter, it may not only be a good investment, but be less expensive and definitely more cost effective than pouring money into the inner-city schools to upgrade the buildings or the teachers when it is really the fellow students who count.

The approaches to integrating the schools without busing involve some economic problems as to where the money is going to come from for housing vouchers or equalization money. There is also a psychological problem in getting the dominant group, meaning middle-class people, to accept poor people in integrated classes.

The abortion SOS has the defect of resistance to birth control, especially at the teenage level, by parents. Subsidized adoptions involve an economic problem. There will be no way of arguing that subsidizing adoption of a deformed black child is a good investment. The justification would be to prevent an abortion. If those who advocate outlawing abortion and replacing it with adoption are sincere, they should support subsidized adoptions in order to make the system meaningful. This part may be less likely to get adopted than having more effective birth control.

The idea of more effective birth control for dealing with abortion is partly an economic problem if the most effective birth control is skin implants, because they are quite expensive. We have a psychological problem when we talk about getting people to use condoms widely in order to avoid AIDS. We also have a problem of getting people to recognize the need for a backup to abstinence and not to look at the backup arrangements as encouraging the dropping of abstinence. This prevents a political problem in getting that kind of program adopted. Subsidized adoptions as part of the abortion SOS costs money, especially if it is to provide practically a lifetime of support for a highly defective child, who might otherwise be aborted, who lives a lifetime of special care. This is an unusual situation. The more common situation is a healthy black baby who is hard to arrange for an adoption. If we ask what is holding back on more effective birth control, especially for teenage pregnancy, then the answer may be economic. If the skin implants can be brought down to the prices that exist in Europe, at about $20 per implant, they could be widely adopted, as contrasted to $600 in the United States. In the past there was a technological problem with regard to preventing AIDS. We do not have a vaccine and condoms are not adequate as a preventative measure. The technology of developing a skin implant that would prevent pregnancy and reduce sexuality is also a technological problem.

Political Policy

Congressional reform in terms of campaign expenditures has the defect that voluntary restrictions may not be adopted. Sometimes voluntary restrictions get adopted by politicians because they want to avoid the stigma of accepting money from lobbyists and interest groups if their opponents are not doing so. A second attraction is that public money is available only to politicians who adopt the restrictions. Public money is likely to be sufficient and save the politicians from undesirable fundraising.

Another drawback is that political action committees can still make candidates indebted to them by spending money to get candidates elected, even if the money is not given directly to the candidates. One frustrating effect of trying to find defects in these SOS solutions is that we then see that they actually are not such perfect solutions after all. The saving feature, as previously mentioned, is that they are still better than existing policy. Voluntary restrictions on PAC campaign expenditures are better than nothing. Likewise, reporting on the contributions is better than nothing. A key criterion should be whether this proposal is better than what we have now in terms of conservative and liberal goals. Nor is this proposal perfect in terms of achieving those goals to the maximum possible or higher.

In addition to political feasibility, campaign reform may have to deal with constitutional or legal feasibility. Individuals cannot be prohibited or subject to maximum amounts in paying for billboards, radio-TV time, or newspaper ads for their favorite candidates. Doing so would violate first amendment free speech rights.

There are many political feasibility problems with registration and voter turnout, with conservatives reluctant to give votes to potential liberal voters. This is a good example of where a proposal is an improvement but is not perfect. There is no way we are ever going to get 100% turnout. On-site registration, though, removes the excuse for not voting that one has not previously registered. Political feasibility is clearly the bigger obstacle to overcome.

The United Nations volunteer force may have problems getting administered and financed. There may also be opposition to getting it adopted in the first place. One might say that any proposal that has not already been adopted might have difficulty getting adopted, funded, and well administered. The technology gap does not always apply nor does the constitutionality of the issue.

The big defect in the North American Free Trade Agreements and other free trade is providing the expanding economy that will in turn provide the jobs for the displaced workers.

METHODS OF GENERATING SOS SOLUTIONS

Economic Policy

The first issue is inflation and unemployment. The key approach here is a package of alternatives for economic growth. The key defect is that the increased productivity leads to displaced workers who need to be taken into consideration. Another defect is that the increased spending to handle unemployment may be inflationary. The counter to this is that the increased spending comes from increased productivity, which means more goods, which should offset the inflationary effect of more money.

Economic growth as the way of dealing with inflation and unemployment can also be considered an example of expanding resources, raising goals, or redefining the problem. The problem used to be how to reduce inflation, or how to reduce unemployment, but not both simultaneously.

Technology Policy

The approach to environmental protection is the technological fix and increasing benefits while decreasing costs. The defects are technological feasibility and the cost of research.

The approach to expanding technological innovation is to encourage competition, which we did not have on the list of approaches previously. The defects are political, and administrative in determining what is a reasonable royalty, and legal if there is an attempt to make the system retroactive.

Social Policy

Regarding public aid in general, we can work in internal public aid as the traditional conservative or liberal issues and arguments, and then talk about job facilitators as the SOS. The approach might be called getting at the causes, meaning that lack of jobs is the cause of poverty and the need for public aid. The possible defects of the jobs approach is that it requires money for job facilitators. There is also a psychological problem with regard to getting motivation for public aid recipients.

Another policy problem is family policy, with an emphasis on the abortion issue. There the approach is getting at the causes, which mainly means unwanted pregnancies. The defect, if we are talking about skin implants, is expensiveness. There is also the psychological problem of allowing or encouraging birth control in view of increased sexuality. These are political feasibility problems. There is a legal problem with regard to parental consent. The AIDS problem has been mixed in with the teenage pregnancy problem here. The two are hard to separate since they are both caused by sexual activities. For now, since there is no AIDS vaccine, like a skin implant, the AIDS problem among teenagers needs to be addressed by abstinence and condoms. Condoms are also relevant to unwanted pregnancies, but skin implants are more relevant. Thus we have lots of defects, depending on what kind of SOS we are referring to. It sounds like a combination of abstinence, implants, and condoms, and defects that relate to economic, political, legal, psychological, and technological issues.

The approach to inner-city schools is a package of alternatives. The defects are largely economic in terms of housing vouchers, redevelopment, and contracting out, which involves some political feasibility problems. There is some psychological resistance to various forms of integration.

Chapter 24

LEGAL POLICY

The seven legal policy topics are juries, crime, business wrongdoing, constitutional compliance, free speech, government and religion, and equal treatment.

For criminal cases conservatives want 6-person juries, majority vote. Liberals want 12-person juries, unanimous vote. Neutrals on all these issues tend to be in between or half and half or some of both. The SOS is videotaping, note-taking, questions from the jury, and training—all to increase the likelihood of convicting the guilty and acquitting the innocent.

On crime reduction, conservatives emphasize more punishment and less loopholes. Liberals tend to emphasize poverty reduction and professionalism. The SOS talks about job opportunities and eliminating the drug market through treatment and education.

On business wrongdoing, we are talking about antitrust, labor, and environmental protection as representing three different periods of business wrongdoing. The best way to deal with antitrust is encouraging competition. For labor, regulation might be needed. For environmental protection, it is a matter of incentives.

On constitutional compliance, the conservative position has been to have judicial review for interference with business. The liberal position has been judicial review for interference with civil liberties. The SOS is socialization to make it part of public opinion that there should be high compliance with the Constitution.

Free speech from a conservative point of view means restrictions on pornography, defamation, and subversive advocacy. The liberal view means no restrictions. The SOS means restrictions where other constitutional rights would be violated, also winning over liberals and conservatives with more free speech for both business and labor.

With regard to the government and religion matter, the conservative position is to allow prayers and Bible reading of an organized nature in public schools.

The liberal position is to not allow this. The SOS position is to emphasize ethical training rather than theology.

On unequal treatment, the conservative position is to allow discrimination or prohibit it, but no affirmative action, or affirmative action but no preferences. The liberal position may include preferential hiring and admissions, at least temporarily. The SOS emphasizes upgrading skills so minorities can better qualify.

LEGAL PROCEDURES

This section provides one civil procedure example and one criminal procedure example. The civil one relates to whether the loser should cover the winner's expenses. The criminal one relates to constructively employing prison labor.

Liability and Damages: Loser Pays

The conservative position is that the loser should pay the expenses of the winner. The traditional position is that each side pays its own costs. At first glance, one might think that having the loser pay would help plaintiffs who are the underdogs in civil cases. The defendant's insurance company would have to pay their expenses. This rule does help plaintiffs in Equal Employment Opportunity Commission complaints, but not in auto cases because plaintiffs do not have any expenses, win or lose. They normally operate on a one-third contingency fee, in which they do not pay attorney's expenses separately.

With each side paying its own costs, then the injured plaintiff does not pay the plaintiff's side. Instead, the plaintiff's lawyer does. But if the defendant wins, the plaintiff's lawyer is not deterred from bringing a case against the defendant, since the defendant pays either way.

The neutral position would be the loser pays half the winner's costs. This still would be a deterrent for injured plaintiffs who are currently paying nothing. The conservative position is to discourage damage suits. The liberal position is to facilitate collecting proper damages. The SOS is the loser does not pay unless the loser acted in an unreasonable manner. An indication of that would be where the loser loses on a summary judgment without the other side having to present any testimony. That way, only unreasonable damage suits would be deterred, not all of them, thereby pleasing liberals. Conservatives should be pleased under such a rule, since it would mean improvement from their perspective on the present system, since the new system would involve the loser paying some of the time.

Guilt and Sentencing: Prison Labor and the Minimum Wage

The conservative alternative would be nothing an hour or maybe $1.00 an hour, some nominal wage. The liberal alternative would be closer to the minimum wage which is now $4.50 an hour; compromise would be something in between, about $2.00–$3.00 an hour. The conservative goal is to reduce prison costs and to increase the deterrence of crime. The liberal goal is that working at a minimum-wage job rather than a no-wage job is a step in the right direction on rehabilitation.

An SOS that would reduce prison costs while at the same time increasing rehabilitation would be to produce profitable products that would sell for more than the minimum wage. This raises political feasibility problems, largely from labor union opposition. The unions would like to have prisoners producing nothing competitive. However, if they do produce something, then those who sell the products should be required to pay minimum wages, so as not to depress the minimum wage. This is like making labor costs higher in order to get producers to be more efficient. This should be seen in the context of segments of the adult population who are capable of being productive but who are not. There are about a million able-bodied people in prisons in the United States who could be earning a minimum wage of about $4.50 per hour, 40 hours per week, for about $10,000 per year.

That is $10 billion per year, which is not that much, considering we have a $5 trillion GNP, although the whole $10 billion would not be taxed away. But $10 billion is enough to pay for half of the anticrime budget. A better way to put it is the $10 billion gets spent and thereby becomes $9 billion for the first round of consumers. If $1 billion is lost on each round of spending, that means $10 billion in spending would generate about $55 billion given the multiplier effect. That is a little healthier addition to the economy. A key object is that prison costs could be lowered from the profits. These prisoners may have learned a trade that will enable them to earn a legitimate income when they get out of prison. The money they are being paid is not a subsidy like public aid. They presumably are producing more than they are being paid. Otherwise they would get fired.

If all prisoners were required to work, then it is a bit like forced labor. The pay should be an incentive to work. Requiring work could be justified on the grounds that it is a learning experience. Even if it is called forced labor, it seems justifiable. The term "forced labor" is a cold war term that the State Department has used in referring to Russian and Chinese prison labor. Every country provides work for its convicts, with the United States doing the worst job in that regard. It is partly a result of our affluence. In developing nations, they cannot operate a prison unless the prison produces profitable products with prison labor. This is not breaking up rocks, which is not profitable.

LEGAL PERSONNEL

Judicial Selection

Conservatives tend to like appointed judges over elected judges. That's the main issue in judicial selection. A lesser issue is short-term versus long-term.

Short-term judges are less likely than long-term judges to side with minority groups in equal protection cases or with other civil liberty matters not so popular among voters.

A key goal of conservatives is to get conservative judges on the courts. A key goal of liberals is to get liberal judges on the courts. The elected long-term judges are more relevant to liberal interests than appointed short-term judges. A middling position might be appointments for long terms, like federal judges, or elected for short terms, like most state judges. The SOS position might be to provide career judges with special training and a promotion system. This is the system in Western and Eastern Europe and most of the world, but it isn't so politically feasible for the United States. Both conservative and liberal lawyers would like to become judges someday, but they aren't going to go back to law school to enter the judges curriculum.

Perhaps the political feasibility problem could be overcome by not making the new system retroactive. It certainly wouldn't apply to any judges currently on the bench. There doesn't seem to be any very meaningful way of making it nonretroactive to aspiring lawyers who aren't on the bench. It could specify that it goes into existence as of a future year and anybody who graduates from law school prior to that year is made inapplicable. This means that they could become judges without following any special curriculum and career path.

This could get some support from lawyer legislators who graduated before that year. A related problem is how to get the law schools to set up a judicial curriculum for lawyers who want to be judges. The only thing we have in the United States along those lines is the judicial college at Reno, Nevada. It is for people who are already judges. We also have judicial conferences that judges attend, in which information is given on new developments. The state of Illinois has a judicial training program for which the state bar association is partly responsible. It lasts about a week or two, which is not the same as the three- or four-year program to become a French judge, although most of those three years involve taking courses that anyone wanting to become a lawyer would take.

A more politically feasible system involves concentrating on limiting judicial arbitrariness through increased codification, flat sentencing, and no-fault liability. All of these decrease judicial discretion. Therefore, it doesn't make so much difference whether judges are conservative or liberal if they don't have much discretion to exercise. Judicial committees on judicial character and fitness help get rid of bad judges. That is a cure, rather than a prevention, that goes with a better selection system. The object is to improve the quality of judges without trying to change the way they are selected, since that has too many political obstacles. It is not just a quality issue. It is a three-pronged approach. One prong is training, which does improve quality. The second prong is easier removal, which improves quality after it has deteriorated. It improves quality by removing bad judges. It is easier to set up removal criteria than selection criteria. The third prong is to limit discretion so the bad judge cannot do much harm. (See Table 24–1 for legal personnel issues.)

Table 24-1
Legal Personnel

ISSUES	CONSERVATIVE	LIBERAL	NEUTRAL	SUPER-OPTIMUM SOLUTIONS	FEASIBILITY
1. ADMINISTERING RIGHT-TO-COUNSEL	1. Low cost and non-disruptive -- -- 1. VOLUNTEERS	1. Accessible and competent -- -- 1. SALARIED GOVERNMENT LAWYERS	-- -- REIMBURSED JUDICARE OR MIXED	1. Salaried base 2. Clearinghouse 3. Training 4. Contracting out 5. Encouraging volunteers	1. Psychological
2. THE ADVERSARY SYSTEM	1. Favor dominant party -- -- 1. PURE ADVERSARY SYSTEM	1. Favor non-dominant party -- -- 1. INQUISITORIAL OR PATERNALISTIC SYSTEM		1. Adversary system but appoint counsel 2. Encourage settlement	1. Economic 2. Psychological
3. ATTORNEY-CLIENT CONFLICTS	1. Profits for law firms -- -- 1. MARKETPLACE	1. Low prices and quality service for clients -- -- 1. GOVERNMENT REGULATION	-- -- REGULATE THEFT	1. Competition by anti-trust 2. First Amendment 3. Expanded quantity of lawyers	1. Legal
4. JUDICIAL SELECTION	1. Conservative judges -- -- 1. APPOINTED SHORT TERM	1. Liberal judges -- -- 1. ELECTED LONG TERM	-- -- 1. IN BETWEEN ON IDEOLOGY: APPOINTED LONG TERM OR ELECTED SHORT TERM	1. Career judges with training and promotion system 2. Limit discretion 3. Removal	1. Political
5. CIVIL JURIES	1. Pro-defendant -- -- 1. MINIMIZE CIVIL JURY	1. Pro-plaintiff -- -- 1. FULL CIVIL JURY	-- -- SMALLER JURY	1. Accident prevention 2. No-fault liability 3. Eliminate judges and lawyers 4. Improve accuracy	1. Technological

Civil Juries

The conservative approach would like to minimize the civil jury, which tends to be too sympathetic to plaintiffs, to operate from a deep-pocket theory. Liberals like the full civil jury. Neutrals will compromise by having smaller juries deciding by less than unanimous vote.

The goal of the conservative in this case tends to be pro-defendant. The goal of the liberal tends to be pro-plaintiff. The SOS has four parts. The first is accident reduction, which cuts down on the number of injured plaintiffs who bring suits. The second part is alternative dispute resolution, which is more a compromise position between the defendant and the plaintiff, although it could be SOS alternative dispute resolution, not necessarily split down the middle alternative dispute resolution.

A third part of the SOS is to have no-fault liability. The plaintiff likes that, since it's easier to prove liability. Some defendants (i.e., insurance companies) also like it, because it puts limits on how much can be collected and tends to eliminate the presence of lawyers. A fourth aspect of the SOS package is to improve jury accuracy by making use of videotaped trials, written instructions, note-taking, question-asking, and jury training.

Judges

The conservative position on judicial review as of the 1990s is either no judicial review or highly restrained, with the professed goal being that the majority of the American people should decide what is constitutional. The liberal position is to have vigorous judicial review out of sensitivity to protecting minority rights. A neutral position might be to have judicial review with a two-thirds concurrence, elected judges, or fixed terms. The SOS is to emphasize the need for socializing and educating legislators, administrators, and the general public into having a higher regard for the Constitution and the Bill of Rights, so that unconstitutional laws will not be so frequently passed and have to be declared unconstitutional. This is getting at the causes, like getting at unwanted pregnancies and abortion.

When judicial review is exercised it can be restrained in the sense of avoiding a declaration of unconstitutionality by way of the following alternative outlets: (1) interpret the statute so as to make it constitutional; (2) avoid rendering opinions from which there is no concrete case, meaning no abstract judicial review—there must be a litigant who is being harmed; (3) do not go beyond what is needed to declare the offending portion of the legislation unconstitutional; (4) there may be a need for a presumption of constitutionality when there is doubt; (5) try to comply with prior precedents rather than overruling; (6) try to comply with lower court decisions rather than reversing; and (7) concentrate on the wording of the Constitution, with intent of the framers as the second most important criteria. The consequences should also be considered, but in light of the idea that that is what the framers would have intended.

Lawyers

The conservative position on providing attorneys to the poor is to rely on a combination of hired counsel, volunteers, and assigned counsel in order to minimize taxes and disruption. The liberal position is salaried government attorneys, in order to maximize access and competency. A neutral position might be volunteers in civil cases and salaried attorneys in criminal cases. The SOS is to work with a base of salaried attorneys but have volunteers recruited through mandatory pro bono. Another SOS would be contracting out legal services for the poor. This provides accessibility and competency that liberals like, while at the same time it is less expensive than tax-supported lawyers and less disruptive.

LEGAL COMPLIANCE

Crime Reduction

Gun Control

The conservative position is as little gun control as possible. The liberal position is sometimes to go as far as outright prohibition of various kinds of guns and ammunition, maybe prohibiting all handguns without a special permit. The neutral position is restrictions like waiting periods or limiting the access of minors to guns. The conservative goal is to prevent people from becoming victims of robberies and burglaries. The liberal goal is to prevent people from becoming victims of burglaries, accidental shootings, or other harm where they aren't committing a crime. The SOS involves emphasizing the need to reduce crime in order to get people to be more willing to accept gun control, and then gun control can help further reduce crime. It should be noted that liberals don't propose gun control in order to reduce the killings that conservatives are concerned with—namely, the killing of a burglar or a robber. The liberals are especially concerned with the killing of the storeowner's wife by the storeowner in a family fight or the killing of the storeowner's five-year-old child, who gets killed playing with the gun, or the killing of some neighbor who accidentally came to the wrong house.

Even though gun control may not have such a big impact on crime reduction, it does have an impact on reducing killings. Also, even though it doesn't have such a big impact on crime reduction, people think they need guns to reduce crime and their thinking causes them to resist gun control. Therefore there must be less anxiety, just as in tariff reduction, if there is to be any legislative adoption. (See Table 24–2 for legal compliance issues.)

Table 24-2
Legal Compliance

ISSUES	CONSERVATIVE	LIBERAL	NEUTRAL	SUPER-OPTIMUM SOLUTIONS	FEASIBILITY
1. GUN CONTROL	1. Prevent victimization - - 1. NO GUN CONTROL	1. Prevent other killing - - 1. PROHIBITION	- - RESTRICTIONS 1. WAITING PERIODS 2. NO MINORS 3. NO AUTOMATIC WEAPONS	1. Crime reduction 2. Gun control	1. Political
2. DRUG-RELATED CRIMES	1. Reduce drug buying and selling - - 1. LAW ENFORCEMENT CRACKDOWN	1. Reduce side effects of enforcement (robbing, assaulting, corrupting, AIDS, overdosing) - - 1. LEGALIZATION	- - 1. PARTIAL LEGALIZATION, E.G., MARIJUANA 2. TREATMENT AND EDUCATION	1. Medicalization. Phase out maintenance prescription from public health. 2. Deprofitize	1. Political
3. STOCK-BROKER SWINDLES	1. Minimize business regulations - - 1. BE LENIENT	1. Deter business wrongdoing - - 1. BE SEVERE	- - IN BETWEEN	1. Encourage competition by banks 2. Salaries rather than commissions 3. No conflict of interest	1. Administrative
4. POLITICAL ACTION COMMITTEES	1. Business influence and freedom from regulations - - 1. UNRESTRICTED AND UNREPORTED SPENDING	1. Decrease business influence and freedom of speech - - 1. SPENDING RESTRICTIONS AND REPORTING	- - REPORTING BUT NO SPENDING RESTRICTIONS	1. Government funding of elections 2. Voluntary restrictions 3. Voluntary business spending	1. Political 2. Administrative

Drug-Related Crimes

The conservative alternative is to allocate more money to law enforcement. The liberal alternative is to allocate more money to treatment and education. The neutral alternative is to allocate less to law enforcement than conservatives want but more than liberals, also less to treatment and education than liberals want but more than conservatives.

The goals may be the same—namely, to reduce the drug problem. This would be an example of where both sides have the same general goal in mind, which makes it a neutral goal. They differ in their perceptions. Conservatives think that law enforcement is worth about at least a 4 on reducing drugs. Liberals think it is worth about a 2. This means it does more harm than good. By lessening competition for the selling of drugs it makes drug selling more profitable. On treatment conservatives might consider the relation score to be a 2 and liberals a 4. Conservatives would argue that providing drugs as part of the treatment by definition adds to the circulation of drugs and thus does more harm than good.

If we convert these scores into part/whole percentages, then conservatives would want to give 67% of the budget to law enforcement and 33% to treatment with the opposite for liberals.

An SOS solution would involve possibly increasing the budget from 100 monetary units to 134 so as to provide more than $67 for law enforcement and more than $67 for treatment.

Another SOS solution might be to improve the effectiveness of law enforcement by having it apply only to illegal drugs, which would not include prescription drugs as part of the treatment process. This would make law enforcement more effective because one redefines the crime partly out of existence. This, in effect, makes law enforcement more effective by spending more money. This is an allocation problem in which we have a tentatively fixed budget. We could reallocate how the money is spent. For example, more could be spent to subsidize those who grow coca or manufacture cocaine to do something else. They would have to be paid more than they are getting for cocaine. This adds another alternative of using subsidies at the source rather than law enforcement.

Treatment could be made more effective by developing drugs that can take the place of cocaine the way methadone takes the place of heroin. Another possibility is developing drugs that create an aversion to cocaine like drugs that create an aversion to alcohol. This raises a problem of incentives to take them. The key thing is the idea of concentrating on improving the perceptions on the relation scores.

If the relation scores can be raised high enough, then the conservatives would be happy not because they are getting more money but because there is more goal achievement. This is where working with the allocation formulas comes in.

This does illustrate the need for being able to vary the basic model in order to have situations where conservatives and liberals agree on the same goals and weights but differ on the perceptions. They could disagree on both the goals and the perceptions. The software needs to be changed to be able to deal better with those kinds of differences. The present software could do it but with a little more difficulty than if the software were changed.

Business Wrongdoing

Stockbroker Swindle

Conservatives advocate relative leniency. Liberals advocate relative severity. The conservative goal is to minimize business regulation. This isn't viewed as criminal activity, but as business activity. Just as Reagan's people were saying that the Iran-Contra coverup wasn't criminal activity, but political activity, the Democrats are seeking to criminalize a business matter.

Liberals, on the other hand, want to deter business wrongdoing, including swindling by brokerage firms. The SOS is to use marketplace forces to bring wrongdoers into line when business wrongdoing is involved. In this context, this might mean to encourage competition by commercial banks. This would put pressure on the brokerage firms to win back customers by getting their houses in order, possibly by more use of salaries, rather than commissions.

LEGAL RIGHTS

Equal Treatment under Law

The conservative position on equal employment opportunity is merit hiring to achieve productivity. The liberal position is some preferential hiring, or what is sometimes called compensatory hiring. The goal is more equity in the distribution of jobs. The neutral position is to seek qualified minorities through advertising, making the location of one's office or factory more accessible, and removing tests that correlate highly with race when other tests might be available that do better on job performance but may not correlate so highly with race. The SOS is to have affirmative action in training, but not necessarily in hiring. This means upgrading skills of minorities so they would be able to qualify under any reasonable merit hiring program, and thus add to productivity and to equity in the distribution of jobs to minorities. (See Table 24–3 for legal rights issues.)

Sexual harassment could come up under equal treatment, but it is not there because it was raised too recently. It could also come up under free speech, where it is present. The conservative position is dependent on how one defines conservative here. We are not talking about conservative male sexism. We are talking about conservative in the sense of being willing to restrict free speech, as contrasted to being liberal on expanding or at least not restricting free speech.

Table 24-3
Legal Rights

ISSUES	CONSERVATIVE	LIBERAL	NEUTRAL	SUPER-OPTIMUM SOLUTIONS	FEASIBILITY
1. ABHORRENT FREE SPEECH	1. Protect from mental upset - - 1. PROHIBIT AND NO FUNDING	1. Creativity - - 1. ALLOW AND NOT EXCLUDE FROM GENERAL FUNDING 2. CLEAR AND PRESENT DANGER AND NO FUNDING	- - 1. COUNTER-DEMONSTRATIONS 2. IGNORE	1. Remove causes -- socialization -- porno, extremism 2. Prosperity	1. Administrative
2. PRAYER AND BIBLE READING IN PUBLIC SCHOOLS	1. Religiosity and ethical behavior - - 1. PRAYERS AND BIBLE READING	1. Avoid dogma and stimulate creativity - - 1. NO PRAYERS OR BIBLE READING	- - 1. STUDENT-LED PRAYERS	1. Ethical training 2. Individual prayer 3. Meditation moment 4. Before and after school hours	1. Administrative
3. EQUAL EMPLOYMENT OPPORTUNITY IN GENERAL (RACE, GENDER)	1. Productivity - - 1. COLOR-BLIND HIRING	1. Equity in distribution - - 1. PREFERENTIAL HIRING OR COMPENSATORY HIRING	- - 1. OUTREACH HIRING SEEKING QUALIFIED MINORITIES (ADVERTISING, LOCATION, REMOVE BAD TESTS)	1. Outreach training to upgrade skills	1. Economic

Perhaps we could say that one side is strong feminists who put women's rights ahead of free speech, and the other side is not antifeminists The other side is people who believe in women's rights, but they believe in free speech more. They are simply the pro-free-speech side. The feminists are not anti-free-speech, they are pro-women's rights, just like they do not like to be called proabortion, but pro-choice. And the antiabortionists do not like to be called antichoice, but rather antiabortion. The important thing is that those who are pro-free speech do not want to see employers fined or enjoined because they allow employees to post notices in the workplace arguing against women's rights. The pro-women forces think this should be a violation of the 1964 Civil Rights Act on equal employment opportunity. The object is how to get women treated with dignity while at the same time preserving free speech. The Supreme Court's neutral position is that if the speaking activities are directed at a specific woman, then harassment may be found, but not if the speaking activities are directed against women in general. The SOS is to increase respect for women through socialization and also facilitating women rising in prominence so they get more respect by virtue of their achievements rather than respect by virtue of some kind of administrative regulation that says women have to be respected or else one gets fired.

Free Speech

The conservative position on free speech in general is willing to tolerate various restrictions, such as pornography and subversion, in order to promote social stability. Other restrictions include libel-slander and commercial speech. The liberal position is unrestricted free speech, with the restrictions only on behavior or when there is a clear and present danger that illegal behavior will result. The neutral position follows for restrictions when other constitutional rights are involved, like privacy, due process, or equal protection. The SOS is to emphasize that free speech benefits conservatives as well as liberals by way of such matters or as unlimited rights to influence public opinion by way of business money. There must be First Amendment protection for commercial free speech, especially in the context of business competition. And virtually unlimited free speech must be allowed to persuade workers not to join unions, including requiring that they come to an antiunion assembly on company time without providing for any opposition speakers. The SOS might also include the need for a broader socialization and education program. This comes out more clearly when one is talking about abhorrent free speech, as contrasted to political free speech, which is what is mainly referred to here, or maybe artistic free speech. It is easy for people to accept free speech in the abstract, but not necessarily concrete examples of Ku Klux Klan demonstrations or demonstrations in favor of atheism, communism, or homosexual rights. Then conservatives may advocate prohibiting or at least exclusion from various funding programs.

The last new item is on abhorrent free speech in the sense of what Voltaire or others would say they thoroughly despise but would defend to the death the right of the speaker to be able to speak. The conservative position is outright prohibition or to make things so inconvenient to come close to prohibition, such as no funding from any source like the National Endowment for the Arts or the Humanities. The conservative goal toward which these alternatives are directed is to protect people from the psychological upset of having ideas that are generally considered obnoxious presented. The liberal position is to allow such speakers mainly on the grounds that disallowing them sets a bad precedent that can easily spread to other less obnoxious minority viewpoints. The neutral position is prohibit when there is a clear and present danger of illegal behavior. The SOS is to remove the causes, which means through socialization and education to remove the potential audiences. Also, to provide a prosperous society so there will not be disgruntled people who may advocate such things as genocide or a dictatorship out of the frustration of being long-term unemployed or having had one's savings wiped out by inflation.

FEASIBILITY PROBLEMS

Law Personnel

Career judges as an SOS may have an insurmountable feasibility problem. The civil jury package has technology problems in reducing accidents.

Law Compliance

There is a lot of police opposition to drug medicalization. Gun control runs into big problems from the National Rifle Association. Not all conservatives are National Rifle Association members', just as not all conservatives are involved in cigarette manufacturing. These are two powerful lobbies that raise political feasibility problems even though a majority of public opinion may be opposed.

The idea of encouraging competition is an excellent way of dealing with consumer fraud. The problem is more of an administrative one. After a while the competitors may start working together to divide up the market or one competitor may dominate the others. It is difficult to keep competition encouraged. The idea of requiring salaries rather than commissions might be possible through the Securities and Exchange Commission.

The problem of socializing the general public and politicians to have a higher regard for the Bill of Rights so there is less need for judicial review has implementation problems. For example, in the schools, no matter how well they are trying to get across the idea of judging people on individual merit, the children may encounter a lot of prejudice in the home or on the streets that the schools cannot sufficiently counteract. Once again an SOS solution does not mean that it brings perfection. If these modules can increase respect for free speech, due process, and equal treatment in the sense that before scores of children and adults were relatively low and now they are relatively high, but not perfect, then the proposal is worth adopting even if it has imperfections or defects, so long as the costs do not outweigh the benefits.

The abhorrent free speech problem is also dealt with by way of socialization.

Law Rights

Prayers and Bible reading are also handled with an education program emphasizing ethical training. There are three different kinds of programs: the first is directed toward the Bill of Rights, the second toward productivity and democratic institutions, and the third toward ethical training based on the Golden Rule. All of this seems almost trite in the sense that these are widely accepted values. The reality is that this kind of thinking is not taught at the preschool or elementary levels, and very little even at the high school level. The school emphasis is both fortunately and unfortunately on reading, writing, and mathematics, and advanced versions at higher levels as contrasted to normative values. Such values are taught in parochial schools. Public schools should not be teaching religious indoctrination, but they can teach what might be called secular normative values. The word "secular," though, has bad connotations, as if it means atheist. It is better to talk in terms of widely accepted normative values.

Upgrading skills to meet merit hiring requirements costs money, but the investment is well worth it. A shortsightedness attitude may be blocking it. There is a need to get across the importance of the concept of productivity spending versus wasteful spending in government expenditures. Upgrading skills is an example of productivity spending. We need a lot more of that. An example of wasteful spending is defense spending in 1993. We need a lot less of that. The entitlements are mainly wasteful spending that should have a needs test and an emphasis on job opportunities.

The main SOS on gays in the military is to judge people on the basis of merit, but at some time in the future, not all at once. This assumes a constitutional feasibility problem. We are in effect assuming that the courts will say that "don't ask, don't tell" is unconstitutional as the federal appellate court has already said. It is not a merit criterion.

The loser-pays rule has administrative problems as to what constitutes suing unreasonably. Defendants may be assumed to have acted reasonably in defending themselves and therefore the defendant will never have to pay the plaintiff's costs. This SOS rule is in effect the federal rule, except the federal rule may need to make an exception that has never been explicitly made, saying that if someone sues on a theory that free speech is being restricted, or due process or equal treatment, then no matter how absurd the claim is, it will not be subject to the loser paying because the government wants to encourage people to be the equivalent of citizen attorneys general in enforcing the Bill of Rights.

Chapter 25

OVERALL POLICY

CONSERVATISM-LIBERALISM AS TO GOALS

Basic Concepts

In a general sense, conservatism refers to preserving the past, and liberalism refers to making changes that are considered modernizing or in accordance with long-term trends. These definitions may be especially relevant to developmental policy studies. They are, however, not sufficiently specific or in conformity with various examples. It is not considered liberal to want to change a left-wing government, or conservative to want to preserve a left-wing government.

Economic conservatism-liberalism refers to the relations between various segments or factors in the economy. Conservatives tend to be relatively more sympathetic to business, whereas liberals tend to be relatively more sympathetic to laborers and consumers.

Conservatism-liberalism on a political or civil liberties dimension refers to the relations between the government and the people. Conservatives tend to have a relatively narrow interpretation of free speech, due process for people accused of crimes, and equal treatment under law including rights that relate to voting, criminal justice, education, employment, and housing. Liberals tend to have a relatively broad interpretation of those rights.

Combining Economic and Political Ideology

If one combines economic and political ideology, at the extremes, being a liberal on both tends toward democratic socialism; being a conservative on both tends toward dictatorial capitalism; being an economic conservative and a political liberal tends toward democratic capitalism; being an economic liberal and a political conservative tends toward dictatorial socialism at the extremes. (See Table 25–1 for economic and political ideologies.)

Table 25–1
Economic and Political Ideologies

POLITICAL	ECONOMIC	CONSERVATIVE (Pro-employer and pro-manufacturer)	LIBERAL (Pro-labor and pro-consumer)
CONSERVATIVE (Restrict civil liberties)		1. Dictatorial capitalism (fascism) 2. Hitler, Mussolini	1. Dictatorial socialism (communism) 2. Stalin, Mao
NEUTRAL (Hold constant civil liberties)		1. Democratic capitalism 2. Bush, Reagan	1. Democratic welfare state 2. FDR, JFK
LIBERAL (Expand civil liberties)		1. Libertarianism 2. Milton Friedman, Ayn Rand	1. Socialist democracy 2. Norman Thomas, Clement Atlee

NOTES:

1. Economic includes economic and technology since they are closely related. Political includes domestic, international, and especially civil liberties (speech, due process, and merit treatment).

2. Each of the six ideologies can generally be subdivided (1) into secular or religious, (2) into whether they emphasize trade-off thinking or mutually beneficial thinking, (3) into whether they have an optimistic or pessimistic view of the future, or (4) into whether they have a strong or weak position on environment, gender equity, or on ethnic equity.

Types of Liberals and Conservatives, Especially in the American Context

The types of liberals are intellectual liberals who emphasize an expanding economy for helping the poor; intellectual liberals who emphasize redistribution of wealth and income for helping the poor; ethnic liberals who emphasize equal opportunity regardless of ethnic affiliation, although they are also liberal on labor and consumers; labor or pocketbook liberals who emphasize the rights of labor and consumers, but who tend to be conservative on civil liberties.

The types of conservatives are libertarians who are conservative on business regulation but liberal on civil liberties; business conservatives who emphasize an expanding economy for helping business; business conservatives who emphasize pro-business taxing and spending for helping business; religious conservatives who emphasize bridging the separation of church and state, although they are also generally conservative on business matters and foreign policy.

CONSERVATISM-LIBERALISM AS TO ALTERNATIVES

Conservative Alternatives

The concept of conservative alternatives in public policy tends to mean various things. A libertarian conservative believes in a minimum amount of government involvement in public policy. The emphasis should be on leaving things to the marketplace regardless of whether one is talking about economic, social, technological, or political policy.

A business conservative wants the government to play an active role toward promoting the interests of business, including bailouts, tariffs, subsidies, tax breaks, and loans without a lot of strings attached.

The religious right wants the government to play an active role toward repressing pornography, abortion, prostitution, homosexuality, and sex outside of marriage while encouraging prayer and Bible reading in the schools.

In the judicial process, conservatives tend to emphasize crime reduction and convicting the guilty. They also emphasize defenses to merchants, manufacturers, employers, and landlords when they might be sued for damages.

Liberal Alternatives

The concept of liberal alternatives in public policy also tends to mean various things. A civil libertarian liberal emphasizes the importance of free speech, separation of religion and government, due process for those accused of crimes, and equal treatment under law.

A labor liberal wants the government to play an active role toward promoting the interests of labor, including higher minimum wages, workplace safety, union rights, no child labor, and overtime pay.

Ethnic liberals tend to be members of minority racial, religious, or ancestral groups. They may be members of other groups that are often discriminated against on the basis of gender, sexual preference, or disability. They tend to emphasize equal opportunity and government help for those who are discriminated against.

In the judicial process, liberals tend to emphasize acquitting the innocent and minimizing wrongful arrests and searches. They also emphasize minimizing defenses to merchants, manufacturers, employers, and landlords when they might be sued for damages.

Neutral Alternatives

The concept of neutral alternatives refers to an alternative that is partly conservative and partly liberal or that is in some sense between the conservative and liberal positions. The neutral alternative may involve the fewest people on a highly controversial issue. This alternative may, however, be the winner in many practical situations because the conservatives and liberals may arrive at a compromise in order to get a policy adopted and implemented.

Super-Optimum Alternatives

The concept of super-optimum alternatives refers to an alternative that can enable conservatives, liberals, and other major viewpoints to all come out ahead of their best initial expectations simultaneously.

CONSERVATISM VERSUS LIBERALISM

Ideas that the Democrats have come up with over the last generation or so that Republicans fought against but then supported include the following: the pro-consumer ideas of Woodrow Wilson and the Federal Trade Commission and the Food and Drug Administration; the labor and workplace ideas of Franklin D. Roosevelt, including fair labor standards, the National Labor Relations Act, Social Security; the Civil Rights legislation of John F. Kennedy and Lyndon B. Johnson in the 1960s.

There are fewer ideas that the Republicans have come up with that Democrats opposed but then have become more supportive of because the Republicans, by definition or almost by definition, are conservatives. Their role is to keep things restrained, not to promote radical change, unless we are talking about the radical right, which has not been the mainstream of the Republican party.

One big exception, although it is not an innovation but more a return, is the idea of privatization. This has been opposed by liberal Democrats in the past as a move toward capitalism that would exploit consumers, workers, and even stockholders. The new privatization includes deregulation, which is good for consumers; it includes contracting out, which may specify more liberal provisions than a bureaucratic government operates, and rely more on profit motives to do well from a liberal perspective. An important example is that Minneapolis turned over its whole public school system to a private contractor. (Minnesota is perhaps the most socialistic state in the United States.) The turnover also was endorsed by the new black woman mayor. This clearly is not some kind of radical right activity. Maybe it is a radical left activity just like deregulation of the airlines was strongly pushed by Ted Kennedy as proconsumer, contrary to what the airlines would now like. They want entry regulations; they want less competition, not more.

Even though Republicans and conservatives do not normally push ideas that Democrats had first opposed and later supported, it is important to indicate to Republicans and conservatives how they benefit from legislation that is oriented toward consumers, labor, or minorities. Consumer legislation promotes more competitive products, labor legislation promotes more profitable automation, and civil rights result in more productive use of the population and labor force.

Some people say that we need to have a whole new category between or in addition to being conservative or being liberal. Here we are not talking so much about an SOS that is a political party or an ideology. There are SOS thinkers within the Democrats and Republicans. Some Democrats are trade-off thinkers like Jimmy Carter, others are more expansionist like Bill Clinton when he was campaigning, and like Robert Reich. Likewise, the Republicans have some SOS thinkers, including Ronald Reagan and some trade-off types, including George Bush.

The environmental "greens" like to think of themselves as being outside the conservative and liberal spectrums, operating on different issues than labor-management consumer-seller, minorities-dominant group. They are concerned with the environment versus the polluters. Some of them are one-issue people with knee-jerk reactions to things like the milk hormone. Most of them are mildly liberal Democrats who view environmental protection as another form of business regulation that cuts into business expenses unnecessarily. It is not something separate from the traditional spectrum, it isn't a new dimension. It is new in the sense of a new purpose for business regulation, but not enough, especially in the United States, to be generating any serious talk about a green party.

Therefore, the idea of needing to win these people over is no different than the normal conservative versus liberal analysis. In talking about "winning" them over, what we are referring to is not the Republicans winning them over to allowing pollution, instead we are talking about the Democrats winning the more extreme environmentalists over to the idea that raising the GNP and improving employment may be more important than getting the last ounce of pollution out of some landfill that has already had 95% of the toxic waste removed.

This is a problem that both political parties have with winning the more extreme elements to the mainstream of the party. Clinton has it on the North

American Free Trade Agreement, with environmentalists who would wreck the whole agreement because it isn't strong enough on Mexico's environmental enforcement. But there are also knee-jerk one-issue labor people who would wreck the whole agreement because it isn't strong enough on Mexico's minimum wage enforcement. In both cases, the adoption and expansion of the economy, at least regarding labor, should make a difference.

The bottom line on this is the importance in a democracy of trying to get consensus, or at least majority support, that is generally not enough. We want to cut down on divisiveness. Some of the examples above show how, with the passage of time, good innovative ideas do get accepted. This is more likely to be true in a democratic society, where debate is vigorous and people feel that they have been given an opportunity to make their points and to get things repealed if they are not working. There will always be some people who, even now, would say that whatever the New Deal passed was communistic, although they would have to be rather old-timers to have personally experienced the anti-Roosevelt hate of the 1930s. There are still some people around who would say that the Civil Rights legislation of the 1960s was communistic, but very few, including Ronald Reagan, who campaigned against it in 1964.

INTERMEDIATE DEFINITIONS

A public policy issue is a subject on which there is substantial disagreement among people as to how the government should be handling a problem that relates to the economy, society, the political system, technology, or the legal system. The key elements are the government as a decision maker and at least some segments of the general public as an evaluator. These are two key elements. The third is a social problem, meaning some aspect of human interaction that is considered to be not functioning as well as it could be.

Defining conservatives would emphasize people who feel that social problems are best handled with a minimum of government involvement in order to promote the interests of business, which indirectly results in promoting the interests of everybody. This definition leaves out conservatives who want lots of government involvement when it comes to social issues, crime, or national defense. One may need to define conservatives just in terms of goals, and not try to work in the alternative of minimum government involvement. Conservatives could then be defined as people who want to promote the interests of business and traditional social values.

Liberals might then be defined as those who are especially oriented toward promoting the interests of consumers and workers and civil libertarian values. Both conservatives and liberals would say that promoting the interests of their respective constituencies promotes the interests of everybody indirectly, with conservatives endorsing a trickle-down theory and liberals endorsing a percolate-up theory.

An SOS alternative is one that is capable of achieving overall conservative goals, even better than traditional conservative alternatives, and simultaneously capable of achieving overall liberal goals even more than traditional liberal alternatives.

A feasibility problem, as it applies to an SOS alternative, is one that relates to putting the alternative into full effect owing to a lack of economic, political, administrative, psychological, legal, or technological feasibility or practicality. The underlying idea behind these objections is that there are constraints that need to be considered and not just goals. An alternative could do well on goals like income, expenses, benefits, or costs, but be subject to some constraints that makes it outside the feasible region of practicality.

An SOS generating approach is a way of thinking that helps lead to specific SOS alternatives for specific social problems. These generating approaches tend to have in common thinking about how conservative and liberal goals can be simultaneously achieved. A key characteristic is thinking in terms of the goals rather than compromising the conflicting alternatives.

GENERALIZED VARIABLES

Overall Goals

One overall conservative goal is to promote the interests of business, especially big business, where there is a conflict between big and little. Another goal is to reduce taxes, but only on domestic programs, not on defense programs or anticrime programs.

An overall liberal goal is to promote the interests of labor and consumers, but also minority groups and the environment. Sometimes these interests conflict, such as where consumers benefit from tariff reduction and certain labor unions do not. Or where consumers benefit from access to wilderness areas and consumers of recreation and environmentalists do not like that. Minority interests can be competitive with traditional union interests.

Overall Alternatives

The overall conservative alternative is to rely on the marketplace, with a minimum of government involvement, but lots of government involvement when it comes to imposing conservative sexual values, or when it comes to repealing proconsumer legislation that may have been adopted at the state level.

The overall liberal position involves emphasizing the government for resolving social problems, including government salaried people.

SOS Alternatives

SOS alternatives fit into various categories, such as expanding the resources so that all sides come out ahead; a technological fix that enables greater profits,

Figure 25–1
Generalized SOS Analysis: Public Policy

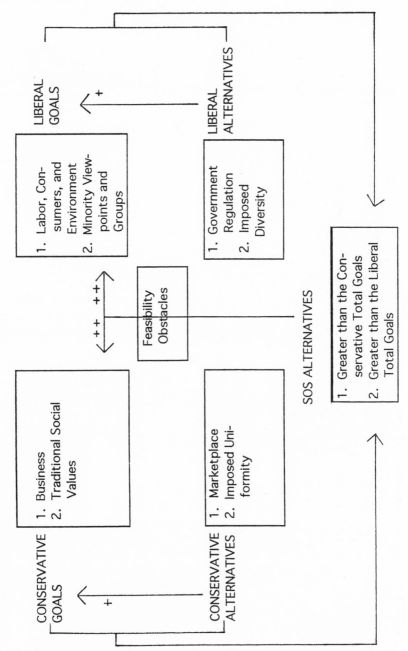

Figure 25–2
Generalized SOS Analysis: Criminal and Civil Cases

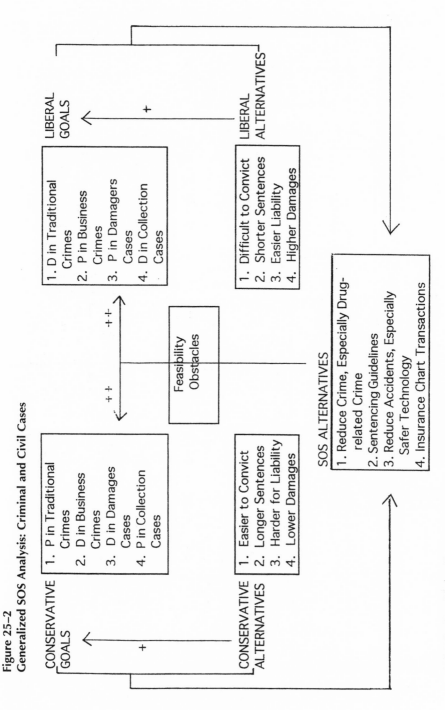

CONSERVATIVE GOALS		LIBERAL GOALS
1. P in Traditional Crimes		1. D in Traditional Crimes
2. D in Business Crimes		2. P in Business Crimes
3. D in Damages Cases		3. P in Damagers Cases
4. P in Collection Cases		4. D in Collection Cases

Feasibility Obstacles

CONSERVATIVE ALTERNATIVES	LIBERAL ALTERNATIVES
1. Easier to Convict	1. Difficult to Convict
2. Longer Sentences	2. Shorter Sentences
3. Harder for Liability	3. Easier Liability
4. Lower Damages	4. Higher Damages

SOS ALTERNATIVES

1. Reduce Crime, Especially Drug-related Crime
2. Sentencing Guidelines
3. Reduce Accidents, Especially Safer Technology
4. Insurance Chart Transactions

NOTES: P = Plaintiff or Prosecutor. D=Defendant

Figure 25-3
Generalized SOS Analysis: Constitutional Cases

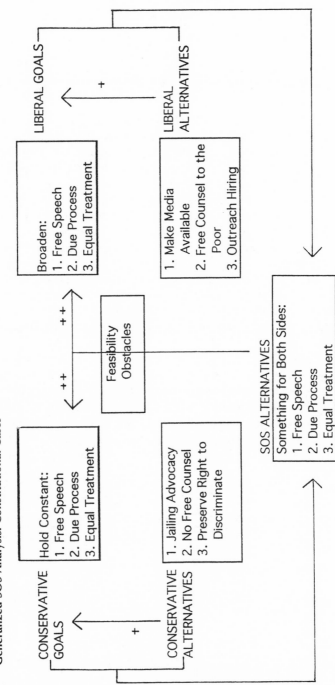

while at the same time a cleaner environment or consumer benefits or labor benefits; combining alternatives fully that otherwise look mutually exclusive; redefining the problem in terms of the goals, such as how to achieve two otherwise conflicting sets of goals simultaneously rather than compromising on the alternatives; developing new forms of interaction like HMOs that are capable of providing increased benefits and decreased costs (the distinguishing characteristic of an HMO is that it is an insurance system run by private-sector providers or suppliers, whereby people pay a certain amount and receive all the service or products they need of a certain kind; the provider has an incentive to reduce the need and also not to be wasteful in providing what is needed); contracting out, which can provide the profit motive of capitalism and the equity of socialism in the contract specifications; competition, which can be profitable to business and generate low prices and quality products for consumers; socialization, which enables people to comply with the law without needing to increase the costs of noncompliance or decrease the benefits or give rewards for compliance; facilitating international trade or domestic trade in order to reduce friction between nations or groups so that they can all come out ahead by buying and selling from each other; big benefits for one side and low costs for the other in bilateral negotiation; a package of alternatives that contains some items that would make conservatives especially happy and some items that would make liberals especially happy; raising the level of the goals to be achieved, including both conservative and liberal goals; the third-party benefactor which is usually the government who gives something to both the conservative side and the liberal side—this is the voucher idea, which is applicable to housing, food, training, health care insurance, school tuition, and other important services that the private sector can provide; removing the causes of the conflict—such as crime reduction, unwanted pregnancies, lack of income due to lack of jobs— regarding the controversies of capital punishment, gun control, abortion, and welfare reform, the sequential SOS that recognizes adopting the SOS all at once might be politically or psychologically not feasible; it has to occur in stages, with gays in the military being an example.

RELEVANT DIAGRAMS

Figures 25–1, 25–2, and 25–3 summarize many of these concepts as applied respectively to public policy in general, civil and criminal policy, and constitutional rights policy.

Going Further ──────────────────

A BIBLIOGRAPHY

If you would like to read further about win-win policy and super-optimizing analysis, various books by people other than myself might be helpful. They include the following books arranged alphabetically by author or editor:

Barfield, Claude E. and John H. Makin (eds.). *Trade Policy and U.S. Competitiveness* (American Enterprise Institute for Public Policy Research, 1987).

Chickering, A. Lawrence. *Beyond Left and Right: Breaking the Political Stalemate* (Institute for Contemporary Studies, 1993).

Cohen, Steven and Ronald Brand. *Total Quality Management in Government: A Practical Guide for the Real World* (Jossey-Bass, 1993).

Common, Michael. *Sustainability and Policy: Limits to Economics* (Cambridge University Press, 1995).

Dobel, J. Patrick. *Compromise and Political Action: Political Morality in Liberal and Democratic Life* (Rowman & Littlefield, 1990).

Kettl, Donald F. *Sharing Power: Public Governance and Private Markets* (Brookings Institution, 1993).

Krone, Robert (ed.). *Total Quality Management* (Symposium issue of *Journal of Management Science and Policy Analysis*, Spring/Summer 1991).

Levine, David I. *Reinventing the Workplace: How Business and Employees Can Both Win* (Brookings Institution, 1995).

Magaziner, Ira C. and Robert B. Reich. *Minding America's Business: The Decline and Rise of the American Economy* (Harcourt Brace, 1982).

Mitra, Gautam (ed.). *Computer Assisted Decision Making: Expert Systems, Decision Analysis, Mathematical Programming* (Elsevier Science Publishers, 1986).

Myers, Norman and Julian L. Simon. *Scarcity or Abundance? A Debate on the Environment* (W. W. Norton, 1990).

Noyes, Richard (ed.). *Now the Synthesis: Capitalism, Socialism, and the New Social Contract* (Holmes & Meier, 1991).

Rehfuss, John A. *Contracting Out in Government: A Guide to Working with Outside Contractors to Supply Public Services* (Jossey-Bass, 1989).

Romm, Joseph J. *Lean and Clean Management: How to Boost Profits and Productivity by Reducing Pollution* (Kodansha International, 1994).

Sawhill, Isabel V. (ed.). *Challenge to Leadership: Economic and Social Issues for the Next Decade* (The Urban Institute Press, 1988).

Susskind, Lawrence and Jeffrey Cruikshank. *Breaking the Impasse: Consensual Approaches to Resolving Public Disputes* (Basic Books, 1987).

Walsh, Kieron. *Public Services and Market Mechanisms: Competition, Contracting and the New Public Management* (St. Martin's Press, 1995).

Zagare, Frank C. *Game Theory: Concepts and Applications* (Sage Publications, 1984).

For further materials by me, the following books might be helpful:

With Miriam Mills, *Developing Nations and Super-Optimum Policy Analysis* (Nelson-Hall, 1993).

Higher Goals for America: Doing Better than the Best (University Press of America, 1989).

Legal Scholarship, Microcomputers, and Super-Optimizing Decision-Making (Quorum Books, 1993).

With Miriam Mills, *Multi-Criteria Methods for Alternative Dispute Resolution: With Microcomputer Software Applications* (Quorum Books, 1990).

Policy Analysis Methods and Super-Optimum Solutions (Nova Science, 1994).

The Policy Process and Super-Optimum Solutions (Nova Science, 1994).

Super-Optimizing Analysis (Symposium in *Public Budgeting and Financial Management: An International Journal*, 1992).

The following chapters in other Nagel books might also be helpful:

"Arriving at Super-Optimum Solutions" in *Research in Public Policy Analysis and Management* (JAI Press, 1995).

"Broadening the Applicability of Multi-Criteria Dispute Resolution" in *Systematic Analysis in Dispute Resolution* (Quorum Books, 1991).

"Computer-Aided Super-Optimizing" and "The SOS Demo Disk" in *Teach Yourself Decision-Aiding Software* (University Press of America, 1992).

"Judicial Process Controversies and Super-Optimum Solutions" in *Computer-Aided Judicial Analysis: Predicting, Prescribing, and Administering* (Quorum Books, 1992).

"SOS Evaluation" and "SOS Causation" in *Evaluative and Explanatory Reasoning* (Quorum Books, 1992).

"Super-Optimizing Analysis and Policy Studies" and "The SOS Process: Generating, Adopting, Implementing, and Facilitating" and "The Need for Improved Policy Analysis" in with Miriam Mills, *Professional Developments in Policy Studies* (Greenwood Press, 1993).

"Super-Optimum Solutions and Public Controversies" in *Social Science, Law, and Public Policy* (University Press of America, 1992).

I have been especially interested in applying super-optimizing analysis to the policy problems of developing nations. Publications in Nagel books along those lines include the following:

"Developing Nations and Public Policy" in *Encyclopedia of Policy Studies* (Marcel Dekker, 1994).

"Improving Public Policy Toward and Within Developing Countries" in *Public Administration and Decision-Aiding Software: Improving Procedure and Sustance* (Greenwood Press, 1990).

"Introduction" in *African Development and Public Policy* (Macmillan, St. Martin's, 1994).

"Introduction" in *Asian Development and Public Policy* (Macmillan, St. Martin's, 1994).

"Introduction" in *Eastern European Development and Public Policy* (Macmillan, St. Martin's, 1994).

"Introduction" in *Latin American Development and Public Policy* (Macmillan, St. Martin's, 1994).

"Introduction" in *Public Administration in China* (Greenwood Press, 1993).

"Preface: Chinese Policy Studies" and "Super-Optimizing Analysis and Chinese Policy Problems" in *Public Policy in China* (Greenwood Press, 1993).

"Super-Optimizing Analysis and Developmental Policy" in *Global Policy Studies: International Interaction toward Improving Public Policy* (Macmillan, St. Martin's Press, 1991).

INDEX

About the Author

STUART S. NAGEL is Professor of Political Science at the University of Illinois, Associate Dean of International Policy Studies, and Coordinator of the Miriam K. Mills Research Center for Super-Optimizing Analysis and Developing Nations. Dr. Nagel has received awards, fellowships, and grants from the Ford and Rockefeller Foundations, the National Science Foundation, the Center for Advanced Study in the Behavioral Sciences, and other prestigious organizations. This is the twelfth book he has written or edited for Quorum.

ISBN 1-56720-118-0

90000>

EAN

9 781567 201185

HARDCOVER BAR CODE